Repeated Takes

2

1 8

Repeated Takes

A Short History of Recording and its
Effects on Music

MICHAEL CHANAN

V

VERSO
London · New York

First published by Verso 1995
© Michael Chanan 1995
All rights reserved

Reprinted 2000

Verso
UK: 6 Meard Street, London w1v 3hr
USA: 180 Varick Street, New York, ny 10014

Verso is the imprint of New Left Books

ISBN 978-1-85984-012-2

British Library Cataloguing in Publication Data
A catalogue record for this book is available from the British Library

Library of Congress Cataloging-in-Publication Data
A catalogue record for this book is available from the Library of Congress

Typeset in Monotype Bembo by Lucy Morton, London se12
Printed and bound in Great Britain by Biddles Ltd,
www.biddles.co.uk

To the girl from Culver City

Music gets around. So does the public.

John G. Paine, General Manager, American Society of
Composers, Authors and Publishers, 1940

*The transmission of events and sounds around our planet has
forced us to concede that there is not just one musical tradition
but, rather, many musics, not all of which are concerned – by
our definition of the word – with tradition.*

Glenn Gould, 'The Prospects of Recording',
High Fidelity, 1966

Contents

Preface

This book fills a strange gap, for despite the mass of writings on cinema, television and other media, and the central place occupied by recorded music in the cultural experience of the twentieth century, there is almost a dearth of serious writing about the record industry (as opposed to a mass of anecdotal stuff about recording artists). A number of books on different parts of the industry have appeared recently, but there is no comprehensive survey to be found on the shelves. I have set out to provide a general history of the medium from Edison's talking tin foil of 1877 to the age of the compact disc. The book is modest in its endeavour and I make no claim to original research, yet the story is in many respects unknown. Without writing a history of music in the twentieth century, I have tried to trace the connections between the development of recording, changes in the interpretation of classical music, and the rise of new forms of popular music. I relate the growth and development of the industry, both technical and economic; the changing quality of recorded sound and the aesthetics of recording; the effects of the microphone on interpretation and performance in both classical and popular music; and the impact of all these factors on musical styles and tastes. I also discuss topics such as the gramophone as an item of domestic furniture; the symbiosis between records and radio; the relationship with the talkies; the development of magnetic recording; disc jockeys and payola; the roles of the A&R man, the recording engineer and the record producer; multitracking, mixing, dubbing, scratching and sampling.

In part this book is a 'spin-off' from a larger work on the social practice of Western music, already published under the title *Musica Practica*, from which it borrows a few paragraphs, and which also deals in greater detail with a number of topics which might otherwise have been included here, such as the development of electronic music and electrophonic instruments.

For information on various topics my thanks go to Glyn Perrin, Steve Stanton, Alfredo Anzola, Theo van Leeuwen and Dave Wren, and to Pat Kahn for several key aperçus. Also my special thanks go to the students at Back Hill who contributed through discussion and essays to the thoughts in this book, especially in the last chapter.

M.C.

I

Record Culture

Thomas Alva Edison's invention of the talking tin foil, for which he borrowed from another inventor the term 'phonograph' ('voice-writer'), dates back to 1877, the year after Alexander Graham Bell, using a word that had been around even longer, patented his first telephone ('distant voice').

There are two ways of seeing this act of invention. In one version, it was the realization of an old dream, answering to ancient susceptibilities. The French photographer Nadar, greeting Edison's invention, said it was as if Rabelais's tale of the sea of frozen words, which released voices into the air when it melted, had passed from the imaginary to the real.[1] Rabelais was dead only thirty-five years when in 1589 the Italian scientist Giovanni Batista della Porta, one of the inventors of the telescope, imagined that he had 'devised a way to preserve words, that have been pronounced, inside lead pipes, in such a manner that they burst forth from them when one removes the cover'. Around the same time a Nuremberg optician suggested enclosing echoes inside bottles, where he thought they would keep for a few hours at least.[2]

Acoustics was not yet a named branch of science – the term was only introduced in the early eighteenth century by Joseph Sauveur, following a century of investigations by Vincenzo Galilei (father of Galileo), Mersenne, Kepler, Bacon and Descartes. More advances followed, beginning in the 1820s, especially on the part of a number of French researchers. The velocity of sound at different temperatures was established by Gay-Lussac, Arago and others; Savart invented a toothed wheel for determining the number of vibrations per second for a given musical pitch; Helmholtz established the laws of harmonics; Lissajous projected light vibrations onto a screen as a series of sinusoidal curves; and the writing of John Tyndall (his book on sound was published in England in 1867) helped to popularize the subject.

But when the moment materialized, the invention of the phonograph proved remarkably simple, almost as if this new knowledge scarcely counted. It was certainly much simpler than that of cinematography fifteen years or so later, for which Edison also shares some of the credit. Although both of them involved assorted precursors, Edison's phonograph of 1877 used little by way of scientific knowledge and no new materials. Two American writers, Oliver Read and Walter T. Welch, authors of the most detailed technical account of the invention, point out that all the basic components of the phonograph were already known. The stylus had been in use since ancient times. The diaphragm or tympanum had been known since the time of Hippocrates, from human and animal dissection. The feed screw was invented by Archimedes. A speaking trumpet was shown by Leonardo in a sketch for a tube communication system for the palace of the Duke of Milan. Cylinders and discs were known from the use of the lathe.[3]

The problem with this account is that it hardly explains why the phonograph was not invented earlier, or leaves you to suppose that it only awaited the genius of the right inventor. But this is bad history. Inventions never just appear out of a vacuum in the mind of the inventor, and there are usually several inventors at work simultaneously on similar endeavours, sometimes in competition and sometimes in ignorance of each other; for it is social, economic and cultural circumstances that motivate the invention and the direction of the inventor's imagination. The phonograph is no exception.

At the same time, because invention is always a matter of trial and error, it is often characterized by the 'happy accident', and in the second version of the phonograph story the invention is a by-product of Edison's work on the telephone, and the accidental result of the close relationship between these two inventions. Edison had started by attempting to extend the reach of the telephone line by producing a device to repeat the signal, on the same principle as his successful telegraph repeater. He then realized, quickly enough, that what he had arrived at was something else, and in an article for the *North American Review* in 1878 he suggested a number of uses for the new invention. The article makes curious reading: here is an inventor, aware that the machine he has just created is remarkable but as yet too crude to be practicable, trying to awaken people's imagination to what it might do:

1. Letter writing and all kinds of dictation without the aid of a stenographer.
2. Phonographic books, which will speak to blind people without effort on their part.
3. The teaching of elocution.
4. Reproduction of music.
5. The 'Family Record' – a registry of sayings, reminiscences, etc., by members of a family in their own voices, and of the last words of dying persons.
6. Music-boxes and toys.
7. Clocks that should announce in articulate speech the time for going home, going to meals, etc.
8. The preservation of languages by exact reproduction of the manner of pronouncing.
9. Educational purposes; such as preserving the explanations made by a teacher, so that the pupil can refer to them at any moment, and spelling or other lessons placed upon the phonograph for convenience in committing to memory.
10. Connection with the telephone, so as to make that instrument an auxiliary in the transmission of permanent and invaluable records, instead of being the recipient of momentary and fleeting communications.[4]

All the uses Edison suggests here have since been achieved, more or less, using one form or recording or another. If it was not at first apparent that the reproduction of music would be the principal focus and determining factor in the development of the new instrument, this was because of the very limited quality of the sound of which, like the telephone, it was initially capable. The sounds we are used to today are in another class. According to Bell's own advertisement of 1877:

The proprietors of the telephone ... are now prepared to furnish telephones for the transmission of articulate speech through instruments not more than twenty miles apart. Conversation can easily be carried on after slight practice and with occasional repetition of a word or sentence. On first listening to the telephone, although the sound is perfectly audible, the articulation seems to be indistinct, but after a few trials the ear becomes accustomed to the peculiar sound and finds little difficulty in understanding the words.[5]

The phonograph was initially no better.

In Edison's original design, the stylus was attached for both recording and replay to a telephone diaphragm, but the electrics made it impractical, and the first machine he actually built was entirely mechanical. The diaphragm he intended to use, which employed carbon granules to convert sound waves into electrical waves, was his own invention. Again he was not the only one to be working on such a device – the need, after all, was plain – and in 1878 the English electrician David Hughes coined the word by which this voice transmitter would thereafter be known: the microphone ('small voice'). Ironically, the electrical microphone played no part in recording for almost fifty years. However, Edison's carbon button was a marked improvement on Bell's magnetic coil device, which worked well enough as a receiver but not as a transmitter; and it allowed Western Union, which commissioned its development, to set up in competition with Bell, although it pirated Bell's receiver in order to do so. The ensuing dispute over patents was quickly resolved and in 1881 the reorganized Bell Company set up Western Electric as its manufacturing arm. Meanwhile Bell himself bowed out of telephones, his attention taken by Edison's phonograph. But Western Electric will re-enter the story in the 1920s, with the development of electrical recording.

The telephone business was quite content with the limited frequency range of the carbon button. It was discovered that the human brain needs remarkably little information in order to understand speech (and recognize voices), and the narrower the bandwidth, the easier to design the equipment, including the receiver; nor did the telephone create the need for a loudspeaker, but only an earpiece. Meanwhile Bell's attempts to improve the phonograph began to pay off, at least in terms of the technical quality of the recorded signal, and by the time he launched his improved machine in 1887, the phonograph produced a better sound than the telephone, even using the tinny horn for reproduction. It was still barely adequate, but a definite break had been made with telephone technology. The key factors in this separation were the mechanical nature of the phonographic recording and the absence of any means of amplifying an electrical signal; neither factor was of any disadvantage to the telephone.

Telephone and phonograph, two of the key inventions responsible for transforming the experience of everyday life in the twentieth century, were thus closely related at birth but technically distinct – the one electrical, the other mechanical. With their almost magical simplicity, and despite their shortcomings, these two inventions rapidly made the names of Bell and Edison world famous, but then they manifested different patterns of industrial development. In marked contrast to the telephone, or for that matter the cinematograph subsequently, the phonograph was distinctly slow to get going (and enriched Edison far less than the incandescent light bulb which he perfected two years later). The telephone saw continuous steady growth from the outset and generated a large support industry. The growth of cinema was even more rapid. The phonograph, however, on top of the usual battles of any new invention over patents, needed a whole series of technical improvements before the original cylinder was replaced around the turn of the century by the 78 r.p.m. shellac disc, and the industry really took off.

The crucial problem that held the phonograph back, until the introduction of the disc, was that every recording was an original: there was no means of mass replication. At best it was possible to record simultaneously on a bank of machines, or use a pantograph to copy them a handful at a time, but these methods were simply unable to satisfy the demand that the invention created. Only the disc made it possible to devise a means of mass production, and even then the technique took a number of years to master. In short, in its original form the invention that promised the repeatable recording but not its replication was able to capture the imagination of a potential market but not to satisfy it.

When it did take off, the record industry, like the medium of film, was immediately international in character. A recording could be made anywhere and then be easily transported across the ocean to be mass-produced in a different location. Certain North American cities, for example, provided a crucial market among the large community of Italian immigrants for records of operatic excerpts recorded back in Italy, where opera was a popular rather than an elitist art form. A record made in Milan in 1904 by Enrico Caruso became the first disc to sell a million copies, thus helping to establish the machine's credentials as a respectable form of diversion – at the same time that the other new medium, moving pictures, was evolving an aura of disrepute. This, according to a writer celebrating the centenary of the invention, 'was the last occasion on which the classical European repertoire had a decisive influence on the development of the record industry'.[6] The claim is mistaken – it ignores the role of classical music in the launch of new formats (the LP at the end of the 1940s, stereo ten years later, and the compact disc, first unveiled in the centenary year of 1977). But the drift that it indicates is correct, for the industry quickly learned to develop a repertoire of its own: above all, it discovered how to transform the 'raw' music of urban and ethnic popular culture into formulaic commodities of mass consumption. It is symptomatic that what by many accounts was the first jazz recording to sell a million copies, dating from 1917, was by a group of five white musicians calling themselves the Original Dixieland 'Jass' Band, who had journeyed north from New Orleans to reap the rewards of success in New York. One must add, however, that what followed was an explosion of new popular musical forms, styles and voices, in which music that was originally marginal ended up by transforming the mainstream. The process was fuelled by two basic factors: the low costs of entry into the business, and the potentially very high rate of profit.

The cylinders which predated discs are intriguing objects, frail and fragile, like faded photographs: seemingly blurred, with sometimes only the barest echo of a sound in evidence. In 1889 Edison's German agent set up his apparatus in a music room at No. 4 Carlsgasse, Vienna, and recorded Brahms playing one of his Hungarian Rhapsodies. At least, that is what his gruff-sounding voice announces – all one can hear after that are some very faint tinkles, which one strains to catch. What it sounded like originally we can only guess; the grooves have been worn away by repeated playing, a liability of the wax which quickly replaced tin foil (tin-foil recordings were destroyed when the foil was removed from the cylinder). No matter. To the enthusiast, 'vintage' recordings are like nothing so much as trophies, or archaeological finds, and in the figure of the collector they clearly promote a certain fetishism. Yet like early moving pictures, they have the grain of history. They seem to belong to a time when music was different, and to offer tantalizing clues to what it was like. I am thinking, for example, of how in 1902 the apparatus was taken to the Sistine Chapel and there, as Roland Gelatt puts it in *The Fabulous Phonograph*, 'the last of the great castrati, Alessandro Moreschi, bequeathed to unborn generations the eerie bleat of the male soprano'.[7]

The impression of a lost history is not entirely illusory. The machine that turned the intangible sound of music into a material object was also to register huge changes in interpretation and performance styles, for which it is largely itself responsible. The difference between a compact disc of Beethoven's Fifth by the latest prize-winner of an international conductors' competition and the original 78s of the recording by Nikisch in 1913, let alone between Moreschi and, say, Michael Jackson – these differences are more than technological, but encompass a stark sea-change in the musical climate, and a profound transformation of musical consciousness.

If at first the phonograph record was little more than a novelty, the stuff of entertainment arcades and 'educational' lectures, it was also an entirely novel commodity: it turned the performance of music into a material object, something you could hold in your hand, which could be bought and sold. The effects of this innovation were both economic and aesthetic, and emerged in stages, revealing different aspects in the process.

Economically, musicians began to experience recording as a new and contradictory form of exploitation, in which other people were always making more from records than they did, although the rewards to be gained with success often outstripped all other sources of musical money-making; a process that also changed the shape of music publishing and the entertainment business. The aesthetic effects stem first from the physical separation of listening from performing, which has several implications. On the one hand, the performance becomes disembodied and transportable; this would alter ways of listening. On the other, musicians are able for the first time to hear themselves as others hear them; this would change the nature of interpretation. At the same time came the effects of the technical constraints of early recording systems, the brief duration and limited tonal range of the record. The results were already becoming apparent when the gramophone was joined in the 1920s by radio, from which in various ways its history henceforth becomes inseparable.

The seeds of broadcast radio were planted in the years leading up to the First World War, reaching fruition in Europe and North America at the end of the war as an indirect result of wartime military investment. The development of amplification and the loudspeaker for the purposes of radio broadcasting, not to mention improvements to the microphone, was also to benefit the gramophone, and by the mid-1920s the record industry began to fight back against radio with the introduction of electrical recording and a huge improvement in the quality of recorded sound. Radio enjoyed the same benefits, and in consequence, records and radio fell upon each other rapaciously. Radio fed off records to fill up air time; records were attracted to radio as an aural showcase. After battles had been fought over the questions of copyright and royalties, both media also provided important additional sources of income for publishers, composers and musicians; opened up new forms of musical activity; and led to major changes in musical style and language. (So did the movies following the introduction of the film soundtrack in the late 1920s – another offshoot of the same technical developments.) Then, following the Second World War, came the multiplication and perfection of recording, replay and transmission systems which is still going on: LP, magnetic tape, stereo, audio cassette, compact disc, digital recording, and the convergence with television, video, cable, satellite and the computer chip. Economically this is a tale of repeated expansion, recession and regeneration, and the transformation of the music business and its markets through the development of novel forms of consumption. The result has been a qualitative alteration in the political economy of music, and its incorporation into the military–industrial complex (several of the major equipment manufacturers are also producers of military equipment).

In the course of this process, the age-old dialogue of musical communication was radically upset. Above all, the technique of reproduction – mechanical, electrical or electronic – creates a distance, both physical and psychic, between performer and audience that simply never existed before, which produces new ways for music to be heard and allows the listener totally new ways of using it. This includes not only records but also broadcasting, which is reproduction at a distance. In the words of Walter Benjamin's crucial essay on the subject, 'The Work of Art in the Age of Mechanical Reproduction', written in the 1930s, the effect is to put a copy of the original into situations that are out of reach of the original itself, like a choral performance played in a drawing room.[8] Nowadays, being further down the same road, we can listen to opera while riding the underground, Mahler while driving along the motorway, or Spanish monks singing Gregorian chant while flying high above the ocean, not to mention John Coltrane, Ravi Shankar, Jimi Hendrix, Youssou N'Dour or Astor Piazzolla. As far as classical music is concerned, even if the work in itself were to remain untouched in this process, the quality of its presence is reduced and denuded, like the image of a landscape on a television screen. In short, the technique of reproduction detaches the musical work from the domain of the tradition that gave birth to it, and destroys what Benjamin calls the aura which signals its authenticity; except that it also creates new types of musical object which do not belong to a particular domain, but rather anywhere that a loudspeaker (or earphones) may be found – some of these recordings cannot be performed live at all. This process also redefines the audience, which comes to be constituted quite differently from before. It is no longer limited to traditional concepts of community; it is not compact but dispersed; it is atomized and, in the end, often divided more by generation than by social class – except, again, that in certain places and certain times, new styles of recorded music emerge which forge new identities within the communities that create them, and then extend themselves across countries and continents as they become diffused by the apparatus of distribution. (I am thinking of the way, for example, that the Chilean New Song movement of the 1960s became the political expression of the whole continent; or of the rapid worldwide diffusion of rap from its genesis among the inner-city urban youth of the South Bronx in the 1980s.)

It is now possible for music of every kind to enter every corner of daily life in every corner of the world. Previously the music entertained by any given social group in any society was essentially its own, speaking its own musical vernacular. It was not unintelligible to outsiders (unless, for ideological reasons, their ears were blocked), for as Benjamin's contemporary T.W. Adorno once remarked, music is indeed a universal language, though without being Esperanto. Moreover, since music is portable and travels easily, no musical culture was ever isolated, and every wave of migration and conquest had the effect of musical innovation. But today the musics of every society and every historical period are instantly available everywhere at the touch of a button. And again the result is that musical experience has radically altered.

Recording has transformed music by changing the experience of the ear. A symptomatic episode in the early stages of this process was the apperception of the Hungarian composers Bartók and Kodály when they made the first field recordings of eastern European folk music in the early years

9

of the twentieth century. The cylinders they recorded would start to degrade with repeated playing. The first task was to transcribe them. When they started transcribing what they had recorded, they discovered that the established musical notation was not equal to the job. It needed modifying in order to capture features like the quarter-tones (the notes between the notes, so to speak) that the phonograph revealed directly to the ear as characteristic of this music, but which 'cultured' Western hearing all too easily failed to register. Listening to these recordings, Bartók said, was like examining musical objects under a microscope. This recalls something else that Benjamin observed, about the way that film enriched our perception in a manner comparable, he said, to Freudian theory. Before Freud,

> a slip of the tongue passed more or less unnoticed. Only exceptionally may such a slip have revealed dimensions of depth in a conversation which had seemed to be taking its course on the surface. Since *The Psychopathology of Everyday Life* things have changed. This book isolated and made analysable things which had heretofore floated along unnoticed in the broad stream of perception. For the entire spectrum of optical, and now also of acoustical, perception, the film has brought about a similar deepening of apperception. It is only an obverse of this fact that behaviour items shown in a movie can be analysed much more precisely and from more points of view than those presented in paintings or on the stage.[9]

Recording has had the same effect on musical apperception. In doing so, it has also radically changed the way in which music is heard by the inner ear, so to speak.

Think of all the things a singer or instrumentalist can do (depending on the instrument) for which a written score contains only the vaguest suggestion, if at all: the scoops, slides and wobbles, and the subtle alterations in tempo or tone colour, which are nevertheless regarded as necessary parts of creative interpretation, whether the music is written or not: without them the performance is liable to sound flat and inexpressive, whatever the music. Think also of the way these features sound in jazz, blues, folk singing, all varieties of ethnic musics, even, if you like, crooning and rock music. For example, the way jazz players treat their instruments, almost singing into them to produce all kinds of 'forbidden' timbres in the same way that the vocalist 'plays' the microphone: timbres which never occur when the same instruments are played in the classical manner, or not until recently, but the avant-garde has been busy reintroducing them.

None of these inflections are easy to notate, if at all. The purpose of notation is to fix the values of a series of components of performance. The symbols used must identify definite values and unambiguous elements, otherwise there is confusion over what they denote and whether the performance indeed complies with the score: hence the tendency in classical music to add verbal instructions (usually using a standardized Italian vocabulary); hence also the arguments and debates between musicologists over the correct performance of 'ancient music', where the notation seems 'incomplete'. But no system of notation can ever be complete; there will always be elements that escape notation because of their subtlety and their spontaneous and elusive nature. The real problem is something else: the eventual loss of the tradition that governed the score's interpretation. The paradox is that recording has not, as one might first suppose, detained this process, but seems instead to have accelerated it, reducing the idea of a traditional style of performance to a chimera.

The advance of notation had the effect of forcing the musical text into a peculiar kind of straitjacket – invisible and enormously elastic – in which many of these elements were either demoted or repressed. Some were removed from the conscious deliberation and control of the composer and consigned to the mystique of performance and the great virtuoso, like the slides and vibrato of a Pablo Casals. Other elements were expelled from the 'civilized' Western musical idiom altogether. The notes of the scale were reduced to what John Cage once called 'those stepping stones twelve in number', thus eliminating the quarter-tones in between – like the inflections that Bartók discovered in eastern European and Mediterranean folk music which became a major influence on his own style of composition. On Bartók's own admission, recording played a seminal role in reawakening his hearing to the presence and significance of these various subtle powers of expression.

The same problem was noted by Federico García Lorca, a musician and collector of folksongs as well as a poet and playwright, who thought the gramophone could be a positive force. 'For ten years', he wrote, 'I've been involved in folklore, but as a poet, not just a scholar … and Falla has already said it: it is not possible to copy down the songs on music paper; it is necessary to collect them with a gramophone so as not to lose that inexpressible element in which more than anything else their beauty lies.'[10] With a few exceptions, he said, Spanish musical folklore suffered unceasing confusion in the business of transcribing melodies, many of which remained uncollected. 'There is nothing more delicate than a rhythm, the basis of all melody, nor anything more difficult [to notate] than a singer of the people who in melodies like these sings in quarter- or third-tones, for which there are no signs in written notation.'[11]

Some of the songs that Lorca collected he recorded at the beginning of the 1930s for HMV, accompanying the singer La Argentinita on the piano. Released in 1931, they were not only an immediate success but several of them were also taken up as fighting songs, with new words, by the Loyalists in the Spanish Civil War, in which Lorca himself was assassinated by the Fascists; 'Anda jaleo' and 'Los cuatro muleros' are probably the best known. Lorca's work was banned in Spain when Franco won, and the records practically disappeared, but they have now been reissued on CD (and make splendid listening). This example must stand in here for the many instances throughout its history when the gramophone, simply by disseminating its wares, has contributed to political movements.

One of the main cultural effects of the expansion of the record industry was indicated by the music critic Jacques Barzun when he wrote that 'This mechanical civilization of ours has performed a miracle ... it has, by mechanical means, brought back to life the whole repertory of Western music – not to speak of acquainting us with the musics of the East.' Formerly, he explained, changes in musical fashion would bury the whole musical past except for a few dozen works. Today, this neglected past has come into its own. 'In short, the whole literature of one of the arts has sprung into being – it is like the Renaissance rediscovering the ancient classics and holding them fast by means of the printing press. It marks an epoch in Western intellectual history.'[12]

It would be difficult to over-emphasize the truth behind Barzun's assertion, in the West at least. The past is returning: to us, if not us to it. The process has gathered pace since the end of the Second World War in the shape of what is known as the early music movement, which has now become one of the major musical trends of our times; indeed it has been reported that Christopher Hogwood sells more records than Luciano Pavarotti. Still, an important qualification is needed: the new audience, according to the Italian composer Berio, has little historical sense. It is not really a 'return to the past', he says, because many of those now listening, say, to Bach are unaware of Bach's existence, and have no historical taste for musical chronology anyway. 'For many young Italian people twenty years ago, the "cool" improvisations "à la Bach" of the blind pianist Tristano and real Bach were practically the same thing. And the same goes for real Mozart and Mozart sung as an eight-voice "ba-da-ba-da-ba-da" by the Swingle Singers' (which implies no disrespect for the Swingles' musicianship – on the contrary, Berio wrote them in to his *Sinfonia*).[13]

The musicologist Joseph Kerman has observed that the historical sense in music is much newer than in literature, which has long possessed canonic texts; or in the visual and plastic arts, where museums and galleries have been cultivated since the Renaissance.[14] In a word, the musical tradition is not one of either texts or artifacts, but rather what Roland Barthes, reviving a medieval term, called *musica practica*: the everyday practice of music, as opposed to the theory; music by ear rather than music by the book; the practice through which it lives and breathes, and is transmitted from generation to generation, and which every generation modifies according to its own needs. Consequently, as Kerman puts it, music is evanescent, and until recently the repertory of Western art music, with some exceptions, did not extend back more than a generation or two at any time. Back in 1477, for example, the composer and theorist Johannes Tinctoris claimed that there was no music worth listening to that had not been composed in the previous forty years or so. Almost a hundred years later, in 1569, a certain Massimo Troiano tells us that Lasso's choir at the court in Munich normally sang music no older than that of Josquin, who died in 1521, and his immediate successors. If the late eighteenth century no longer spoke this way about Palestrina, Corelli or Handel, says Kerman, it was only in the nineteenth century that a new historical attitude fully emerged, and Haydn, Mozart, Beethoven, Weber and Rossini are not supplanted by the next good composers to come along. Instead their music was accorded a place in what then became a more or less permanent canon.

The essential change is not difficult to identify: it belonged to the institutionalization of bourgeois culture and its claims to universality, which includes taking possession of history. But the consequent canonization of the great composers has been challenged by the effects of recording on the available repertoire, especially since the Second World War. In the 1930s, the canon, according to Penguin Books' *Lives of the Great Composers* in three volumes, comprised twenty-nine names. They end with Debussy, Wolf and Elgar, and prior to Bach include only Byrd, Purcell and Palestrina (omissions include Vivaldi and Mahler). The era of the long-playing record, however, began to break the mould. In spite of the continued over-representation of the canonic composers in the record catalogues, it is no longer possible to limit 'the greats' to the previously established list – nor to see the music of the nineteenth-century bourgeoisie as the peak towards which all previous music unknowingly aspired. From Perotin and Landini, Machaut and Dufay, to Josquin, Jannequin, Tallis, Lassus, Dowland, Gesualdo and Monteverdi, the number of once-forgotten claimants to recognition begins to weaken the very idea of a canon. This is better understood as the constant renewal of music to be found since the beginnings of modern notation in a succession of paradigmatic works by paradigmatic composers. However, this is not a question of theoretical constructs but of actual practice: the constantly evolving daily practice of music-making through which musical traditions are passed from generation to generation. Again, a question of *musica practica*.[15]

At the same time, the record industry has hugely expanded a corpus of music equivalent to the yellow press, pulp novels and comics brought about by technological advances in the print industry in the latter part of the nineteenth century. Indeed among French music publishers the generic term for this sector of commercial music production is *musique-papier* – music that is effectively worth little more than the price of the paper it is printed on. This kind of output, already well developed in the nineteenth century, nowadays accounts not only for 90 per cent of the market but constantly assails us in the form of sonic wallpaper. It is almost entirely ephemeral (which is not the same as evanescent). This was the phenomenon that Adorno, the most stringent critic of the culture industry – and one of the group at the Frankfurt Institute for Social Research between the wars who coined the term – analysed in terms of 'perennial fashion'. Its basis is economic: competition on the culture market has proved the effectiveness of certain techniques (syncopation, semi-vocalized instrumental playing, impressionistic harmonies, etc.) and these techniques are then kaleidoscopically mixed into novel combinations, says Adorno,

> without there taking place even the slightest interaction between the total scheme and the no less schematic details. All that remains is the results of the competition,

itself not very 'free', and the entire business is then touched up, in particular by the radio. The investments made in 'name bands', whose fame is assured by scientifically engineered propaganda; and even more important, the money used to promote musical bestseller programmes like 'The Hit Parade' by the firms who buy radio advertising time, makes every divergence a risk.

Standard procedures that have been perfected over long periods of time produce standard reactions. Not only that, but the deviations are as standardized as the standards. The result is that everything is always new and always the same.[16]

Unfortunately, despite his pioneering critique of the culture industry, Adorno is not the best guide to the aesthetics of popular culture, for he discounts the real distinctions which nevertheless develop between and within the genres of popular music. This neglect, shared by authorities who are ideologically his opposite, conceals the enormous capacity of popular music of every kind for regeneration, a capacity that has been fuelled by recording. It is to make the same mistake as supposing, for example, that ethnic musics are essentially remnants of past musical cultures that have survived into the present. If there is one thing in common between the different musical traditions nowadays labelled as 'world music', it is that they are all in a state of flux – often explosive – as they re-create themselves through the very encounter with other musics which the age of electro-acoustic reproduction has brought about.

The truth is that many traditional music cultures already present a history of cultural encounter, for few were untouched by the histories of colonization, ancient and modern, which always carry music with them. But it is also true that the gramophone was responsible, almost from the start, for re-creating the repertoire it recorded in its own image. The process began with early record producers scouting for talent and choosing artists whom they considered to suit the medium, but they could also be more proactive. In India, for example, on the eve of the First World War, according to the memoirs of the grand-daddy of record producers Fred Gaisberg, The Gramophone Company set up what he calls 'training centres' to turn out popular recording artists: the company engaged musicians to teach them and to set poems to music for them to sing, thereby generating a supply of two to three thousand new songs every year.[17] Like the same kind of output wherever it occurred, these songs were highly formulaic. The result was to help secure a near monopoly for the company in the production of popular recorded music in India which had a strong influence on the emergence of the Indian film musical in the 1940s and lasted until the coming of the cassette. But in every continent, whether by this kind of deliberation or by a kind of musical Darwinian selection, the gramophone began to shake up popular music from the moment of its arrival, and the contemporary shape of music worldwide is the result. Ironically, perhaps, the paradigm for this process is found in the United States, and is exemplified by the evolution of jazz and blues into the myriad forms of urban popular music, both black and white, from rock 'n' roll to rap. For neither jazz nor blues would have acquired their universal appeal and global reach without the record industry, which served, symbiotically with radio, as their principal means of dissemination.

Still, part of what Adorno argued remains largely true: that the greater part of the music engendered by mass production is composed almost as mechanically as it is reproduced. Indeed the term 'Tin Pan Alley' – originally a nickname for the street in New York where the new commercial music publishers of the 1890s had their offices – has long been identified with the practice of 'manufacturing' songs by assembling ready-made parts in new permutations. But the most extreme case is piped music and its progenitor the Muzak Corporation, set up in 1934 to provide music over telephone lines for distribution by loudspeakers at the destination. Or as a company vice-president put it in 1977, 'functional music as a tool of management in environmental situations. We furnish music in work areas, primarily in offices and factories ... sequentially programmed in such a way as to have an ever-rising stimulus curve.'[18]

The original idea, she says, was the brainchild of a Signal Corps officer in the US Army called Squire back in 1922, when radio was still in its infancy, who devised a scheme for sending music from phonograph records to domestic telephone subscribers – '[he thought] it would be great for housewives'.[19] Not in fact a new idea, but the revival of a promotional gimmick of the early years of the telephone, when subscribers were offered relays of concerts and operas. The 1930s brought investigations into the physical effects of music by behavioural psychologists, who demonstrated the beneficial result of hearing music in the background; in England a study by S. Wyatt and J.N. Langdon called 'Fatigue and Boredom in Repetitive Work' became influential, and stimulated a wartime government request to the BBC to broadcast appropriate music in the afternoons to combat fatigue on assembly lines ('Music While You Work' continued until the 1950s). In America, Muzak began by 'transmitting in New York on direct power lines, originally just to hotel dining rooms and restaurants' and then switched to the workplace after it was bought up by a senator who was also a director of Encyclopaedia Britannica. It succeeded over the years in branching out into selling 'atmosphere' music to factories, restaurants, banks, hotels, salons, clinics, swimming pools, stadiums, parks, even garbage dumps, and since the end of the Second World War the business has spread worldwide. According to the French economist Attali, music here becomes the object 'of a treatment akin to castration, called "range of intensity limitation"' which, far from stimulation, consists in a dulling process. The music to be used is classified by genre, length and type of ensemble, and is nowadays programmed by a computer into sequences of 13.5 minutes on 8-hour tapes to suit both the locale and the time of day – not too much brass for breakfast, songs with string accompaniment for lunch; for the factory or office, encouraging rhythms at 10.30am and in the middle of the afternoon. As another Muzak executive says, 'We do not sell music; we sell programming.'[20]

The gramophone record itself is only a single element in the industry that has grown up around it, which not only creates the commodity but also the conditions of its purchase. The techniques of advertising and marketing, which feed the flow of magazines for record collectors, turn it into a business of promotion, manipulation and 'hype' whose function is not only the creation of demand but also of the model consumer. The ingenuous words of a columnist in *The Times* celebrating the centenary of Edison's invention reveal how far this seduction went:

> There is something intrinsically pleasurable about the whole process of selecting, buying and playing a record. Indeed the dedicated hi-fi enthusiast probably derives as much pleasure from browsing through his collection, extracting the record from its sleeve, carefully cleaning the surfaces, and adjusting the controls of his hi-fi, as from listening to the music.[21]

It emerges that in the 'classical' market too, the effects of reproduction include changes in musical perception that are not so easy to celebrate. People buy more records than they can listen to, observes Attali; they stockpile what they think they'll find the time to hear, and when they listen to them, as often as not it is either as background music, or else, conditioned by the propaganda of the market, they sit in front of their hi-fi sets like recording engineers, in acoustical judgement.

This is not just a caricature from the pages of hi-fi magazines. A mutation of musical communication has occurred in which live perform-ance has become a mere adjunct to most people's musical experience, which now comes to them overwhelmingly through loudspeakers and even earphones. Our musical experience is now predominantly what Pierre Schaeffer, the pioneer of *musique concrète*, called 'acousmatic': sounds that one hears without seeing their source. The modern mother is invited to lull her baby to sleep with a cassette, instead of singing a lullaby herself. The integrity of the musical work of the past, its intimate unity with the time and place of performance, what Walter Benjamin called its aura, has been destroyed. Music has become literally disembodied, and the whole of musical experience has been thrown into a chronic state of flux. In these circumstances, in which ubiqitous mechanical reproduction pushes music into the realms of noise pollution, it often seems that musical values must inevitably become relative. And this is both a symptom and one of the causes of the condition of postmodernism.

Within this uncontrollable acoustic chaos, recording has two quite distinct effects. On the one hand, the individual record remains fixed, and robs the performance of its sense of spontaneity. By making a perform-ance repeatable, it gives it an authority that is entirely foreign to its nature – or was, until it began to affect the art of interpretation. As Attali puts it, 'little by little, the very nature of music changes: the unforeseen and the risks … disappear in repetition. The new aesthetic of performance excludes error, hesitation…'[22] It freezes the work; it reifies the human voice and hand. A new kind of performer is needed, the virtuoso of the repeated take. The effect is different in different musical camps. In pop music, this tendency leads to products that depend entirely on recording technique, and which cannot be performed live at all.

Paradoxically, however, recording also returns to *musica practica* some-thing of its primacy, because it encourages imitation; and this effect is also different in different camps. In jazz, recording played a crucial role in the rapid and extremely wide diffusion of the music; many jazz musicians who grew up in the 1920s and 1930s have spoken of how they first developed their instrumental technique by copying records. But the role of the record was not to substitute for the written score, which did not exist in jazz; it communicated what cannot be indicated in any score, the nuances of articulation and timbre which are among the central stylistic concerns of jazz. The aim of jazz is to achieve a sense of the spontaneous through sophisticated and controlled improvisation, to be a music which never stands still; the record is a means to an end.

In the case of pop music, it becomes an end in itself. As Tin Pan Alley takes second place to Top 40 radio, and sheet music loses its position as the main distributed form of the pop song, it is the record as a musical object which becomes the primary form in which the song circulates. Again, the untutored learn by playing along with the record and imitating it. As the rock critic Simon Frith has written, 'Rock history has always been about musicians finding their own voices in the process of trying *unsuccessfully* to sound like someone else.'[23] Yet this only makes the style and intonation of the singer ever more important, often much more so than what is being sung; and the record industry encourages this kind of naive talent precisely because, in being untutored, non-professional and unorganized, it is easy to exploit.

In classical music, the record ends up engendering the appearance of a new category, the 'historical recording', in which yet again the qualities of performance are generally more important than what is performed: the resurrection of an old recording in a previous format, which now acquires, if not the aura, then at least the sheen of authenticity. Fostered originally by radio stations like BBC Radio 3, who were able to draw upon their own archives, the record companies then began to follow suit. The whole business is now highly ecological. Every time a new format is introduced, the previous format becomes an archive to be recycled, by reprocessing old recordings and reissuing them. Not only that, but the archives seem to grow ever larger, as old unissued recordings are discovered and brought out for the first time. The result is another potential change in musical consciousness, for as we shall see later, it gives back to us the history of recording as a history of interpretation.

★

Is it only coincidence that over the same period as the introduction of the new technology of reproduction, the Western musical tradition experienced a revolution in its every aspect? Figures like Debussy, Schoenberg, Berg, Webern, Bartók and Stravinsky turned it inside out and upside down, which not only left it utterly transformed but also became paradigmatic for the whole modernist movement. At the same time, popular music underwent an unprecedented explosion as a new Afro-American music burst forth and rapidly spread abroad, which reintroduced in the process many of the elements of expression that had become lost to the classical tradition. I hardly want to suggest that technology was the sufficient cause of these profound transformations, but neither is it neutral, or merely secondary to aesthetic and even spiritual processes. In the view of Simon Frith, recording enabled aspects of performance previously unrepeatable, like improvisation and spontaneity – to be reproduced precisely, 'and so enabled Afro-American music to replace European art and folk musics at the heart of Western popular culture'.[24]

For Adorno, the introduction of the gramophone was a crucial determinant of the musical process in the twentieth century, just as photography was of painting. The liberation of painting from objective representation constituted a defence against the mechanization of representation by photography and the consequent cheapening of the image. In the same way, art music reacted against recording and the attendant commercial degradation of music by freeing itself from the traditional harmonic idiom. Because the music industry was handed over almost entirely to the disposal of 'artistic trash and compromised cultural values', which catered to 'the socially determined predisposition of the listener', radical music was forced into complete isolation – Adorno is thinking essentially of Schoenberg, whose response to these conditions was the most thorough-going and uncompromising, and whose music was for many years unrecorded.[25] In this equation, the abandonment of tonality equals the abandonment of representation and atonality equals abstraction. But this is only part of the story. Walter Benjamin remarked that 'much futile thought had been devoted to the question of whether photography is an art. The primary question – whether the very invention of photography had not transformed the entire nature of art – was not raised.'[26] Could the same not be said of recording – that it has transformed the very nature of music?

If, following recent writers like Jacques Attali, one thinks of music as a barometer of wider cultural forces, there have been two main phases. The first corresponds to the process of modernization from the late nineteenth century to the 1930s; the second, which follows the Second World War, ends up in the cultural stage that has been called the postmodern. To follow David Harvey's incisive analysis in *The Condition of Postmodernity*, the process involved the transformation of the daily experience of time and space which is integral to the development of industrial capitalism, from steam ships, railways and the telegraph, to jet air travel, communications satellites and the digital computerization of information. As modern technologies of communication have progressively shortened the horizons of time and space, says Harvey, 'so we have [had] to learn how to cope with an overwhelming sense of compression of our spatial and temporal worlds'.[27] Here, then, is one of the fundamental causes of both our modern disenchantment and the artistic revolution of the twentieth century. How could the old conventions survive when, as the painter Léger put it, 'A modern man registers a hundred times more sensory impressions than an eighteenth century artist'?[28] At a critical moment, in the years leading up to the First World War, the sense of plight overwhelmed each of the traditional forms of artistic expression in turn: not just music but painting, sculpture, dance, drama, the novel, poetry and architecture, all experienced the process of disruption and renewal identified with modernism. The whole business was thrown into relief by the birth of a new aesthetic medium which was itself a technological product of the process of modernization: the medium of the film provided novel means for reconstructing the experience of time and space in terms of each other. Recording is an integral element of this process because, like photography and the telephone, it conquers time and space. It separates the place and time of audition from the place and time of performance, paradoxically giving the experience of modernity a sound in the very act of preserving the voice that fades as it sings.

Modernity lies in the reputation of the effects of modernization. What we now think of as the media are implicated as both symptoms and agents of the whole process. 'If there had been no railway to conquer distances', writes Freud in *Civilisation and its Discontents* (which dates from 1930), 'my child would never have left his native town and I should not need the telephone to hear his voice; if travelling across the ocean by steamship had not been introduced, my friend would not have embarked in his sea-voyage and I should not need a cable to relieve my anxiety about him.' At the same time, new techniques remove the limits of human powers, whether motor or sensory, and extend their range. In the photographic camera, says Freud, we find 'an instrument which retains the fleeting visual impressions [of our eyes], just as the gramophone disc retains the equally fleeting auditory ones', adding that both are thus materializations of the power of recollection, of memory.[29]

In the second phase, now known as postmodernism, which has been creeping up since some time after the mid-point of the century, the Freudian memory effect has been overlaid with another factor: the domain of recorded sound has become a kind of continuous present, in which, as old recordings are recycled, memory can be confounded. The condition can also be heard in the cacophony and confusion of contemporary music of all genres bombarding us from all sides, an increasing proportion of which is recycled. But this recycling takes different forms, from the nostalgia racks in the record stores to the inventive recycling of movements like hip-hop. Recent innovations like synthesizers, sequencers and samplers have only intensified the effect by creating their own virtual sound-space where musical sounds – and noise of every kind – become the raw material for reprocessing. On the one hand, the technification of music has not only refashioned the process of listening, but as a result of excessive amplification is also liable to physically damage our hearing. (A recent report places disco music at an intensity of 115 decibels, or 35 decibels higher than the level at which tinnitus, or permanent noises in the ear, begins to become a risk.)[30] On the other hand, it increasingly throws everything back into the arena, as the ease of reproduction allows the circulation of music to escape the control of the market and discover new forms. In short, the old hierarchies of aesthetic taste and judgement may have broken down but music continues to breathe and to live according to its own immanent criteria.

2

From Cylinder to Disc

The most frequently cited precursor of the phonograph is a device built by Léon Scott, a French amateur scientist who in 1855 invented an instrument to make a visual tracing of sound vibrations, which he called the phonautograph, or sound-writer; it was manufactured by a Paris firm for some years as a scientific instrument for laboratory research. The mechanism consisted in a membrane stretched over the small end of a cone hinged to a wooden lever; at the other end of the lever a pig's bristle was suspended over glass or paper covered with lampblack, such that by speaking into the cone while the glass or paper was moved beneath the bristle, a tracing of the pattern of the sound waves would be produced. Scott's device belonged in turn to a long line of experiments concerned with acoustical analysis which would also issue in the telephone. Bell, in 1874, built a macabre version, using a dead man's ear rigged up to a metal horn with an armature and stylus attached to the ossicles. Three years later, another French amateur presented a paper to the French Académie de Sciences describing a process by which a phonautograph could be made not only to trace a sound but to record and reproduce it. Charles Cros was a poet and patron of a literary circle which met at the Chat Noir, the famous Parisian cabaret frequented by the young Debussy, where Satie was employed for a period as a pianist. Unfortunately, Cros never succeeded in attracting the funds necessary to get his invention made.

Back across the Atlantic, Edison had set up the prototype of the modern research laboratory, the famous 'invention factory' at Menlo Park, New Jersey, where he worked with a team of assistants on various projects simultaneously. It is unlikely that Edison knew about the work of Cros, whose proposal was not published until a few months after Edison's first provisional patent. According to Read and Welch, there is little similarity between the device proposed by Cros and the one built by Edison's assistant John Kruesi. Nor is there much similarity between Edison's machine and that of another precursor, a certain F.B. Fenby of Worcester, Mass., who was granted a patent in 1863 for a complicated electro-magnetic device which was also never built but about which this time Edison must have known, for it was Fenby who coined the word 'phonograph'.[1]

Edison, then, was the first to come up with a working prototype. Using a sheet of tin foil wrapped around a cylinder (later replaced by wax), the recording needle was mounted on a screw, so that turning the handle inscribed a spiral groove. Reversing the process, the needle reproduced the wave form inscribed in the groove, and a faint and distorted sound could be heard. Edison's groove was vertically cut; this is known as the hill-and-dale method: Scott's phonautograph and the machine designed by Cros used the lateral cut which would later become standard.

This device, crude but hugely impressive, not only made Edison's name world famous within a matter of months, but it also served to attract the funds that he spent in developing the incandescent light bulb over the next couple of years. But it took almost a decade before Edison's competitors had sufficiently improved the phonograph to re-launch it on the market. The problem was more than technical. Investment in the initial phases of the telephone was underwritten by the immediate functions it served within the infrastructure of communication and social circulation. The telephone, a method of sending the human voice down the wire in place of Morse code, followed the existing model of telegraphy. The telegraph had hugely reduced the time required for communication across great geographical distance, promoting the expansion of the market by speeding the flow of commercial intelligence and international news. The telephone began more modestly, by introducing simultaneous two-way talk within local areas, but this did more than just create new forms of social interaction; it stimulated both the diffusion of information and the growth of local business. The phonograph seemed to promise something similar, but it failed to deliver.

The phonograph served very few immediate practical functions – only Edison's sentimental macho claims: 'We will be able to preserve and hear again ... a memorable speech, a worthy singer ... the last words of a dying man ... of a distant parent, a lover, a mistress'.[2] Most of the uses that Edison imagined were far in advance of its capabilities, for the prototype suffered from the same technical limitations as the first telephones. It is possible that the vocation of the gramophone lay in music partly because music provided a degree of familiarity sufficient to make the imperfect early recording seem, as it were, complete. But this took more than ten years to become evident, and in the meantime Edison lost interest to the point of letting go of control of his patents. (His attention was taken up mainly by electricity. The light bulb was a far more practical form of electric lighting than the arc light, introduced over the preceding decades, and hence the crucial stimulus for the electric power industry. The company that Edison set up to promote electric lighting by building power stations to supply electricity was the ancestor of General Electric. In a word, the light bulb had a rapid multiplier effect, as the expansion of the electricity supply industry in turn stimulated the electric motor and the electrical appliance – both industrial and domestic – and then, with the invention of radio, when the incandescent bulb led to the valve and electrical amplification.)

Nevertheless the phonograph attracted the attention of Bell, who wrote in a letter to his father-in-law a few months after Edison's patent, 'It is an astonishing thing to me that I could possibly have let this invention slip through my fingers when I consider how my thoughts have been devoted to this subject for so many years.'[3] At his new research laboratory in Washington, he and his assistants slowly achieved crucial improvements, like the floating stylus, and a means to turn the cylinder at a constant speed with an electric motor (clockwork motors came later, when electric ones proved too expensive for the early market). The improved Bell machine, the cylindrical 'graphophone', was introduced in 1886, as a dictation machine. His backers managed to buy into Edison's patents, so that he could not block them, and set up companies to manufacture the new model – including the Columbia Phonograph Company. The venture misfired: the machine was far too impractical for the purpose. Growing up under their noses, however, among the showmen who operated in the penny arcades and amusement centres, was a different idea: the coin-in-the-slot machine. Credit for the prototype of the jukebox goes to the manager of a phonograph agency in San Francisco called Louis Glass, who in 1889 equipped his machines with coin-operated listening tubes, took out a patent and introduced them to entertainment saloons. It was this relocation of the market that saved the business from going under and began to push the phonograph in the direction of music. By 1891, Columbia had issued a ten-page catalogue of recordings, ranging from marches by Sousa to comic monologues and 'artistic whistling'.

The telephone too gave evidence of a market for music, a by-product of its appeal as an item of luxury consumption, with a number of experimental relays: in 1880 a concert in Zurich was sent over telephone lines to Basel, fifty miles away; the following year an opera in Berlin and a string quartet in Manchester were transmitted to neighbouring cities, and in 1884 a London company offered, for an annual charge of £10, four pairs of headsets through which subscribers would be connected to theatres, concerts, lectures and church services. Nor were these the only examples. One can think of the phenomenon as a precursor of broadcasting: in Paris and Budapest, on the same principle, all-day news services were available. (The London service lasted until 1904, but the telephone news lines lasted into the inter-war years.)[4] The musical appeal of the phonograph, then, with the superior sound of the improved model of the late 1880s, needs no special explanation. The repertoire, on the other hand, was different from the telephone relays because the phonograph reached out to a popular audience. And then, of course, because the recordings had to be short, popular tunes performed by strong voices and loud instruments were especially suited.

Edison now re-entered the business, supplying cylinders for the coin-machines. (He also applied the same model of exploitation to his next big invention, the technique of moving pictures, and thus, leaving the problem of projection aside, produced the kinetoscope, or 'what-the-butler-saw' machine, thereby further promoting the amusement arcades and accelerating the coming of cinema.) In London, Edison's English agent invited distinguished personages like William Gladstone and Robert Browning to listen to the phonograph and record their voices. The composer Arthur Sullivan gave the most prescient testimony: 'I am astonished and somewhat terrified at the results of this evening's experiments – astonished at the wonderful power you have developed, and terrified at the thought that so much hideous and bad music may be put on record forever!'[5]

The machine was still far from perfect. In 1888, according to a writer in *Scientific American*, the mechanism was 'not yet reduced to that simplicity and perfection of operation necessary for its general sale'.[6] It could not, for example, compare with photography after George Eastman introduced his first push-button Kodak Camera in the same year, advertised with the famous slogan 'You press the button, we do the rest'. But improvement of both the machine and its method of manufacture continued, and produced a spectacular fall in price; an advantage that the manufacturers supported with a supply of pre-recorded cylinders to play on them. In 1888, at $150, domestic purchase was rare, but by 1891 there was sufficient business for the publication of a trade journal called *The Phonogram*. In 1893, the Columbia catalogue ran to thirty-two pages, and listed marches, polkas, waltzes, vocal selections, foreign language courses and recitations. Machines with the new electric motors were still expensive, but by 1894 the latest model with clockwork spring motor was down to $75, and by the turn of the century a serviceable Edison phonograph was only $7.50.

It was Emile Berliner, a German immigrant to the United States, who achieved the improvements that made it possible, as he himself put it, to 'make as many copies as desired', and thus for singers and performers to 'derive an income from royalties on the sale of their phonautograms'.[7] The most important of his innovations was a method of duplication. This consisted in first etching the recording by chemical means onto a metal disc, then producing a reverse metal matrix and using this to stamp the copies. The 'golden discs' that later came to be awarded to the best-selling recording artists are not merely symbolic: gold was found to be the best metal for the master discs.

Berliner was the son of a German–Jewish banker who had worked for Bell Laboratories, went back to Germany to set up a telephone company with his brother Joseph in Hanover, and then returned to America where he set to work on recording. He filed his first patent in 1887, under the name 'gramophone'. The method differed from Edison's device not only in using discs but also lateral cut. A year later he produced his first test recordings and, in 1889, licensed a German toy-maker to manufacture small hand-turned models for the novelty gift trade. The discs to go with them were single-sided seven-inch plates, as they are still called in German, lasting two minutes each; these machines soon turned up all over Europe. In America, the first Berliner discs appeared in 1894, a year after Berliner set up the US Gramophone Company. The simple machines on which to play them sold for a mere $12, much less than cylinder machines.

The discs were originally produced in a hard, vulcanized rubber known as ebonite, a substance resistent to chemical attack and an effective electrical insulator, which was also used for telephone receivers before the adoption of the plastic known as bakelite. Ebonite had the advantage over wax of not wearing out so quickly, but was difficult to press. Berliner found an alternative in the form of a material employed in making buttons by a company in New Jersey called Durinoid. Instead of rubber, the material used shellac, mixed with a number of other substances, to form a lacquered plastic which allowed thousands of discs to be pressed before the stamper showed any signs of serious wear. Shellac itself comes from the secretion of a tropical beetle, the lac, common in India and Malaya; a substance known from early times and used by the ancient Egyptians and Chinese as both a glue and a polish. Shellac discs survived almost unchanged until the 1940s, when the Allied countries were cut off from the sources of supply in the Far East and found a replacement in vinyl, which had been developed in the early 1930s.

Cylinder machines still had certain advantages. One enthusiast, a New York Italian called Bettini, had devised an improved recording mechanism, although his machines and cylinders were costly and restricted to the luxury market. But phonographs fitted with electric motors to drive them were widely available, and the gramophone did not provide effective competition until Berliner attached his own turntable to a cheap spring motor to give it a steady speed. The first spring-driven gramophones were produced in 1896, using a motor developed by a New Jersey engineer called Eldridge Johnson, who ran a machine shop which had a sideline in building prototypes for inventors. Berliner contracted a New York advertising man to market the new model, which sold at $15. Over the next few years, Johnson played a key role in resolving the conflict over rival patents between Berliner and the Bell interests, by which the latter tried to prevent Berliner from using wax to cut his discs.

The solution to the problem of mass reproduction involved the separation of the process of recording from that of reproduction. By 1901, when Berliner joined Eldridge Johnson in the launch of the Victor Talking Machine Company, the mould was already cast. Not only was music more important than speech, but a model of consumption was established which

treated the record like a book, and not like, say, a photograph. The gramophone became an instrument for playback, and a different machine was
needed for recording, which was not marketed to domestic purchasers.
The technical possibilities of amateur and domestic recording had to wait
for the techniques of magnetic recording to reach fruition fifty years later
– while photography became a popular art form.

The advantage of discs over cylinders was decisive. After battles over
patents had been lost and won, the leading companies settled into a cartel
with pooled patents, and the product was progressively standardized by
combining the best features from different systems: pressings in shellac
from a reverse metal stamper of a wax-recorded master, employing a
floating stylus; further technical improvements followed at irregular
intervals, as the new cartel responded to market pressures. In Europe, the
gramophone business was established from the outset along international
lines. In 1898, when The Gramophone Company was formed in England
to exploit the European rights on Berliner's patents, the manufacturing
plant for the operation was located in Hanover, next door to the Berliner
telephone company; it was financed by German capital, and used hydraulic
presses imported from the United States to manufacture and export shellac
discs from masters recorded in different cities throughout Europe and even
further afield.

The best inside account of these developments – though still rather
flimsy – is the memoir by Fred Gaisberg. Gaisberg began his career at the
Graphophone Company, then went to work making cylinder recordings
for Bell's partner Tainter, and ended up in 1896 with Berliner, for whom
he opened what he claims to be the first recording studio a year later in
Philadelphia. He then went to England in 1898 as 'chief recorder and
artist scout' for the new Gramophone Company. He soon began to make
trips through Europe, recording singers in Leipzig, Vienna, Budapest, Milan
and Madrid in 1899, Moscow and Warsaw in 1900, and again a year later,
in between music-hall artists and the like in London. By 1900, the
company's catalogue already offered 5,000 titles, with separate lists of
English, Scottish, Irish, Welsh, French, German, Italian, Spanish, Viennese,
Hungarian, Russian, Persian, Hindi, Sikh, Urdu, Arabic and Hebrew
records. By 1910, a year after Edison was obliged to shut down his cylinder
phonograph plants in Europe, the Gramophone Company had factories
making discs as far-flung as Riga in Latvia, serving the Russian market,

and Calcutta for the East, as well as plants in England, France, Spain and Austria.

Initially, the rather narrow bandwidth of the acoustic needle and the horn favoured the singing voice but was unkind to instruments, especially in groups. It was singers, therefore, who were the first to benefit from the decisive improvements introduced by Berliner, and operatic singers more than popular singers because their trained voices recorded better. According to Roland Gelatt, chronicler of *The Fabulous Phonograph*, it is 'generally agreed today' that Caruso's Milan recordings of March 1902 'were the first completely satisfactory gramophone records to be made'; or at least, Caruso's strong tenor voice (with its baritone quality) helped to drown out the surface noise, so that even on the inadequate apparatus of the time, his records sounded rich and vibrant. Gaisberg tells us that for his ten records in March 1902 Caruso was paid a flat sum of one hundred pounds (at a time when a classical accompanist in a London studio was paid 2s 6d an hour). This was considered excessive by Gaisberg's bosses, but by the time Caruso died in 1921, the gramophone had earned him over two million dollars.[8]

Operatic voices and excerpts played a special ideological role in the early gramophone business. In 1905, the Victor Talking Machine Company of New York took out a series of four advertisements in the trade journal *Talking Machine World*, adorned with photographs of their recording artists. The blurb explained, 'Three show pictures of operatic artists, one shows pictures of popular artists. Three to one – our business is just the other way, and more, too; *but there is good advertising in Grand Opera.*'[9] In other words, the promotion of cultural prestige was a practical business proposition, and it was the records made by the greatest opera singers of the day that set the musical seal of approval on the gramophone. These celebrity recordings (many of them recorded by Fred Gaisberg), which Victor labelled Red Seal, commanded premium prices. Chaliapin's first pressings issued in 1903 were sold in the United Kingdom at twenty shillings, but were quickly snapped up by eager buyers.

The portability of the early recording apparatus enabled agents of the record companies to travel around persuading distinguished singers to record something. The recording process was simple – the singer directed their voice towards the horn. The results were pretty much a gamble. Nellie Melba made a private recording to send to her father in Australia.

She was persuaded to record commercially, and her first records in 1904 had special labels on mauve paper and were priced at a guinea each – a shilling more than Chaliapin or the great Tamagno, the famous *tenore robusto* who had created the role of Otello in Verdi's penultimate opera. Even the aging Adelina Patti, a favourite singer of Verdi's, was persuaded to record.

These early recordings were made in any convenient location, often in hotel rooms. But soon the first recording studios were opened, which improved the results to the extent of providing a separate and quiet location for the recording, though without as yet much in the way of acoustic design. In Paris, among the first to record in a studio was Debussy, accompanying the soprano Mary Garden in some songs of his and an excerpt from *Pelléas et Mélisande*. Bit by bit, recording technique improved, and around 1911 came the first just acceptable orchestral records, although the orchestra was reduced in number and orchestral balance was impaired. Nevertheless, when Arthur Nikisch recorded Beethoven's Fifth Symphony in 1913 with the Berlin Philharmonic, this was comparable in terms of prestige to the records of Patti or Tamagno a decade previously. By this time, Victor's Red Seal catalogue contained some 600 recordings, and they had published an illustrated book of 375 pages called *The Victor Book of the Opera*, which included the stories of the operas and the texts of the recorded arias, and sold for seventy-five cents. Moreover the price of records had fallen significantly, with serious effects in the music industry. Here it was in popular music that the effects were most strongly felt. Publishers, in order to compete with the growing popularity of gramophone records, were forced to cut the price of sheet music; composers and songwriters saw their royalties reduced, without yet seeing very much benefit from mechanical reproduction fees. When radio broadcasting developed in the 1920s, the struggle over the allocation of royalties only intensified.

This sequence of events amounts to the discovery of a new economic law, to go with a new kind of commodity, namely, that of technical linkage, where the commodity takes on a double form – like record player and record – and the market for one is interdependent with that of the other. This in itself is nothing new. There was always a link, for example, between the sale of musical instruments and the consumption of sheet music. What is new is the technification of the process, and the resulting organization of the industries concerned.

Nowadays we think of this link as the relation of hardware and software, but this is a phenomenon that appears in various different guises. The first technology where this relation arose, therefore conceptually the first step towards the distinction, was the telegraph, which created a new kind of commodity in the shape of the message sent down the line, or rather the time it took to send it: the telegraph was the first technology to establish information as a commodity by measuring it. With each new medium since then have come new variants in the character of the linkage, for software takes various forms.

There are important differences between carrier and content. In photography, for example, the camera creates a demand for photographic film, as Eastman demonstrated with the Kodak. The success of the first models, which required that the entire camera was sent back to the factory, where the film was removed, processed, printed and returned with the camera loaded with new film, provided Eastman with a platform for advances in the production of roll film, the basis of the company's future as a monopoly. The phonograph appeared at first not dissimilar: it carried signals by means of fixing them in a novel kind of technical object. In part, this object was like photographic film: a blank on which the user of the instrument inscribed the signal to be reproduced. The phonograph industry, however, was to follow a different pattern from photography. The photograph, once it is printed, no longer needs the camera. In the case of the phonogram, the recording is of no use without the instrument to play it on. The difference is significant.

Technical linkage, then, leads directly to commodity linkage, which takes different forms, like cameras and film, or gramophones and records. Since you cannot have one without the other, this gives rise to a general principle, namely that manufacturers of any new kind of hardware have to concern themselves with the production of the appropriate software without which the hardware has no market. Thus the early producers of cine gear were also film producers and distributors – the very distinctions took time to appear.[10] And the early recording companies made both phonograph and phonogram, record player and record.

Radio, on the other hand, was a different situation. Broadcasting is not like selling either photographic film or records, nor like charging for admission, or even supplying relays to telephone subscribers: broadcasting comes free to anyone with a receiver (until the coming of pay television and subscription channels). The first manufacturers of radios therefore not only had to set up radio stations and produce programmes, but they also had to produce them gratis, because there was no way of selling them. To maximize profits they needed to divest themselves of this function. This accounts for the indirect forms of finance that broadcasting rapidly proceeded to evolve: advertising, the licence fee, or state funding. If the preferred method of American operators was advertising, this reflects the advanced stage of development of the American advertising business, where the first modern agencies date back to the 1840s. American business culture was thus already steeped in the idea of aggressive marketing and quick to spot new opportunities. Commercial radio began to take shape in 1922 when a station owned by AT&T introduced what it called 'toll broadcasting' – that is, sponsorship. But advertising has a peculiar effect. It begins by making a commodity out of the airtime that the advertiser purchases in order to reach the audience, through sponsorship or spot commercials. It ends up by making the audience itself, its size and its social composition, measured by audience research techniques and expressed in ratings, into the commodity that the advertiser buys from the broadcaster, thereby financing the programmes. We shall see later how this affects records and music.

For the early record companies, once they realized that they had to produce recordings too, the main obstacle they encountered to the development of the business was the absence of any method of replicating the cylinder on which the recording was made. On top of which the quality was poor, and novelty value alone attracted little by way of risk capital. As a result, the early growth of the record industry was largely self-contained and did not link up with other forms of entertainment or industrial capital. On the other hand, the business was at first unfettered by problems of musical ownership and the issue of copyright. When the Berne Convention on international copyright was drawn up in 1886, the gramophone was regarded in the same light as musical boxes and Barbary organs. The manufacture of these mechanical instruments was a mainly Swiss industry, and the Convention agreed that mechanical reproduction of music should not count as infringement of copyright, a provision of value to the Swiss industry which did little harm to the interests of publishers or composers. If anything, publishers generally thought that there was good advertising in records, which would result in increased sales of sheet music. The result was that new businesses were free to develop all sorts of mechanical instruments: not only phonographs and gramophones but also the automatic player piano called the pianola, which used perforated rolls and for many years rivalled the gramophone in popularity.

As the century turned, however, and the record industry began to take off, both publishers and judges were prompted to change their attitude towards 'mechanical music'. The French Revolution had introduced the concept of performance rights, since when publishers and composers in several European countries had formed societies to collect them. Now they found that recorded performances were unprotected, and were increasing fast. In Britain, when the appeal courts heard a test case for infringement in 1899, the publishers lost. By 1905, a French court was to rule against unauthorized reproduction of songs and music, and in Italy a year later the Italian Society of Authors and Composers won a suit for royalties on record sales. The same year, however, a Belgian appeal court reversed a similar decision in the case of *Compagnie Générale des Phonographes, Pathé Frères and Société Ullman* v. *Marcenet and Puccini*, on the grounds that the complainants were without rights in the matter so long as the Berne Convention remained unmodified.[11] When the Berne Convention met in Berlin in 1908 the situation was rectified: as well as performing rights, composers and thereby their publishers were now to be given protection against reproduction of their work by mechanical means.

In Britain the law was brought in line by a new Copyright Act in 1911, but the United States, which remained aloof from the Berne Convention, was even quicker off the mark. A number of commercially successful American composers, including John Philip Sousa and Victor Herbert, had watched events in Europe closely, lobbying for the revision of American law and urging the formation of an organization to secure enforcement. As a result, a new Copyright Act introduced in 1909 included provisions for both performing rights and mechanical reproduction rights. In certain respects the 1909 Act was more rigorous than any other copyright law of the time. It provided, for example, for a minimum damage claim against anyone proven of violation, and established a fixed royalty on each record, originally set at two cents. But in the attempt to balance the interests of the publishing and recording industries it also instigated a system of compulsory licensing, which subsequently became universal, under which, once a songwriter allowed their song to be recorded then anyone else could record it as well, subject only to the payment of the required royalty. As a couple of Canadian writers put it, 'This meant that record companies never had to compete for a song, only for the performance of a song.'[12] Five years later, in 1914, Herbert was one of the prime movers in the formation of ASCAP, the American Society of Composers, Authors and Publishers, created to pursue collection of the new rights. The full consequences of this system, however – including the rights of broadcasters to use records which are available on public sale, and the practice of cover versions by contracted artists – would only emerge much later, when signing up the top artists became more important to the record industry than the supply of music, which was easier to acquire.

From the account of Fred Gaisberg it is pretty clear that these first years of international success were based on a modest amount of both capital and technical expertise. Yet despite its late start, the gramophone industry quickly established itself at the same time as cinema and in much the same way – for cinema was also international from the outset – as a paradigm for the development of popular culture in the twentieth century. A certain amount of trial and error was necessary. When the Lumière Brothers launched their Cinématographe, and sent trained agents around the world in 1896 to present the wonder of moving pictures, their main object was to sweep up on the fascination that the new invention created everywhere before rival American inventors caught up with them. If, in adopting this strategy, they did not foresee the huge industry that cinema would grow into, then, considering the career of the phonograph at the time, their attitude was not unreasonable. When Gaisberg started travelling round the world on behalf of The Gramophone Company a few years later, however, largely following the same imperial trade routes, he was able to organize the local phonograph agents he encountered almost everywhere into an international network on which the company's future monopoly power was based. In short, it was the embryo of a new kind of transnational corporation, which has ended up in the creation of a global market – a market dominated from the start by a handful of major companies, which then went on to develop intricate cross-interests in all manner of related (and sometimes unrelated) sectors.

However, the spread of the phonograph was by no means even. Outside Europe, The Gramophone Company had set up a manufacturing plant in Calcutta in 1908, but elsewhere activity was sporadic. In West Africa, their agents were operating in countries like Ghana, Nigeria and Sierra Leone before the First World War, importing records for the amusement of the colonial classes. In East African countries like Uganda, Kenya and Tanganyika, they would also find a market for imports from the studios in Bombay. However, although the first field recordings by ethnomusicologists south of the Sahara date from the same time as Bartók's recording expeditions in eastern Europe, it is not until the 1930s (and again with the exception of India) that recording of indigenous popular music was undertaken commercially. Even then the master recordings had to be sent to Europe for pressing into discs. Or take the case of Venezuela, which has recently been documented by the film-maker Alfredo Anzola. The story is told in a film about his father, Edgar Anzola, a pioneer of Venezuelan cinema, who in the 1930s became one of Venezuela's first producers of both records and radio. (The film is called *El misterio do los ojos escarlata* – 'The Mystery of the Scarlet Eyes' – after the title of his highly popular radio drama series of the 1930s.) According to Anzola *père*, in an interview he gave late in life, the first phonographs arrived in Venezuela before he was born in 1893, cylinder phonographs which passers-by could listen to for a quarter at the stalls in the Plaza Bolivar in the centre of the capital. But the records he produced in the 1930s, which he recorded in the studios of the new Radio Caracas, had to be sent to the United States for pressing. Sixty years later, when his son, to accompany the film, re-issued a selection of these records on CD, the same thing happened again: the transfers to digital tape were made in Caracas, but the CD was mastered and pressed in America.[13]

3

'Polyhymnia Patent'

The audible limitations of the early phonograph were musically restrictive, and remained so, despite a constant stream of improvements, until the introduction of electrical recording in the mid 1920s, when the disc was joined to amplification and the loudspeaker. The principles of electrical recording were not new. Envisaged by Fenby in 1863 and considered by Edison in 1877, a method of magnetic recording was proposed in 1888 by one Oberlin Smith and a prototype along these lines was built in Denmark in 1898 by Valdemar Poulsen – the first wire recorder, which he named the 'telegraphone'. Ancestor of the magnetic tape recorder, it was partly the lack of a means of amplification that prevented successful development of the instrument at the time, the same reason that Edison had abandoned it, with the result that the phonograph became separated from telegraphy and the telephone. But in the meantime, telegraphy led to radio, and radio to the principles of amplification.

The technique of radio transmission (or wireless telegraphy) was first developed in the final years of the nineteenth century by Guglielmo Marconi, an Italian with family connections in England where he found support from the Post Office, the War Office and the Navy. It crossed the Atlantic through the activities of American Marconi, a subsidiary of Marconi's British company. Soon, in place of Marconi's interrupted wave, carrying the Morse code signal in a series of bursts, the Canadian experimenter R.A. Fessenden (who had worked for Edison and then Westinghouse) contrived to send a continuous wave, upon which sound captured by a microphone was superimposed in the form of modulations. (Fessenden's method is known as AM, for amplitude modulation; FM, or frequency modulation, was devised in the 1930s and adopted by the nascent television industry, but not exploited for radio broadcasting till some time after the Second World War.) As the media historian Erik Barnouw recounts, 'On Christmas Eve 1906, ship wireless operators over a wide area of the Atlantic, sitting with earphones to head, alert to the crackling of distant dots and dashes, were startled to hear a woman singing; then a violin playing; then a man reading passages from Luke. It was considered uncanny... '[1]

In the same way that some form of microphone was integral to the telephone, some form of amplification was integral to radio, but workable systems took some years to develop. Fessenden's work incorporated the valve invented by Alexander Fleming in 1903, which was adapted from Edison's incandescent light bulb. Three years later, Fleming's valve became in turn the basis for Lee de Forest's triode, the prototype of the radio valve which magnifies weak signals without significant distortion, the key invention for future developments, on which all amplification systems were based until the coming of the transistor in the 1950s. De Forest had earlier worked for Western Electric, the Bell Telephone Company's manufacturing subsidiary which ran its own research activities, but he developed the valve independently, demonstrating his invention by means of transmissions in New York and from atop the Eiffel Tower in Paris; like Marconi and Fessenden, he made sales to the Navy. In Europe, the work of the German physicist Karl Braun on the electrical properties of crystals meant that radio sets equipped with earphones could be constructed both cheaply and easily, thus creating a movement of radio aficionados. Later, with the introduction of electrical recording, crystals would also be used in gramophone pick-ups, and then in microphones.

By the time the United States entered the First World War, de Forest was transmitting in New York on a fairly regular basis, putting out a variety of material, including music from gramophone records, political speeches, election returns and even once an opera at the Metropolitan. His listeners were not only wireless operators, but the new breed of mostly self-educated electrical mechanics, grand-daddies of the modern radio ham; and in certain places on the eve of the First World War, says Barnouw, 'the air was a chaos of crackling codes, voices and music'.[2] On the outbreak of war, the military stepped in and everywhere the airwaves were banned to amateurs. The incipient free radio movement was suppressed, but as a result of wartime investment, huge technical advances were made and more and more people were trained in the relevant skills; at the end of the war reconversion to civilian uses provided the infrastructure for the development of regular radio transmissions, and broadcasting, a word that until then had meant 'to scatter seeds', acquired a new meaning.

Early radio sets were almost as acoustically limited as telephones, either because of poor microphones, or the limitations of early receivers. Crystal sets became widespread in the early 1920s, in which the weak signal was just strong enough to hear through earphones; some sets were equipped with three or four pairs, and families listened together in their parlours. The first benefit to the listener of valve amplification was that the signal could be used to drive a speaking horn of the kind used by the latest phonographs. The first models were boxes with a horn attached to a magnetic-coil driving unit. The more expensive models were free-standing cabinets, considered by dealers and department stores in the same way as furniture, like the latest phonographs, which already hid their folded horns away inside large cabinets with doors which were opened when you played them.

The prototype for the mechanism employed in these receivers was the moving coil transducer developed by the English physicist Oliver Lodge in the late 1890s, when he was conducting experiments in radio similar to those of Hertz and Marconi. The drawback of the coil-driven horn was that increased amplification also meant increased distortion. Engineers were already at work on alternatives, with the prototypes of the first hornless speakers under construction in various research laboratories in the early 1920s. They included C.W. Rice and Edward Kellog at General Electric, whose design, described in a paper to the American Institute of Electrical Engineers in 1925, provided the basis for all subsequent baffle-mounted speakers.[3] Here, the driving unit is attached to a cone made of thick paper, attached round the outside to a baffle; the paper vibrates in sympathy with the driving unit and thus produces strong and clear soundwaves. The Rice–Kellog dynamic speaker transformed the radio set, which became smaller, clearer and stronger all in one go. It was the growing competition from radio that goaded the record companies to adopt electrical recording in self-defence. The outcome was to intensify and complicate the relationship between the two media.

★

The record industry at first regarded radio as a threat: it promised to compete with gramophone directly on its home ground of domestic entertainment. The gramophone first entered the home as a novelty among the monied classes in the 1880s. Carolyn Marvin, in her entrancing book *When Old Technologies Were New*, quotes a couple of stories culled from the *Electrical Review* in 1888 and 1889 about the phonograph and courting couples. In the first, a suspicious father places a phonograph under the sofa and records an intimate exchange between his daughter and her new beau, which he plays to the family at breakfast. In the second, it is the young lady who uses a phonograph to catch her man:

> 'Did I ever say all that?' he asked despondently as she replaced the phonograph on the corner of the mantle-piece. 'You did.' 'And you can grind it out of that machine whenever you choose?' 'Certainly.' 'And your father is a lawyer?' 'Yes.' 'Mabel, when can I place the ring on your finger and call you my wife?'[4]

Discussions about the phonograph approached it as an invention of great social importance, says Marvin, in which praise for its technical fidelity concealed a more complicated social agenda. There were fanciful speculations about what kind of world it would be if the phonograph had existed in the past, and pointed comments about how the preservation of the sound of Beethoven playing the piano would have banished all the debates about interpreting his metronome marks. In short, the phonograph prompted the idea that sound recording was a means of preserving truth for future generations, and thus 'provided a focus for concern about cultural stability in an era of rapid change'.[5] Music was not nearly as important in this regard as speech, which the telephone propelled towards a new form of social presence. To follow Robert Hopper, in his engaging book *Telephone Conversation*, the impact of the telephone on interpersonal communication, and hence on social interaction, created a new consciousness about spoken language, new patterns of verbal interaction and new forms of social exchange.[6] It is not an accident that the popular name for the phonograph was the 'talking' machine. But the parallel impact of the phonograph on musical communication was never far away.

As the phonograph entered the bourgeois home, there was speculation about its contributions to a middle-class ideal of family life. According to the London magazine *Science Siftings* in 1900, for example:

Nothing is more wonderful, nothing more fascinating than the exploits of a well-trained phonograph. Faithfully melodious, it reproduces again and again the strains sung or prose tit-bits recited in domestic circles; and this sort of thing gives the phonograph a sentimental value that it is difficult to appraise. Appealing thus, to the deepest laid instincts in our nature, there can be no doubt that the phonograph – well made, and put on the market at a price which is reasonable when considered in respect to the mechanical nature and detail of the instrument – will come into world-wide demand. No well-kept, intelligently cared for home will be considered complete without its phonograph.[7]

These speculations are overtaken by the separation of recording and playback which turned the gramophone into a means of consumption of prerecorded discs, but the machine loses none of its fascination – such fascination that in praising its fidelity no one complains about the imperfection of the reproduction. A rare piece of writing to hint at a possible explanation is found in Thomas Mann's novel *The Magic Mountain*, first published in 1924, on the eve of electrical recording, when he recounts the arrival of a new gramophone – one of the latest models with an electric motor – at the Berghof Sanatorium. A new device for the entertainment of the patients, it was not an optical toy like the stereopticon or the kaleidoscope which they discovered one evening in the salon, and greeted with applause, and those simple devices were not to be compared with it – they were outclassed, outvalued, outshone. 'Newest model,' the Hofrat said, 'Latest triumph of art ... a Stradivarius, a Guarneri; with a resonance, a vibration – *dernier raffinemang*, Polyhymnia patent, look here in the inside of the lid ... The truly musical, in modern, mechanical form...'

Mann manages to capture the power attained by the reproduction in spite of its imperfection:

> They listened, their lips parted in smiles. They could scarcely believe their ears at the purity and faithful reproduction of the colour of the wood-wind. A solo violin preluded whimsically; the bowing, the *pizzicato*, the sweet gliding from one position to another, were all clearly audible. It struck into the melody of the waltz, '*Ach, ich habe sie verloren*'; the orchestral harmony lightly bore the flattering strain – enchanting it was to hear it taken up by the ensemble and repeated as a sounding *tutti*. Of course it was scarcely like a real orchestra playing in the room. The volume of sound, though not to any extent distorted, had suffered a diminution of perspective. If we may draw a simile from the visual field, it was

as though one were to look at a painting through the wrong end of an opera-glass, seeing it remote and diminutive, though with all its luminous precision of drawing and colour. The vivid, consummate piece of music was reproduced in all the richness of its light-hearted invention.[8]

The clue is in the last couple of sentences. The reproduction is imperfect, but complete; a reduction of the original, lacking only in body.

Mann describes the way that his protagonist, the introspective Hans Castorp, gives up playing patience and becomes absorbed in this 'sar-cophagus of music', the gramophone. His favourite records are *Aida*, *Prélude à l'après-midi d'un faune*, *Carmen*; his best time for listening is in the evening, after everyone else has gone off to bed: 'He found there was less danger than he had feared of disturbing the nightly rest of the house; for the carrying power of this ghostly music proved relatively small. The vi-brations, so surprisingly powerful in the near neighbourhood of the box, soon exhausted themselves, grew weak and eerie with distance, like all magic.' In this very self-absorption, Castorp develops the symptoms of what a later generation calls the audiophile.

> He bit his lips in chagrin when the reproduction was technically faulty; he was on pins and needles when the first notes of an often-used record gave a shrill or scratching sound … Sometimes he bent over the whirring, pulsating mechanism as over a spray of lilac, rapt in a cloud of sweet sound; or stood before the open case, tasting the triumphant joy of the conductor who with raised hands brings the trumpets into place precisely at the right moment. And he had favourites in his treasure-house, certain vocal and instrumental numbers which he never tired of hearing.

Indeed Castorp became so wrapped up in this private experience of listening to the gramophone that he dreamed of the thing.

> He saw in his sleep the disc circling about the peg, with a swiftness that made it almost invisible and quite soundless. Its motion was not only circular, but also a peculiar, sidling undulation, which communicated itself to the arm that bore the needle, and gave this too an elastic oscillation, almost like breathing, which must have contributed greatly to the *vibrato* and *portamento* of the instruments and the voices. Yet it remained unclear, sleeping as waking, how the mere following out of a hair-line above an acoustic cavity, with the sole assistance of the vibrating

membrane of the sound-box, could possibly reproduce such a wealth and volume of sound as filled Hans Castorp's dreaming ear.[9]

The only thing that Hans Castorp has in common with Antoine Roquentin, the narrator of Sartre's novel *Nausea* (which dates from 1938), is that both are the most intense introverts; their musical tastes, however, are poles apart. Symbolizing the distance between the last great epic novelist of the old school and the prime mover of existentialism, what absorbs Roquentin's ear are American 'coon' songs, like 'Some of These Days'. But both find similar self-absorption in their favourite records, and the same escape from the awfulness of immediate existence. 'Madeleine turns the handle of the gramophone ... another few seconds and the Negress will sing. It seems inevitable, the necessity of this music is so strong: nothing can interrupt it, nothing which comes from this time in which the world is slumped ... ' Roquentin is struck by the strange disparity between the power of the music and the material object holding the groove; in his nauseous state it makes him anxious: 'it would take so little to make the record stop: a broken spring, a whim on the part of Cousin Adolphe. How strange it is, how moving, that this hardness should be so fragile. Nothing can interrupt it but anything can break it.' But the effect is devastating: it banishes his nausea: 'It filled the room with its metallic transparency, crushing our wretched time against the walls. I am *in* the music.'[10]

He is telling the truth. An elusive truth about an experience that is nonetheless common to our modern reproductive culture. This machine and these strange objects, which resemble nothing that has gone before, transport us beyond the everyday world and the physical limits of our existence. Only make no mistake: this is not Caliban's island, full of noises that give delight and hurt not, a brave kingdom where we shall have our music for nothing. There is a heavy price to pay.

What happened to musical culture in the space between Mann and Sartre, Castorp and Roquentin, is that recording transformed it. Figures are hard to come by, but several references in the scant literature all indicate that from very early on the sales of the popular repertoire far outstripped, *in toto*, those of the classical. Although it was opera singers like Caruso who first achieved the greatest sales, this is because opera was international; popular music at the beginning of the century was rather less so. While composers for the musical theatre, like Offenbach, Lehar and Sullivan, could score foreign successes, the informal genres of café entertainment, music hall and vaudeville were dominated in each country by the local vernacular, the work of local producers, both songwriters and publishers. The scales were tipped, however, by the simple demand that mechanical reproduction created for more and more music, beyond the capacity for any national music industry to supply. The same thing happened in cinema.

The one exception was the United States, where the late nineteenth-century development of popular entertainment circuits had stimulated a wave of new activity among music publishers. In the 1890s, when they began to gravitate to 28th Street in New York, a columnist in the *New York Herald* likened the noise going on there to the clashing of tin pans, and the term 'Tin Pan Alley' took root. This new breed of publishers, many of them songwriters themselves, proceeded to develop new formulae to govern the production of songs expressly designed for commercial exploitation. The heyday of Tin Pan Alley was the first decade of the century, when almost 100 songs sold over a million printed copies each. The gramophone would extend Tin Pan Alley's market, but also take up and disseminate an entirely new musical repertoire from a marginal source, forcing the publishing trade to adapt its thinking. By the mid 1920s, a new musical idiom, based on jazz and the blues, had taken over large parts of commercial popular music, and was beginning to invade foreign shores.

Black American music began to make its presence felt more widely in the years that followed the American Civil War, through forms ranging from the spiritual in the 1870s to ragtime in the 1890s. In a situation in which the bitterness of southern whites towards their emancipated slaves hardened into the segregation laws, music became a vital form of assertion of black indentity. Some of it got written down by educated black musicians like Scott Joplin in the 1890s or W.C. Handy a dozen years later, providing Tin Pan Alley with the means of appropriation. Joplin, for example, by showing how to notate ragtime, provided the source of what the black writer Nelson George calls 'the most popular "pop" style' of the first two decades of the twentieth century, which was 'utilized profitably by any number of white composers'.[11] Irving Berlin, for example, wrote

'Alexander's Ragtime Band' in 1911 – around the same time that W.C. Handy began to write down the blues.

Jazz first emerged around the turn of the century in New Orleans, where it was fed by a rich local musical tradition which had been fostered by the period of French rule. Here plantation slaves had been allowed the cultural expression of their African origins which was denied by Anglo-Saxon slave owners. Moreover, New Orleans was a highly musical city – it supported three opera companies and its first black symphony orchestra was formed in the 1830s. The first jazz musicians were semi-professionals – they listed their skilled trades as their primary occupation. They made music in the marching bands, and were hired to play in the tradesmen's clubs, at the picnics that were one of the features of New Orleans life, at weddings and funerals. The more they began to rely on music for their livelihood, the more dependent they became on the club owners, and on vaudeville and medicine shows and the show people who ran them. But since the music was improvised, they escaped the reaches of the music publishers, and the idiom was able to develop in conditions of direct relationship to its audience. As a result, the economic basis for the growth of jazz lay, like its vocal counterpart, the blues, in the various forms of low-class musical entertainment; in particular, as dance music on the black entertainment circuits, as a component of vaudeville, and in cabaret (which would later evolve into the jazz club).

Jazz and blues, with their roots in improvisation and oral tradition, initially lacked notated forms at all. The first written blues (using the twelve-bar shape which would later influence rock 'n' roll) were published around 1913–15, rapidly followed by the first recorded blues. It is commonly reported that the first jazz records were made in New York in 1917 by a white ensemble calling themselves the Original Dixieland 'Jass' Band. In fact, as Christopher Small comments in his study of Afro-American music, *Music of the Common Tongue*, ragtime and the kind of instrumental novelty numbers that formed part of the ancestry of jazz were being recorded as early as the 1890s.[12] If the white Dixielanders were widely distributed and promptly imitated then this only confirms that the new music was already in the air and its exploitation on record only awaited the signal of success – whereupon the dissemination of the new idiom was extremely rapid. In the process the music prospered, but it was also transformed. In the shape of white imitators and commercial genres, it would lose its edge as the music of an oppressed people giving voice to their being and their soul; at the same time, black musicians, forever re-asserting their identity, would repeatedly reclaim the music for their own and propel jazz constantly forwards. But even in the white commercialized forms in which it first spread abroad, jazz was both infectious and threatening to established social mores. Walter Benjamin, reporting from Moscow in 1927, comments on the confusion that jazz had caused within the Communist Party. On the one hand, it was extremely popular, which Benjamin considered 'not surprising'. On the other, it was regarded officially as a symbol of the decadence of bourgeois society, and dancing to it was forbidden. 'It is kept behind glass, as it were, like a brightly coloured, poisonous reptile, and so appears as an attraction in revues.'[13] This was not so very different from its reception by white 'society' in New York or London, except that dancing was allowed.

Jazz musicians provided backings for the classic blues recordings of the 1920s, which followed the discovery of a record market among the black population. This market for what were called 'race records' took shape in 1920 when Mamie Smith scored an unexpected success with a couple of recordings on the new Okeh label. The term 'race' was not a derogatory one at that time; on the contrary, in the black press of the 1920s prominent black leaders were referred to as race spokesmen, although a year later, when W.C. Handy set up one of the first black record labels, Black Swan (which was bought by Paramount three years later), his sleeve advertising boasted 'The only records made entirely by colored people' and 'The only records using exclusively Negro voices'. The economic basis of the explosion of the race market was the low costs of entry into the business. According to one source, at the beginning of the 1920s each disc cost twenty cents to manufacture and it needed a sale of only 5,000 copies to cover the costs of production.[14] By 1927 some 500 race records were being issued each year, although many were of inferior technical quality. As a recent reviewer observes, they were often 'so cheaply made that they would sometimes wear out after just fifty plays … Small wonder … that the records have become such rarities.' Indeed, since unsold records were destroyed, only the very biggest hits have survived in appreciable numbers.[15]

Singers like Mamie Smith, Sophie Tucker, Ma Rainey and Bessie Smith were vaudeville artists who did twelve-bar, somewhat urbanized blues with the backing of a jazz pianist or a small band. Confronted by the limits of recording, many blues singers responded by simply stringing together a few stanzas on the same subject, but the best attempted some kind of narrative continuity and unity. In this way the ten-inch, 78 r.p.m. disc gave a home to the genre called the 'classic blues'. The record companies sponsored and encouraged the blues partly because the songs were based on folk material, and therefore did not cost them copyright; indeed it permitted them to copyright what they recorded as new songs and secure royalties from them, a practice that developed apace when the majors entered the market with their own specialty labels. Musically, however, recording promoted the blues because it extended the reach of those parts of the music that were beyond the capacity of the printed form – especially the intonation of the voice, its tone-colour and its nuances. Records carry the performance to the hearing of those who have never witnessed the performer live; they have documentary value, but what they document, which could never be documented before, is the performance rather than the piece. As Evan Eisenberg puts it in his book *The Recording Angel*, 'Whereas Bessie Smith had needed to go on the road with Ma Rainey in order to learn from her, Victoria Spivey and Billie Holiday and Mahalia Jackson could learn from Bessie Smith by staying put in Texas or Maryland or Louisiana and playing her records.'[16] What they learnt this way was therefore not only songs but also a way of singing, which could not be communicated on paper, and over which, once acquired, they retained control.

Even when the music publishers reasserted their hold over the recorded repertoire, musically their control was limited. According to another writer, black audiences at whom these records were aimed preferred a jazz backing, and the publishers lacked the wherewithal to provide it. The publisher's arrangement, says Mike Hobart in an essay called 'The Political Economy of Bop', could only constitute the broad outline of performance: the proper emphasis and inflection could only be provided by musicians versed in the idiom, in other words, the players in the studio. 'Even in the most regimented contexts, the musician retains a degree of autonomy that is denied in musical forms that can be fully expressed in notated manuscript.'[17]

This was even more true for instrumental jazz, for which, though smaller than that for the classic blues, there was a proven market. But here the record companies were as much at sea as the publishers, lacking the knowledge to make detailed and precise commercial judgements. Musical numbers were often 'composed' just before a recording session: first because record companies did not like to pay royalties unless they had to, and published tunes were therefore avoided; second, because the band was often not a permanent performing group but rather, as on Jelly Roll Morton's New Orleans Red Hot Peppers records of the 1920s, the best musicians available for a given session. So as Eisenberg puts it, 'even regular performing bands, when they recorded, often put aside their well-worn, worked-out routines and threw together fresh ones. A skeletal tune, all ribs and riffs, left plenty of room for powerful new muscle.'[18] In these circumstances, musicians like Morton, or a few years later Louis Armstrong, had an unprecedented degree of autonomy over their product in the recording studios. Away from their regular employment in pit orchestras and dance bands, playing in ensembles that only existed in the studio, they were free to determine the values of their music themselves. For this reason, in Eisenberg's view, records not only disseminated jazz, but 'inseminated' it – made it what it became (a pity about the phallocentric metaphor).

Until the end of the 1940s, says Francis Newton in *The Jazz Scene*, the ten-inch three-minute 78 r.p.m. single side was almost the only format in which jazz was recorded, 'perhaps because the 12-inch, five-minute record was too expensive, perhaps because longer pieces, which involved changing records and breaking continuity, were unsuitable for dance music, almost certainly because it was the cheapest economic unit of record production'.[19] The need to squeeze the music onto the side of a 78 r.p.m. record had a number of different effects, damaging to classical and popular music alike. Since few pieces in the classical repertoire were short enough, tempi were often adjusted, repeats deleted and sections excised, with evident compromise in matters of style and interpretation. But in popular music too, the duration of the record is a highly artificial length of time, shorter than both the normal duration of a single dance and the improvised performance of the folk singer, let alone a protracted jam session. According to the jazz professor David Baker, if three-minute records meant that the solos were of great brevity, then this brevity forced them to be concise, terse and economic, even to the detriment of musical logic. At any rate, they were usually non-thematic and non-developmental, 'because playing thematically demands time for a solo to breathe'. On a three-minute record, he explains, 'if it took forty seconds to play the head (the melody, that is – and everybody recognised the melody) and forty seconds to play the melody on the out-chorus, that didn't leave much in the middle to do. So you didn't lose the audience, because by the time they could get lost, the melody was back again.'[20]

This was very different from live performance, but it also had beneficial effects. As Newton sees it, with the music compressed into the three-minute limit 'musicians were obliged to invent an extremely dense, formally strict, concise form'. They did so with extraordinary success, and 'Constant Lambert was quite right to claim that no orthodox composer could compete with Duke Ellington within this length'.[21] In time this would lead paradoxically to what Baker calls a certain conservatism. 'You can listen to Charlie Parker, who had one of the most inventive minds in the history of music, do three different takes on the Savoy recordings ... and he plays essentially the same solo. Yet in live performance, you heard virtually nothing of the same content in replays of the same piece.'[22] Perhaps a better way of explaining this is in terms of the need in the studio for a measure of time economy. Once an arrangement worked it was a waste of time to develop it any further when repeated takes were necessary for either technical or artistic reasons. Shooting film works the same way.

There were other limitations – acoustic ones. Baker comments on the inability of the early systems to record certain instruments properly, like the string bass, which had to be replaced with other instruments like the tuba. For the same reason a musician called Charles Stroh had invented a special violin for recording, with a diaphragm and horn instead of the normal body, on the strength of which he became a director of a new record company set up in London by Louis Sterling, the future boss of Columbia. These problems affected the instrumental composition of the jazz ensemble, and did not disappear with the electrical systems of radio and electrical recording. In Germany in the 1920s composers like Kurt Weill concerned themselves with questions of how best to score music for the radio. In the 1930s, the needs of guitarists in popular bands in America elicited the electric guitar, with the famous electric bass guitar designed by Leo Fender appearing in the 1950s, when it helped to generate a totally new style of pop music.[23]

There was also the problem of the limited dynamic range of the early gramophone, which affected solo playing by forcing musicians to stay at one dynamic level. The inability to record shading and nuance, says Baker, 'forced the jazz player in the beginning to play much the way boogie-woogie players did: loud, fast, and, in a word, one-dimensionally'.[24] Yet the record also encouraged solo improvisation, and for the same reason – as a solution to the limited technical capacities of the time. The contrapuntal ensemble music of New Orleans jazz was difficult to record, and without the eye to tell the listener who was playing what and when, difficult to listen to. The solo was the obvious musical solution, and paradoxically therefore, the studio was a good laboratory in which to develop the necessary skills.

Indeed the absence of an audience, in other respects a negative factor, allowed the recording session to become an extension of the process of rehearsal, with all the freshness that this brings to the music. And as long as white record producers assumed that black music was crude stuff which required few niceties of direction, the musicians were relatively free to develop their style on their own. The records widely regarded as best exemplifying these conditions are Louis Armstrong's Hot Five series for Okeh records. The Hot Five was almost exclusively a studio band, where Armstrong, who had played second cornet in Oliver's Creole Jazz Band, emerged as a band leader free from the distraction of playing it up for a white audience. In short, if the white take-up of jazz created a problematic relationship to its audience, the recording studio seemed to offer a momentary release.

Recording similarly affected the blues. The creation of a classic repertoire in the form of recordings out of what is essentially an oral tradition had a decisive effect on the future development of the form, by establishing a formulaic vocabulary which made it easier for publishers and their song-writers to imitate. But the effects reached far beyond the control of the market. First there is evidence, according to Paul Oliver, of the influence of recorded blues on folk traditions; and the high proportion of homes with phonographs, even in rural areas, 'probably did much to disseminate blues and to harden its form'.[25] According to one source, between 10 and 20 per cent of rural black Americans in the 1920s had phonographs, and a larger proportion owned records; neighbours without phonographs bought records and played them on their friends' machines.[26] Since the record players were driven by spring motors, the smaller models could be taken along to picnics, parties and other social gatherings, so the music circulated far more widely than simple statistics might suggest.

Oliver adds that the record company talent scouts – precursors of the Artist & Repertory Man – had the role of both promoting the form, and also, 'by the limitations of their taste and spheres of contact ... limiting the range of singers who recorded the material they put on wax'.[27] In other words, anyone seeking 'unpolished' blues would not find it on commercial records, any more than on the radio. The breadth of the folk repertoire is preserved only in field recordings by collectors like Lawrence Gellert and the Lomaxes, father and son, who organized a team of field collectors in the 1930s for the archives of the Library of Congress.

Another writer, Harold Courlander, goes further, arguing that records and radio 'introduced into the development of Negro musical traditions a new element which ought to be called "feedback"'. The process turned the blues into a new vernacular, the lingua franca of North American popular music.

> A traditional type of folksong was picked up by a recording artist and sung in a new way. If the record became popular, a new generation of singers began to utilize some of the personalized contributions of the recording artist. In time, this new version, or elements of it, became, once more, folk music ... One result of this activity is that we may hear cowboy tunes that are reminiscent of Negro blues; blues that sound like the songs of the Golden West; hillbilly tunes and instrumental combinations that gallop through mountainized versions of *John Henry* or *John the Revellator*, with jugs, jews-harps and washtubs; jazzlike treatments of old religious songs; Calypsoish skiffle bands in New Orleans and Mobile; and gospel songs with a suggestion of *Moon Over Indiana* in them. This sort of thing is, of course, not essentially new. Musical acculturation between deep sea sailors and Negro stevedores, between Negro churches and white churches, and between Negro and white railroad workers has been going on for a long time. But the pace and acceleration of cross-fertilization in recent years has probably never been equalled.[28]

Christopher Small, who quotes this passage, argues that recording played a different part in Afro-American music from its role in the classical tradition. First, for the classical musician, playing from the score, the work exists independently of any possible performance of it; the performance is only one instance of it. The classical musician does not feel constrained by this fact: the performer lives for the moment in which the music breathes life, knowing that no two performances are ever quite alike. Consequently, the classical musician (notwithstanding Glenn Gould – but more about him later) becomes suspicious of the permanence of the record. As early as 1919, Busoni, one of the greatest piano virtuosi of the day, complained about the strain and artificiality of recording: 'Not letting oneself go for fear of inaccuracies and being conscious the whole time that every note was going to be there for eternity; how can there be any question of inspiration, freedom, swing or poetry? Enough that yesterday for nine pieces of four minutes each (half an hour in all) I worked for three and a half hours!'[29]

For Afro-American culture, on the other hand, the record is a means, frequently the only means, through which the music is propagated. Posterity does not come into it. In one respect this attitude harks back to the place and forms of music-making in Africa. The African musician's primary responsibility, says Small, is to the occasion and to those taking part in it, and the musician adapts the performance accordingly. As a rule, there is no final form for a piece, which is rather a matrix that can shift and change. Change is constant and often rapid, with new pieces appearing and disappearing in quick succession, although there is always a pool of pieces and songs that retain their appeal (and even these will disappear without regret once they have outlived their social usefulness). Notation, if used at all, has only limited utility, since a fully notated arrangement defeats the purpose.[30] This is like jazz, and completely different from the European tradition of written music which has allowed what the composer–conductor Lukas Foss once called the very unmusical idea of dividing what is essentially indivisible – music – into two separate processes: composition, the making of music, and performance, which is also the making of music. In the African and Afro-American traditions, composition and performance are part of a single act.

If this is no more than the difference between the Western tradition of written music and any oral musical tradition, it accounts for the divergence that results in the encounter with recording. Music in Afro-American culture is essentially an activity constituted by impermanent objects, and the record comes to be treated in the same way. As a matter of fact, says another writer quoted by Small,

> many Afro-Americans in general still tend to regard phonograph recordings more as current duplications (soon to be discarded as out of date) which enable them to reach more people simultaneously than as permanent documents. Euro-Americans, on the other hand, started record collections and archives, which eventually came to include the music of Afro-Americans.[31]

It is only necessary to add that in a consumerist culture, this attitude towards the record as a temporary object of attachment has the fatal flaw that it turns the consumer into the prey of the commercial music producer.

4

Recording Electrified

From the beginning of the century to the start of the 1920s the record industry enjoyed steady growth. Beyond the classical repertoire, the catalogues included popular songs and 'novelty' recordings, march bands and an increasing number of musical theatre hit songs. Since the gramophone followed where Tin Pan Alley led, the growing vogue for rhythmic dance among America's monied classes brought the infiltration of new dances employing Afro-American rhythms: two-step, cakewalk, turkey trot, one-step and the foxtrot. Most of the musicians were white but a few, like the band that accompanied the Castles – America's leading exponents of ballroom dancing – and which recorded for Victor, were black. Victor, valued at $2.72m in 1902, was worth over $33m in 1917. In 1920, Columbia's gross income before tax was $7m, while Victor was making enough to pay out $9m for a 50 per cent interest in the British Gramophone Company with its HMV label, which improved its access to the world market.

The economics of record production during this period are easy to comprehend. The low cost of entry into the business stimulated new labels, catering for relatively small markets, and a distinction appeared between independent companies and the majors. Britain, on the eve of the First World War, had almost eighty record companies, the United States by the end of the same decade almost two hundred. A good many of them, like the Okeh label which was later acquired by Columbia, specialized in 'minority' tastes, especially blues and jazz, known as 'race recordings'. There were also some technical improvements. Columbia introduced a (supposedly) silent record surface developed by engineers in its British branch.

Victor responded by improving the surfaces of its own records and introducing double-sided discs.

The 1920s, however, saw conditions becoming seriously unsettled, the market not nearly as secure as it seemed. The industry was hit by overproduction, falling sales and competition from the new medium of radio, which forced the majors to restructure. In 1922, the American firm of Columbia, in a bid to retain its solvency, sold its prospering British branch to a consortium headed by its general manager in Europe, Louis Sterling. It also put its busy Dictaphone business up for sale, but it was too late. Columbia went into receivership in late 1923 and was subsequently bought up by its erstwhile British subsidiary. Nor did conditions improve: 1924 saw a precipitous decline in sales, and the race for an effective system of electrical recording was on.

Behind this collapse was a curious failure to register the logic of the technology. In the early stages of the industry, the record companies were mostly owned and run by inventors and engineers, stock-market speculators and advertising people, who had little connection with the impresarios involved in publishing, theatres and artist management. They concentrated on international expansion and technical improvement. The business was geared to the manufacture, first, of industrial equipment used to produce records; second, of consumer furniture to play the records on; and third, the records themselves. From the consumer's point of view, the primary commodity consisted in the record; you only had to buy the equipment to play them on once (until you were persuaded that you had to upgrade it). However, from the producer's perspective, records appeared almost as a sideline to promote the sale of furniture, an impression reinforced by the growing splendour of the cabinets in which the gramophone was housed, which incorporated the results of research into the acoustic properties of the horn. The majors, to acquire control over the necessary components and techniques, engaged in cross-licensing agreements, merging when necessary to acquire patents and gain access to technologies. (The same pattern continues to the present, but within parameters much wider than the early years.) But since the separation of recording and playback which solved the problem of mass production, research and development too was fragmented. The result, as Victor's chief engineer of the time later conceded, was a piecemeal approach: 'A complete theory connecting the great series of disjointed facts was still lacking. Development along empirical lines had reached its utmost and the art of sound reproduction had come practically to a standstill in its progress.'[1]

At any rate, it was not the record companies that took the first steps towards electrical recording, but those involved in the development of radio. Research was in progress at Bell in 1919, but it was two British experimenters, Lionel Guest and H.O. Merriman, who gave the first public demonstration of an electrical recording system the following year when they recorded the burial of the Unknown Warrior in Westminster Abbey on Armistice Day. The results were of limited quality, but the two leading record companies in Britain, HMV and Columbia, were sufficiently impressed to conduct – unknown to each other – their own secret experiments, although neither came to fruition. One of the weak links was the microphone. Microphones in the early 1920s were little more than telephone mouthpieces, still using carbon technology. The first effective alternative was a condenser microphone developed at Bell Telephone Laboratories which went into commercial production in 1922 and became widely used in radio. The main advantage was a reduction in distortion and a smoother bass response, but its application was not universal and at the inception of electrical recording some record companies opted for improved versions of the carbon microphone.

The work of Guest and Merriman applied electrical principles to recording but not to playback; their records were made to be played on existing equipment. Electrical playback posed certain technical problems, to do with matching the different sub-systems in the process, and the difficulty of designing a system both reliable and convenient for the user proved more difficult than anticipated. At Western Electric, a research team headed by J.P. Maxfield realized that little was to be gained unless playback was also electrical; otherwise an enormous horn, at least nine feet long, would be needed to register the improvements in recording quality that could be achieved by electrical means. (In fact loudspeakers with large exponential horns were designed for the reproduction of the Movietone talking pictures.) The idea – later called 'backwards compatibility' – was not to alter the disc format but to electrify the recording and playback process in such a way that the new system could still play discs that had been recorded acoustically and acoustic machines still play electrical recordings. Microphones and amplifiers, together with appropriate speakers, not only extended the frequency range of the recorded signal by a factor of four – strengthening the bass as much as the treble – but also permitted a degree of control over loudness and tone.

Maxfield and his team came up with a workable prototype electrical recording system in 1924 and invited representatives from Victor to a demonstration. Western Electric, the manufacturing and licensing division of AT&T, offered Victor the use of patent rights on a royalty basis, but Victor, the industry leader, facing lethargic sales and in fear of radio, dithered. Meanwhile test records were sent to Columbia in London and Louis Sterling was stirred into action. Learning that the struggling American Columbia had also been offered patent rights, but their bankers had balked at Western Electric's price, and since Western Electric would only license foreign production through a US affiliate, Sterling arranged an American loan to purchase a controlling interest in the namesake company in New York. Victor promptly relented and entered the deal, and the two companies then agreed on a joint strategy, which included selling off existing stock cut-price, before the commercial launch of electrical discs in 1925. Sterling made Columbia's fortunes through the deal – Columbia UK, that is. In stark contrast to its American counterpart, Columbia UK went on a buying spree. It acquired Nipponophone of Japan, the German Lindström company, which included German and Italian labels, and the French company of Pathé, together with Pathé Orient and its other Far Eastern branches, and by 1928 had nineteen factories operating or under construction.

The whole episode left an indelible mark on industry lore, for Victor, the industry leader, had been seriously weakened. Profits had fallen from $23m a few years earlier to a mere $123,000 in 1925, although it pocketed orders worth $20m within a week of launching the new system, and its shares began to climb again. But its survival as an independent company was now in question. No major company could any longer afford the risk of not buying into or investing in one line of innovation or another. Indeed this has become a major driving force within the industry, responsible for the proliferation of formats and the rise of new companies quick to exploit them, and with an attendant failure rate due to backing the wrong horse – where now is the eight-track cartridge?

Electrical recording was not just a major step forward in quality; it entailed alterations in both recording practice and the listening experience with

far-reaching implications. According to Read and Welch, the process involved a paradigm shift in the thinking of recording engineers and record
companies. What all acoustic recording engineers were striving for was
greater faithfulness to the source. With electrical recording, they began to
think in terms of creating an aural image. In this they were heavily influ-
enced by radio.

Acoustic recording, say Read and Welch, had generated an unattainable
ideal of realism. But while Edison devoted intensive study to the reproduction of overtones, with the aim of achieving greater brilliance of sound,
differences of opinion arose over the value of reflected sound in the
recording process. In live performance, good acoustics are those where a
measure of resonance contributes to the richness of the sound. Edison, say
Read and Welch, looked upon this reflected sound as 'muddying up' the
reproduction. At Victor and its European affiliates, however, and other
companies like Fonotipia in Italy, engineers found that it helped to allow
a certain amount of ambient resonance, especially if you were trying to
record a large band or orchestra, in order to facilitate instruments that
were further away from the recording horn. Columbia in America tried
to record more reflected sound as a means of getting more bass.[2] Sometimes, whether by careful calculation, or perhaps more often by a fortunate
chance placement, a highly desired 'forward' effect would be achieved,
giving a feeling of presence. Electrical recording brought this effect under
startling new control. According to Gaisberg, the first test pressings made
for Western Electric at the Pathé plant in New York impressed veterans of
the business who chanced to hear them, with their increased volume and
the sibilance of the sound – and this was when they heard them reproduced acoustically.[3] This backward compatibility was crucial to the
successful introduction of the new system.

Another testimony is that of Akio Morita, the founder of Sony, for
whom the experience was decisive. The son of a Westernized Japanese
business family – products such as soy sauce and sake bearing the family
name had won a gold medal at the Paris international exposition of 1899
– he had grown up listening to Western classical music on an acoustic
Victrola. 'Then, when I was at junior high school, an electric phonograph
was imported to Japan from the United States and it was inevitable that
we would get one ... I will never forget the fantastic sound that came
from the new electrical machine – in comparison of course, to the old

mechanical machine. It was a completely different sound, and I was absolutely astounded.' He became obsessed with it, not least because it 'could take the same old scratchy, hissing records we knew so well and make them sound marvellous'. Within months he had managed to build a crude electric phonograph on his own. 'I even made a crude recording of my voice and played it back on my own electric phonograph.'[4] His schooling and the war over, Morita set up Sony's ancestor, the Tokyo Telecommunications Engineering Company, in 1946.

Electrical recording rapidly brought important changes in recording practice. The recording machine could now be removed from the same space as the performers, thus bringing about the design of the modern recording studio with its separate control room, which became the domain of the engineer. The amplifier could be used to modulate the loudness and tone of the performer, while in the studio itself, instead of the musicians directing their sound into a recording horn at full volume, the microphone would free the performers by permitting more natural positions for singers and instrumentalists. In short, electrical recording was conducive to a more relaxed and artistic performance. At any rate, this, according to Read and Welch, was the theory. Moreover it would not be too long before it became possible to use multiple microphones and mix them together during recording, thus compensating, so it was said, for imbalances. From these improvements, they say, came the idea of the reproduction of sound as the creation of an image, a form of projection like the cinema; in other words, a kind of illusion. Advertisements promised to transport the concert hall into the living room or vice versa, but in practice the process was to lead, especially in the case of radio, to the creation of 'calculated effects, of a specious and spurious type of reproduction', which Maxfield himself was soon to criticize.[5]

The advertisements were not just making it up. Two quite contrary philosophies of recording developed. One was based on the conception of bringing the listener into the studio or auditorium. In this method, the microphone was placed at a distance that included the natural room resonance of the studio, or acoustical reflections of the auditorium. An almost unavoidable characteristic of broadcasts of actual performances, the most grievous source of difficulties (say Read and Welch) in the recording of resonant halls or studios, was that multiple reflections resulted in complex wave formations which would mask certain tone colours and muddy rapid passages. The contrary philosophy was the 'close-up' radio broadcast, where small groups of performers would use a small, acoustically dead studio and work close to the microphone. Carried to an extreme, this technique resulted in the vocal 'distortion' of the crooner accompanied by heavy, lush background music, producing an effect of artificial intimacy as if the singer and the song are transported into the presence of the listener.

The only thing missing from this account is an appreciation of the role that is played by the character of radio as a live medium. Radio operates in the present tense, records reproduce a past moment. Radio is ephemeral, records preserve the evanescent. For the recording engineer, the record is not a live medium but precisely a record, which reproduces an original sound. For the broadcaster, the sound at source has no independent integrity and everything is malleable. From here it is only a short step to the notion of radio as a form of aural theatre, exemplified in its populist mode by the rise of the soap opera and the serial in the 1930s, which, modelled partly on cinema, seeks to create an illusory soundscape, palpable but invisible, like a fifth dimension. And this is enough to explain the disregard of numerous radio engineers for the niceties of faithfulness to some unattainable naturalism, and their readiness, on the contrary, to shape a sound which is not intended to be heard other than through a loudspeaker. Here, then, for the first time, there emerges a controversy about the nature of the recording process which has hardly subsided today.

It is hardly an accident that waiting in the wings, ready to pounce on Victor in its hour of trouble, was the new radio giant, RCA. A crucial and uncomfortable symbiosis was to develop between the growth of radio and the record industry, above all in America, where commercial broadcasting was given free play to determine the conditions of the transaction. Records and radio both provided employment to supplement a musician's livelihood. Radio constituted an acoustic showcase for record companies to display their wares. But the power of radio rendered the equations of supply and demand unequal. Radio provided the listener with music much more cheaply than record players (and until the introduction of electrical recording, a higher standard of reproduction) because it was only necessary to pay for the radio set – the music came free. To begin with, when early broadcasters used records as a matter of course, without thinking to pay anything apart from their purchase price, it was like free advertising. But after radio took off, then its growing use of recorded music threw the record companies into a schizophrenic frenzy. The potential value of the practice, if the broadcasters could be made to pay their dues, would be worth millions, although litigation to make them do so would be a costly drain on the record companies' coffers. At the same time, the record companies began to find that the popularity of record programmes on the radio was an excellent guide to sales potential, which tended to mitigate their opposition. The point was demonstrated by Victor in 1925, when it made an arrangement with AT&T to waive the customary advertising fee in return for an hour of the 'world's greatest music', and John McCormack's performance of Irving Berlin's 'All Alone' sold, within one month, a quarter of a million records, a million copies of the sheet music and 160,000 player-piano rolls. But this was in the short term. By the end of the decade, instead of radio boosting record sales, the Depression hit and the record market collapsed.

RCA was a product of military pressure at the end of the war to keep the control of broadcasting in national ownership. Because one of the major suppliers, American Marconi, was a British subsidiary, the US Navy intervened on grounds of strategic interests and contrived its take-over in 1919 by a new enterprise, the Radio Corporation of America. The incident was a crucial episode in the gestation of what an American President, Dwight D. Eisenhower, would later call the military–industrial complex. The major shareholder in RCA was General Electric, together with Westinghouse, AT&T and a company that had been using radio communication to link its agricultural empire in Latin America, United Fruit.

This cartel was primarily devoted to the production of broadcast equipment and radio sets – the new hardware; but the prosperity of their business was beset by the problem of technical linkage between hardware and software. They could not avoid setting up radio stations and undertaking the finance of broadcasting – in other words, the provision of the appropriate software – as a necessary expense, a loss leader, for who would buy the sets without something to tune in to? It is one thing for a tribe of individual operators to each transmit a potpourri of live and recorded sound for an hour or two; this is not yet full-blown broadcasting.

Broadcasting is the transmission of a regular service to a general public, and this costs money. In due course they would divest themselves of these stations, as their need to finance them was rendered unnecessary by RCA's creation of the commercial broadcasting networks.

There were actually plenty of people in the United States ready and willing to try to enter radio: when the boom began in 1920, some five hundred licences were granted within a year. Soon there was growing chaos on the airwaves caused by the multiplicity of transmitters crowding each other's signals, until Washington stepped in with the creation of the Federal Radio Commission in 1927. These were circumstances in which regulation was supported by powerful commercial interests. Some stations, like AT&T's WEAF, had found ways of defraying their operating costs by hiring out their transmitter to any firm or organization wishing to provide programmes, thus initiating the practice of sponsorship, but national advertisers were reluctant to buy time from individual stations with no discernible audience. Hook-ups, which began in 1923–24, and then became organized into networks, persuaded them that there was a new mass public in process of formation.

The big corporations changed tack, and in 1926 the board of RCA decided on the formation of a dedicated commercial broadcasting company, NBC, funded by advertising, to be owned jointly by RCA, General Electric and Westinghouse. AT&T withdrew from the arrangement, satisfied that its own best interests lay in provision of the cabling systems that the growing networks would inevitably require; the others were later edged out, leaving NBC a wholly owned subsidiary of RCA. A year later NBC had two national radio networks in operation, and acquired a competitor when the Columbia Record Company set up CBS (Columbia Broadcasting System), which they soon abandoned, however, to fend for itself. Later a third major competitor was created when NBC was forced by anti-trust legislation to sell off one of its two networks, which in 1943 became the American Broadcasting Company, ABC.

Radio in the United States quickly succumbed to the control of the commercial networks, stimulating the production of music for unreflective and uncritical consumption in the established manner of Tin Pan Alley. In the old cultures of Europe, on the other hand, especially with the example of revolutionary Russia on its borders, high military and civic echelons concerned with certain facts about mass susceptibilities quickly saw the advantage of keeping radio under tighter, more direct control. This factor made it possible for a few well-placed individuals with more enlightened or progressive ideas to conceive of cultural purposes for the medium. In both Germany and England, civic and government radio stations acted independently to put art music on the air. In Germany, young composers like Paul Hindemith and Kurt Weill were encouraged with commissions, and even the music of Schoenberg was occasionally broadcast. Many musicians, wrote Weill as early as 1926, live entirely off their radio work, and for many others it provides an indispensable supplement to their concert and theatre earnings.[6] Here for the first time one can see a recurring pattern: public service broadcasting under a more or less liberal regime becomes a more creative space for contemporary music than commercial broadcasting, or the record industry (which is not prone to recording music for which the market is unproven).

In Britain, where the first broadcast concert dates from 1920, when the Marconi Company began transmissions from a studio in Chelmsford, the BBC not only took over the Henry Wood Promenade Concerts and subsidized symphony orchestras in the provinces, but also in 1930 established its own showpiece orchestra in London under the baton of Adrian Boult, which quickly developed the most adventurous repertoire of any orchestra in the country. This was the year that CBS across the Atlantic, in pursuit of cultural prestige, began to carry the Sunday afternoon concerts of the New York Philharmonic, turning their maestro Toscanini into a household name throughout the country (seven years later he was poached by the rival network, NBC, with their promise to create an orchestra especially for him). But Toscanini and his various paymasters never allowed the same air-space for new music as Boult and the BBC.

These cultural broadcasts promised to create new audiences, and they have certainly done so. Today a single transmission of a new work by a contemporary composer is liable to reach a larger public than could have heard a piece by Beethoven during the whole of his lifetime. (Now that there is television as well, it is also true that more people see a single performance by the punk violinist Nigel Kennedy than ever knew the name of Paganini, whose renown as the most famous musician of the nineteenth century was celebrated in music-hall songs.) But this twentieth-century public is of a different kind to that of Beethoven's or Paganini's time: it is atomized, fragmented, dispersed. In the record stores, consumer tastes are divided up into separate categories, from 'classical' to 'easy listening', 'popular' to 'nostalgia', although, according to one writer on the subject, it was radio rather than records that redrew the map of musical production and consumption, creating unified markets for commercial exploitation by defining various areas of taste. In Paddy Scannell's account, this outcome, at least in Britain, was the consequence of policies consciously argued over and carried out by the BBC, which became by far the largest single provider of music in Britain or any other country at that time.[7]

At first the effects of radio on established interests in the music business were detrimental. In 1925, when there were just over two million licence holders in Britain, the government-appointed Crawford Committee on the future of radio heard evidence from the music publishers of a fall in the sales of sheet music. Radio, the Committee was told, had cut down the life of a popular song; it was leading to fewer live concerts, destroying the amateur and pushing the professional musician out of work. The record companies expressed similar fears of the effects of unfair competition. The same dire predictions were repeated ten years later to the Ullswater Committee, and the failure during the 1920s of several concert organizations, culminating in the collapse of the British National Opera Company in 1929, seemed to confirm these prognostications.

But the evidence is equivocal. A year earlier, the editor of the staid and conservative *Musical Times* perceived a rejuvenation of the audience at the Queen's Hall Promenade Concerts, which the BBC had taken over in 1927 after their previous sponsors, the music publisher Chappell's, lost £60,000 in three years and decided to pull out. And while it is true that a serious decline was registered in the number of music societies across the country – from some four thousand in the late 1920s to less than two thousand in 1935, for which Sir Thomas Beecham blamed the recession, entertainments tax and the rival distractions of mechanized music – in fact the BBC kept many of them alive by paying for broadcasting rights; it also helped to maintain city orchestras in Manchester, Birmingham and Belfast. For his part, Beecham placed his bet on records and set up an orchestra of his own, the London Philharmonic, to benefit from recording contracts with the new combine, EMI. Created in 1932, EMI was the product of a merger between The Gramophone Company, which controlled HMV and Zonophone, and Columbia, which also controlled several labels, in response to the collapse of the record market in the Depression.

In America too the Depression had a decisive effect, by accelerating a process of integration and merger which had begun during the 1920s. In the process of creating a rapidly expanding mass audience, the radio corporations began to prey on other enterprises within the sphere of cultural production which they perceived as servicing them. Asserting their imperialist instincts they initiated a new phase of expansion, signalled by RCA's acquisition of a couple of music publishers in 1927. Hollywood, as the talkies were introduced, did the same. The object was to secure control of copyrights. According to one Merlin Aylesworth, the first president of RCA's filial NBC, giving evidence to a Senate committee, 'It is necessary for us to be in the music business to protect ourselves ... the movies have bought most of the music houses ... we have got to get control of the music situation. It is a simple business proposition with a little touch of sentiment in it.'[8]

This kind of competition between and within the media for control of different sectors is still the daily pattern of the culture industry under late capitalism: one of the latest examples, as I write, is a takeover bid for Paramount by the American cable television operator Viacom. Back in the late 1920s, Paramount had purchased a 49 per cent interest in CBS, thus securing the future of NBC's principal rival. At the same time, while Western Electric was developing a film sound system with Warners and Fox, RCA took over a number of second-rank film interests and in 1928 created RKO Pictures in order to gain a foothold in the same market with a rival system developed for them by General Electric. The following year they acquired the Victor record company. According to some accounts they were interested not so much in the phonograph as in using its plant for the manufacture of radio receivers; what followed were the first fully electric radiograms.

Victor's take-over by RCA at the beginning of 1929 saved it from the effects of the Wall Street Crash. But the Depression blocked the recovery of the record industry, and sales of records and record players plunged (this occurred in Europe as well). Annual record-player sales in the United States declined from nearly one million in 1927 to a mere forty thousand in 1932; the sale of radio receivers over the same period trebled. Records, after peaking in 1926 at 128 million fell to a mere 6 million six years later.[9]

The Edison company discontinued record and phonograph production, in favour of radios and dictation machines, immediately after the Wall Street Crash. A few months later the Brunswick–Balke–Collender company, long-time suppliers of billiard parlours and bowling alleys, which started manufacturing phonographs in 1916, delivered its failing record business into the hands of Warner Brothers Pictures. However, Warner's soon got rid of Brunswick to the American Record Company, producers of bargain discs sold in chain stores like Woolworth's. Meanwhile Columbia UK got rid of American Columbia, which passed first to Grigsby–Grunow, a company that manufactured radios and refrigerators. Two years later, in 1933, Grigsby–Grunow went into receivership and Columbia was up for sale again. Nine years earlier the company had changed hands for $2.5m. Now the American Record Company bought it for a song and a dance: $70,500.

RCA had tried to invigorate business by introducing a new long-play format in 1931, for use in radio, where it provided a means of transcription that allowed material to be prerecorded and exchanged between different stations. First employed in America for the distribution of commercials, the format was sufficiently effective to be taken up worldwide. The BBC used long-playing transcription for the distribution of programmes to the branches of the Empire radio service. In Latin America, it served to consolidate the spread of commercial radio, under North American tutelage. (One of the producers working with RCA in the United States in the mid 1930s, making commercials for broadcast in Latin America, was Edgar Anzola, the pioneer Venezuelan film-maker and record producer whom we encountered earlier.)[10] According to one testimony, it was not technical factors that held back the launch of long-playing records on the domestic market. The Cuban writer Alejo Carpentier, who was not only a novelist but also a music critic, commenting on the new vinyl microgroove format in 1951, described what had happened fifteen years before. The original long-playing disc, he said, had only one main defect: it emphasized the bass, producing 'a certain sonic opacity' which got worse towards the centre of the spiralling groove. But this was remedied by the introduction of new techniques of equalization, and by 1935 the LP, with its convenient and unbreakable discs made of plastic-coated metal, a duration of up to fifteen minutes per side, and widely used by radio stations, was ready for commercial launch. The delay, he says, can only be explained by fear on the part of the big companies of the huge investment that conversion to the new format would entail.[11] In short, as a domestic product the equipment was more than could be borne in a market buffeted by a depression from which it had not yet fully recovered.

In the worried view of J.P. Maxfield, writing in 1933, radio had a deplorable effect upon popular music. Close microphones induced performers, as Read and Welch put it, 'to accentuate the trends in popular taste towards acceptance of the unreal'.[12] Microphones play tricks that recording horns are not capable of, and the sound emerging from the loudspeaker parts company with the sound heard by a listener present in the studio. Since the listener to a broadcast or recording is increasingly unlikely to know what the artist (or even an artist like them) sounds like live, the sound coming from the speaker becomes the be-all and end-all of the process of reproduction, and new criteria appear for the evaluation of the result. These include a new emphasis on the stronger bass and sheer volume rendered possible by the new dynamic speakers.

Microphones did not do away with problems of balance but redefined them. In Maxfield's account, since the microphone (which he still calls the 'pick-up') is acoustically dead, the only method of controlling the balance is by the relative distances of the various instruments from the pick-up; and balance is immediately lost if any instrument changes its loudness. Worse still, since there is no sense of acoustic perspective (which he understood perfectly well to depend on some form of binaural or stereo recording), the result is that instead of the sounds of different groups of instrument blending, as they do in a concert hall, the loud instruments tend to drown out the weaker ones, again destroying the proper balance. The difficulty was not to be solved simply by using multiple microphones, since several microphones could mean several different sets of reverberation, producing unnatural side effects, such as phasing problems, which added to the fuzziness of the sound image. The problem was compounded by the vagaries of domestic listening, in which the sound could be further muddied – so the theory went – by the superimposition of the acoustical properties of one room upon those of another. Technically, therefore, the dead studio technique was correct, and engineers like Maxfield designed their equipment so that no distortion was introduced whose purpose was to compensate for errors within the system itself. Others thought differently, and designed their systems intentionally to offset deficiencies, some purposely to exaggerate the new ability to reproduce not higher tones but lower ones.

There was another problem: electrical recording improved the frequency range of the recorded signal, to something approaching ten thousand cycles, or within an octave of the upper limits of human hearing. But the dynamic range – the ratio of the loudest sounds to the softest – remained restricted, consequently confining the musician's expressive compass.

Musicians, who are ear specialists, naturally developed new techniques to cope with these problems, which were sometimes at odds with those of the engineers. At first, Maxfield recounts, they would sometimes use different, that is, less powerful instruments for recording from those they would employ in a performance for a live audience. At times it was difficult, in Maxfield's experience, to induce the players of louder instruments like brass and tympani to play with anything like their normal power, even when the recording session was in a full-size theatre. On one occasion, it was only after the brass 'had been told three times that the violins were outplaying them that they became angry enough to really produce the volume necessary for the proper natural balance'. As for singers, even they began to develop a 'mezzo voce', a half-voice, 'even for classical numbers where a large part of the emotional content resides in the volume range'.[13] It is this technique that in the hands of popular singers is called crooning – except that crooning is more than a technique, but a style, modelled on the intonation and phrasing of certain jazz singers, typically sliding up to notes rather than hitting them square, and with a sensual, ululating tone that comes from deep in the throat.

If musicians developed new techniques to cope with the limitations of early electrical recording, the results of a single microphone could sometimes be extremely felicitous. Ernest Lough, who as a fourteen-year-old in 1927 was the boy soprano on a famous recording of 'Oh for the Wings of a Dove', explained in a recent television documentary how the recording was made, in London's Temple Church, using a single microphone placed between the church organ and the choir stalls; he himself was placed not in front but behind the choir, raised up.[14] Unquestionably the huge success of this record is partly due to the perfect balance, which gave a wonderful floating quality to the boy's beautifully controlled voice. Here the engineers, using one of HMV's first mobile recording trucks, clearly tried to employ the acoustic – reflected sound and all – rather than suppressing it. Lough's account, however, reminds us of another limitation of the day: if the engineers pronounced a take to be good, the performers were unable to hear the result until a pressing was made. Of course in a sense this was not a limitation at all: it was quite conducive to the act of performing. But it left the musician to have to trust the judgement of the engineer, who was now surrounded by cables, dials and switches.

There were those who, in the face of this accumulation of apparatus, regarded electrical recording as an irredeemable process of distortion which, worse still, as Read and Welch observe, fed back into live performance.

> The insinuating sotto voce, over amplified sounds, made by 'Whispering' Jack Smith and Little Jack Little represented only the more obvious misuses of the microphone techniques eventually to be foisted on the public. Rudy Vallee was to popularise the term 'crooner' and open the doors of the recording studio to a flood of trick stylists from radio. This trend became an epidemic. Soon stage appearances had to be bolstered with public address systems for without amplification the crooning Mills brothers and Miss Poop-poop-a-do could not have been heard beyond the third row.[15]

In short, compared with the limitations of the old acoustic process, the cure had proven worse than the disease.

The position has a certain logic. As another commentator puts it, 'Whether perfect, pluperfect, or imperfect, any recording is a distortion of reality, just as a newsreel is a distortion of a news event.'[16] To put it another way, recording, like news gathering, is not a transparent process, but the manufacture of a product out of a certain type of raw material. But in that case, to designate the results of the process as distortion may be missing the point. In particular what it fails to take into account is, first, that in the musical response of popular singers to the microphone there were none of the inhibitions that afflicted classical musicians, trained to obey the discipline of a conductor's baton; and second, that popular singers, as a result, treated the microphone as an instrument in its own right.

Consider the case of Rudy Vallee, saxophonist, bandleader, composer and singer, who made his first film, *The Vagabond Lover*, in 1929, and was one of the earliest radio and screen entertainers to become a public idol and generate mass hysteria in his audience. Famed as one of the first to exploit the new crooning voice, in the days before the microphone became an essential part of the popular singer's trade he used a megaphone to project his soft, soothing and rather nasal tones. If it is therefore difficult to say which came first, the desire to croon or the instrument that made it possible, the truth is that the microphone arrived on the scene with a kind of symbolic fitness – like the piano, say, in the eighteenth century, of which Arthur Loesser has written that it not only encompassed every kind of music making, from the most private to the most public, but with its multitude of precisely engineered moving parts also came to exemplify the modern age of machinery.[17] The microphone is analogous in its hunger for music of every scale and genre, and its exemplification of the electrical age.

5

Enter the Talkies

In the United States, the accomplishment of electrical recording accelerated the race for talking pictures. It had long been a dream to marry film and sound. Edison had tried to pair the phonograph with the kinetoscope and since then several attempts had been made to synchronize film with records, but until the 1920s none were to overcome the two fundamental problems: the imprecision of the synchronization, and the absence of amplification – an indispensable requirement in a medium that was consumed collectively in large spaces. The development of radio provided the solution to the latter problem; the former would be solved by the development of sound-on-film, whereby signals from a microphone were used to modulate a light beam which could be photographed, laid alongside the picture on the same film strip, and then reproduced through a photoelectric cell. But the story is a complicated one, with several rival systems being developed on both sides of the Atlantic, and not all of them were photoelectric. The Danish experimenter Poulsen, who had produced the first magnetic wire recorder in 1898, was partly responsible for a photoelectric system that was used for a number of years in France and Britain; but in 1923, with his co-worker P.O. Pederson, he also developed a magnetic sound-on-film system which would only be put to commercial use thirty years later. Even in America four major rival systems were developed, three of them under the aegis of the same company, Western Electric, and one of them using discs.[1]

Western Electric's dominance in the field stemmed from its acquisition in 1912 of rights on de Forest's Audion tube, the key to amplification. Its immediate interest was the construction of amplifying repeaters for long-distance telephone lines, the core business of its parent company AT&T. Discovery of the photoelectric effect (in which certain substances release electrons when struck by light) goes back to 1839 and is credited to Edmond Bequerel; the prototype of the photoelectric cell was developed by two German scientists (Julius Elster and Hans Geitel) in 1905, and several attempts at sound-on-film systems incorporating the device were made in the years following the First World War, including one designed by Lee de Forest. Severely hampered by lack of finance, de Forest entered into co-operation with another experimenter, Theodore Case, who had started working in the field during the First World War. A rather better entrepreneur than de Forest, Case ran his own research laboratory where he brought the system to perfection, or at least a high level of practicability, using microphones, amplifiers and loudspeakers licensed from Western Electric.[2] It was this system that was adopted by William Fox, given the trade name Movietone, and publicly launched in 1927. However, Western Electric was also responsible for the disc-based method known as Vitaphone, the first system to be launched commercially, with the backing of Warners, which was then a small company trying to muscle in on the Hollywood majors. The first feature using this system, *Don Juan*, was shot mute and then post-dubbed with music and sound effects; it was premiered in August 1926, followed by *The Jazz Singer* over a year later, in October 1927.

It is clear from these developments that the process of research and development had reached a new level, in which the only real players were the electrical combines and a few established research laboratories. (In 1925 AT&T ranked with United States Steel as the largest private corporation in the world.) Even then, backing was needed from potential users – in this case the film studios – before a prototype could become fully functional, since the adoption of sound involved re-equipping both studios and theatres.

It is hardly an accident that the first sound films were not so much talkies as primitive musicals, which meant, as far as Warners was concerned, film records of musical acts of the kind successfully exploited on the radio. The American film theorist Rick Altman quotes the advance annoucement in which Albert Warner declared that 'the perfected radio music program will begin a new era for moving picture patrons throughout the country'. These radio programmes were an outgrowth of the record industry, and so were films like *The Jazz Singer*. As one reviewer put it, it was scarcely a motion picture, but 'should more properly be labelled an enlarged Vitaphone record of Al Jolson in half a dozen songs'[3] – which did not, however, prevent its huge success.

The Movietone system clearly had a number of advantages over Vitaphone. With discs, even when the problem of how to start in sync was solved, the system remained problematic: what happened when the needle jumped or the film sprockets tore? Moreover, normal disc life was only about twenty playings, and discs were liable to break. (When Warners finally abandoned the system, they cited the costs of the extra discs needed to cope with these problems as one of the reasons.) With the Movietone system, sound and picture, being carried on the same film strip, could not lose synchronization; in the case of the film breaking and frames being lost, an equal amount of sound would also be lost; there was no extra trouble or expense involved in handling or shipping the film; and the fact that picture and sound were recorded in the same camera made for more compact and portable equipment. However, while this was an advantage for newsreel work, it was less satisfactory in the film studio. Since sound and picture were recorded on the same negative, they had to be developed together; as the optimum contrast for picture and sound were different, the quality of both was compromised.

The third system developed by Western Electric overcame this problem by recording on a separate machine, synchronized with the camera by a special motor, and using its own film stock. The greater bulk and complexity of this double system was offset on a controlled sound stage by the greater quality. Since picture and sound were only combined on the final print (which was projected in substantially the same manner as Movietone), optimum quality could be maintained for each. This was the system that most of the major players finally agreed upon in 1928. The double system also allowed the development of equipment and techniques for mixing, dubbing and re-recording – the first models were introduced in 1930 – which soon became standard procedure in feature film production.

Talking pictures brought refinements and advances in recording technology, from microphones to loudspeakers. The first speakers, introduced by Western Electric in 1919, and designed by a team led by Frank Jewett, used a large folded horn driven by a moving coil attached to a metal diaphragm. This was the first public address system, and in 1922 AT&T

used a long-distance telephone link to broadcast President Harding's address at the burial of the Unknown Soldier in Washington live to crowds in New York's Madison Square Gardens and San Francisco's Auditorium. Clear reproduction for large indoor audiences was thus available several years before an effective technology of talking pictures. Smaller versions of the same system were used for a period in domestic radio sets, but the standard design subsequently adopted for loudspeakers in radios, gramophones and television sets, in which a paper cone mounted on a flat baffle is driven by a freely suspended moving coil, was the work of Edward Kellog and others at General Electric, and formed part of a fourth sound-on-film system which General Electric developed for RCA, known as Photophone.

The sound film, like radio, also stimulated the development of new microphones. These come in several families and, because of the fundamental properties of the transducer – that its mechanism is always reversible – are usually paired with different types of earpiece or speaker, and sometimes other devices. Crystal microphones dated back to a prototype developed by the French physicist Paul Langevin in 1917, in the course of his work on the uses of ultrasonics in submarines; the technique was improved by an engineer at Western Electric, A.M. Nicolson, just after the war. While technical problems hindered commercial application before the end of the 1920s, this work also produced a crystal gramophone pick-up, which was first demonstrated in 1925 and then became standard. Alternatively there was a new kind of diaphragm-and-moving-coil microphone, which originated in a design dating from 1919, based on discoveries by William Siemens in 1877 and Oliver Lodge twenty years later; these found application in recording studios in a version designed by an engineer at EMI, Alan Blumlein. Or else there were ribbon microphones, developed by an RCA engineer, H.F. Olson, which first came on the market in 1931, while ribbon-driven loudpeakers were produced in Germany some years earlier. Each type had its own characteristics, which suited different kinds of sound source or location; as the advantages of each usage emerged, new models were introduced to enhance these usages, which improved on their sensitivity or their directional capabilities.

Edison had improved the sensitivity of the carbon microphone in the course of developing a sound-on-disc system for motion pictures which he launched, unsuccessfully, in 1913. But the standard studio microphone of the 1920s was the condenser type, developed by a team of engineers at the Bell Telephone Laboratory over a couple of years and launched in 1922 for use in radio studios. It was this microphone, with its sensitivity and smooth bass response, that led to the effects practised by radio which J.P. Maxfield bemoaned as bad habits, precisely because it was only effective at a close distance from the sound source (which in turn encouraged crooners). Nevertheless, it was also the microphone adopted in Hollywood for use with the double sound-on-film system.

Here it immediately raised new problems of sound perspective, highlighted by mismatches between sound and image. Often the microphone had to be so close to the actor that it could not be kept out of the field of vision in a medium shot, thus forcing dialogue into close-ups. Editors then forced the spectator to jump from long shot to medium shot and thence to close-up 'on important business'. To compensate for the stilted results, the studios adopted multiple microphone set-ups: in order to maintain intelligibility of dialogue as the actors moved around (because unfortunately film actors do that), a number of microphones were spread around the set, and the recording engineer chose the best, that is, most intelligible sound. The results were still disconcerting. According to an RCA sound technician called John Cass, writing in a technical journal in 1930, 'quality and volume remain constant while the cutter jumps from across the room to a big close-up'; at such moments the viewer becomes aware of 'witnessing a talking picture', a condition that indicates 'that the illusion has been partially broken'.[4] There were many who complained that artistically, cinema had taken a step backwards.

The resulting soundtrack, said Cass, was a blend of sound that yielded no definite point of audition 'but is the sound which would be heard by a man with five or six very long ears, said ears extending in various directions'.[5] Another writer in the same journal puts the blame on the intrusion of the radio industry:

> In some ways it is unfortunate that the radio industry supplied most of the experts to the film industry. In radio broadcasting it usually is desirable to present all sounds as coming from approximately the same place – that of the microphone. And so levels are raised and lowered to bring all sounds out as approximately the same volume, the microphone being placed as near as possible to the source of the sound. But in talking picture presentations, it is very desirable to achieve space effects, and dramatic variation of volume level.[6]

J.P. Maxfield, who as head of Western Electric's outfit on the West Coast debated the problems in several journals during the 1930s, advanced the cause of the single microphone, arguing that a single microphone placed near the camera's line of sight automatically co-ordinated sight and sound by reflecting the character's movements towards and away from the camera. The effect was not just a matter of volume, he explained, which by itself was an insufficient marker of distance, but was due to the importance of changes in the ratio of reflected sound to direct sound at different distances for determining perception of sound scale, which, Maxfield argued, should dictate the proper microphone placement for the scale of the image.

But if this was the theory, then as Altman points out, Hollywood practice led in a different direction. When new microphones became available in the early 1930s, which were not only lighter and more compact but also, unlike condenser microphones, needed no preamplifiers to cope with the weak output, a new practice developed: the microphone was slung on a boom, which could be moved about to follow the actors, pausing at the appropriate point to capture the dialogue from the optimum angle just outside the camera's field of vision. The advantages were decisive. First, the boom simplified the process of shooting, by eliminating the time required for multiple camera and microphone set-ups, so it was economically preferable. Second, it rendered the soundtrack susceptible to greater control in post-production, when the synchronous track would be mixed with music and sound effects to be married to the final print. But this had a radical influence in determining the function and status of the soundtrack in the talkies, with profound effects not only on film aesthetics but also upon the modes of hearing of musical reproduction. The common term 'background music' is misleading: it is not in the background, it has no place. It is disembodied, but not in the same way as on a record. The music on the record is disembodied because it is a mechanical memory; the music that floats through the film is disembodied because it comes from nowhere.

As Altman explains, with a single immobile microphone such as that championed by Maxfield, the spatial characteristics of the pro-filmic scene were already inscribed on the soundtrack. That is to say, the acoustic properties of the view represented by the camera were recorded with the picture.

A character receding or turning away from the mike was recorded with a higher
ratio of reflected to direct sound; similarly the size of the room had its effects on
volume, reverberation, and frequency characteristics. With the new system, however, the microphone is perpetually kept within approximately the same distance
of the speaker, thus cancelling out nearly all the factors which the earlier system
retained.[7]

Coupled with devices for mixing, equalization and the addition of reverberation, the first of which were introduced in 1930, Hollywood was thus
assured not only of the economic benefits but also of the requisite control
for treating sound in the same way as the picture, and constructing it
according to the same rationalized principles of montage. The method
allowed the creation of a clean, clear and continuous soundtrack oblivious
to the shifting image scale but attuned to the same narrative principles:
intelligibility and continuity of dialogue and plot. The function of music
in this scheme is partly to serve as a discreet commentary, guiding the
spectator in the process of empathy with the actors, and partly to evoke
responses and emotions which are not otherwise there. But now the microphone is no longer a substitute for the human ear, and need no longer
pretend to occupy a real position. If the camera pretends to behave like
the eye of God, going everywhere and anywhere, then the microphone
becomes God's equally disembodied ear. Hence the kind of film music
that is like the music of the spheres constantly playing in the background.

If all this is the negation of Maxfield's principle, it works because it
creates an idealization which has the powerful effect of suppressing the
signs of fabrication and maintaining the status of the fiction. For the one
thing that Maxfield overlooked was that the film studio is a totally different kind of space to the recording studio, let alone the concert hall. It
does not have acoustics in the same sense; in fact acoustics would only get
in the way. It is not a space where a performance is given for a microphone to capture and a disc (or other form of carrier) to transcribe, but
a factory for the manufacture of parts to be assembled subsequently into a
totally constructed aesthetic entity. In the well-known account by Walter
Benjamin, the shooting of a film, especially a sound film, affords a spec-
tacle of an unprecedented kind. If theatre is a space where the spectator is
invited to witness a dramatic illusion, in the film studio, the illusionary
nature of the activity is of the second degree, for the apparatus required to

produce it has penetrated so deeply into reality that 'the sight of immediate reality has become an orchid in the land of technology'.[8] The same is true of the sound of this reality, for which it is equally impossible to assign the spectator in the studio a position; in this case not even a position in line with the microphone would do, for, as Maxfield also explained, human ears are selective, microphones are not.

It is only a corollary of this that the kind of realism inherent in Maxfield's single-microphone principle was in fact neither appropriate nor acceptable to Hollywood. For one thing, what is the point of aiming to record spatial perspective in the dead, unnatural acoustic of a studio? The objective only makes proper sense when filming on location, which was pretty much an impossibility before direct portable sound-filming equipment appeared in the 1960s. There are a few highly significant exceptions, such as films by Jean Renoir (*Toni*, 1934) and Michael Powell (*The Edge of the World*, 1937), shot entirely on location and using authentic sound, which demonstrate in the depth of their social portrayal a form of realism completely alien to Hollywood, in which the quality of the soundtrack, with its sounds recorded *in situ*, plays a crucial role. Hollywood could easily have done the same had it wanted; it preferred to construct the soundtrack in post-production through re-recording, mixing and dubbing. If *Citizen Kane*, dating from 1941, is the foremost paradigm of the dramatically as well as musically composed soundtrack, with great attention paid to acoustic perspective, then the practice reached the point where virtually no sound recorded synchronously with the camera survived into the final mix, which consisted entirely of sounds dubbed in during the course of post-production.

Second – and this factor was equally determining – the problem is not just one of fitting the microphone to the sound source to match the image scale, but also that of matching the final mixed soundtrack to the space in which it is designed to be heard, the picture palace where the film is projected, which not only posed technical problems in the design of adequate amplification and loudspeakers, but represented a space that Hollywood devoted to illusion, fantasy and escapism, where reality was left outside in the cold and the wind and the rain. If music was an essential ingredient in this illusion (and it always had been; silent movies had never been projected silent, they always had some kind of musical accompaniment), then Hollywood soon found the highest expression of this integration in the musical, which released the screen from the constraints of a realist aesthetic by creating, through the soundtrack, a different kind of space, with a different kind of narrative logic. While the early sound film presented problems in the melodramatic use of soundtrack music, both technical and artistic, the musical as a genre licensed a domain of unreality in which actors burst into song and dance to the accompaniment of invisible orchestras and choirs as naturally as walking and talking. Here Maxfield's principle was simply vaporized away, for everything in this soundscape is necessarily conceived in terms of ideal balance and harmony. The record industry was thankful. The popularity of Hollywood musicals helped it rebuild its fortunes.

The musics worst affected by the Depression in America were jazz and black music. The race labels and innumerable bars and cabarets catering to black audiences closed down, the musicians forced out of work. This did not impoverish the music, which continued to develop in direct contact with its audience, but as the small independents were eliminated, the range of recorded music was seriously narrowed. Meanwhile, radio stations found that low-cost live broadcasts from the big ballrooms gave excellent ratings, and the result was a boost for a new kind of big band playing in a new style called 'swing'. Benny Goodman, the name most closely associated with the beginnning of the craze, formed his first band in 1933 when he was asked by Columbia to organize musicians for a jazz recording date intended for the British market. The band was then featured on a series of late-night networked broadcasts and in 1935 went on tour. The tour was a disaster. The broadcasts had gone out too late in the evening to reach a young enough audience to build up a public following. In California, however, where the broadcasts were received at an early evening hour, the band scored a hit and a new fashion took off. Three years later, when Goodman played Carnegie Hall, half the band had left to form their own swing orchestras. It was also partly on the back of swing – and with the spread of the jukebox – that the surviving record companies began to recover.

The Depression also put a stop to classical music recording in the United States. According to one source, even a popular classical album sold hardly more than five hundred copies, so companies like Victor and

Columbia stopped recording any themselves and imported them from Europe instead. In Europe the market had also seriously declined. In 1930 the combined net profits of the two major English manufacturers, The Gramophone Company's HMV and Columbia, totalled £1.42m; the following year a mere £160,000. A merger followed, and the creation of EMI (Electrical and Musical Industries). The Gramophone Company brought labels and manufacturing plants throughout Europe; Columbia brought its various German, Italian, French and Far Eastern labels. The new combine therefore only had Deutsche Gramophon, with its Polydor label, and a few small independents, as European rivals, and immediately dominated the record industry worldwide beyond the Americas.

Several factors helped the European record business to weather the Depression, and even to broaden the recorded repertoire. If radio was less well developed, the monied classes were more cultured, sustaining a small market for classical recordings, as a budding producer who worked for HMV set out to demonstrate in 1931. 'I devised a plan', wrote Walter Legge many years later, 'which the company could not very well reject: to collect subscriptions in advance for great recordings of unrecorded works and make the records only when the requested number of subscribers had been enlisted, not only to cover the costs but also to yield the company a reasonable profit.'9 First came the Hugo Wolf Society, with a six-album set which needed five hundred subscriptions at thirty shillings each – a target achieved within a matter of weeks; followed within less than a year by the Beethoven Sonata Society. Three years later HMV reported sales of three special sets of Beethoven sonatas played by Schnabel running at £24,000 in Britain and £80,000 worldwide. Meanwhile the method was adopted in France, where it produced Wanda Landowska playing Couperin, Scarlatti and Bach's Goldberg Variations on the harpsichord – the ancestral recordings of the early music movement. Before the Second World War brought the Society recordings to a halt, the recorded literature had been expanded to include Albert Schweitzer's first recordings of Bach's organ music and Pablo Casals playing the unaccompanied cello suites, Fritz Kreisler playing Beethoven's violin sonatas, Bruno Walter conducting Mahler's *Das Lied von der Erde*, Beecham's recordings of Delius and Sibelius, and the Glyndebourne Opera performances of Mozart conducted by Fritz Busch. All of them remain classic recordings of permanent musical interest.

There was room here for competition, which came in the shape of a new price-cutting company called Decca. Originally the trademark of a manufacturer of portable phonographs much favoured by British soldiers in the First World War, the record company dates from 1929 when the business was bought by a London stockbroker called Edward Lewis. Lewis built up the company by acquiring UK re-pressing rights for popular releases from America on the Brunswick and Melotone labels, and classics from Polydor in Germany. Three years later he launched the American namesake, poaching Jack Kapp from Brunswick to run it, who brought a bevy of Brunswick artists with him. The first advertisements for Decca in America announced exclusive contracts with popular artists like Bing Crosby, the Dorsey Brothers, Guy Lombardo, Fletcher Henderson and the Mills Brothers, and records costing thirty-five cents instead of seventy-five cents.

Two years after the American launch, Decca UK announced an initiative in the classical market: a new series of cut-price recordings by the likes of Henry Wood conducting the Queens Hall Orchestra and Hamilton Harty conducting the London Symphony, the Boyd Neel String Orchestra and the Griller Quartet. Critics disparaged the recordings as 'rackety, harsh, and overamplified'. Decca went out and found the expertise to improve the quality of its recordings in a small company called Crystalate, which it bought in 1937, where another pair of English recording engineers, Arthur Haddy and Kenneth Wilkinson, had produced improvements to the condenser microphone, and developed moving arm cutters for engraving master discs which set new industry standards.

Another factor here was the activity of the BBC, and the advantages that accrued from both the BBC's own research and development programme and the example of its Music Department. The latter, where producers were trained musicians, established new standards of studio practice, especially in regard to acoustics and microphone placement, while engineers worked on new microphone technology, sometimes adapting models made by others. For example, they built their own preamplifiers for use with condenser microphones produced by Western Electric. But the BBC also constituted a market for small firms at home producing specialized equipment; like Garrard, which launched a record-changer in 1932, went on to develop transcription turntables for the BBC, helped to pioneer the domestic hi-fi market after the war, and ended up being taken over by Plessey.

The 1930s was the decade that saw the rise of the engineer – people like the aforementioned Haddy, who in the 1940s led Decca's R&D team and in the 1950s became their recording manager. Indeed attached to these various names are biographies that can tell us a good deal about the developing web of industrial connections. Another example from the same group, where records link with radio, is the case of a certain Frank Lee, who started out in the HMV artists department in 1927, moved to Decca when HMV made him redundant, then in 1935 joined the advertising agency J. Walter Thompson. The American advertisers had opened a studio in London to service the new commercial radio stations beamed to England from the continent, Radio Normandy and Radio Luxembourg.[10] These stations, set up to get round the ban on commercial broadcasting in Britain, used transcription recording for a purpose later performed by tape: to allow the physical separation of programme production from transmission. Radio Luxembourg, which was to survive in one form or another until the early 1990s, was the first radio station broadcasting in Britain to challenge the BBC and its music policies, thereby inducing major changes in public taste, especially with the rise of rock 'n' roll in the 1950s.

In the United States, in the leftward democratic turn created by Roosevelt's New Deal politics, the radio networks began to come under attack for their crass commercialism. One critic described the phenomenon of commercial radio as 'like a grotesque, smirking gargoyle' set atop the skyscrapers. 'The gargoyle's mouth is a loudspeaker, powered by the vested interests of a two-billion dollar industry, and back of that the vested interests of business as a whole, of industry, of finance. It is never silent, it drowns out all other voices, and it suffers no rebuke...'[11] In response to such criticism, and under pressure from federal government to satisfy lobbyists on behalf of 'educational radio', NBC and CBS both undertook cosmetic, if costly, initiatives in cultural programming, which naturally included classical music. In 1937 NBC scored off their rivals when they persuaded Toscanini to return to the United States to head a specially formed orchestra of his own, to wit, the NBC Symphony. Given Toscanini's highly publicized repudiation of fascism in both Germany and his native Italy, their initiative had significant political overtones. The business magazine *Fortune* found its own reasons for why the NBC–

Toscanini venture made good sense. What it boiled down to was the 'startling fact' that 39.9 per cent of the US population 'have heard of the name of Arturo Toscanini; and of those who have heard of him, no less than 71 percent can identify him *as an orchestral conductor*'.[12] Certainly, as far as *Fortune* was concerned, this was a mass audience. The venture had almost come to nothing before it got off the ground, when Toscanini was alerted that to form 'his' orchestra, NBC was poaching the top musicians from leading orchestras across the country. (But then the same thing had happened in England when the BBC Symphony Orchestra was formed in 1930.)

For most musicians in the United States considering their jobs, it was difficult to say which was the greater evil: radio, records – or the film industry. To speak, as people do, of the arrival of the talkies rather than the sound film hides the devastating effect that soundtrack music had upon the employment of silent-movie cinema musicians; an effect that was compounded by the Depression, which kept audiences for other live entertainments at home listening to radio and records. Most of the lost employment in hotels, cafés, bars and the cinemas was never regained; the musicians were increasingly replaced by jukeboxes. The jukebox is an automated version of the original nickelodeon, the coin-in-the-slot mechanical gramophone dating back to the 1880s which had disappeared from circulation around 1920. It first reappeared in 1927, on a fairly small scale – one source says 12,000 machines in three years[13] – and then began to take off in 1933, with the repeal of Prohibition, when it began to proliferate in bars, drugstores and diners. By 1936, Decca alone operated 150,000 of them, which took 40 per cent of its record output. By 1939, when the total number of jukeboxes was around a quarter of a million (according to one source – another places it higher), it took thirteen million discs a year to nourish them, or 60 per cent of record sales.

Fearful for the loss of jobs, the American Federation of Musicians (AFM), the musicians' trade union, mounted a million-dollar campaign against mechanized competition in 1930, without gaining much ground. From the point of view of the rank-and-file musician, the main antagonists were the record companies. Records promised worldly success, but when it came to remuneration, the performing musician was always at the bottom of the pile. A top-rated mainstream bandleader could make good earnings. In Britain, Jack Hylton once gave details of how much he earned

in his heyday in the 1920s and early 1930s: he drew £29,000 from HMV
in recording royalties for 1929, and a guaranteed £58,000 for the next
two years from Decca.[14] However, Hylton was not only the unchallenged
emperor of European dance bands, but also a shrewd businessman. The
deal for many artists was nowhere near so good, especially if they were
black. In Billie Holiday's account:

> My friends are always telling me, 'You should be rich, Lady. I just paid ten bucks
> for a couple of your LPs.' I always say, I'm grateful you like my songs – even
> those of twenty years ago. I have to tell them it ain't going to bring me a
> quarter. I made over 270 songs between 1933 and 1944, but I didn't get a cent
> of royalties in any of them.[15]

Nor has the situation improved very much over the years. In the mid
1960s, Ornette Coleman reported that he had 'never received a royalty
cheque large enough to pay his phone bill', yet one of his records was re-
issued three times, selling 25,000 copies.[16] Even the most commercially
successful still only received a small percentage on the sale of the record.
Frank Sinatra kept only 6.66 per cent of $11m worth of sales between
1941 and 1946; even the Beatles got only 8 per cent – while EMI got 40
per cent and the retailers kept 26 per cent (leaving 28 per cent for 'others').
It is possible, says Christopher Small, who quotes these figures, 'to propose
a rule of thumb, that if an artist or group makes a lot of money it is only
after a lot of other people have made a lot more money first'. Thus, Elvis
Presley may have become a millionaire, but in the late 1950s his records
accounted for nearly 25 per cent of Victor's total record sales, much as the
Beatles carried EMI in the 1960s.

There are two issues at stake here, jobs and royalties, where the interests
of different parties are at odds; and the 28 per cent labelled 'others' includes
the rights and royalties attached to the author's copyright which histori-
cally united the interests of composers, songwriters and publishers. The
American Society of Composers, Authors and Publishers (or ASCAP), the
trade organization set up in America on the European model to fight for
these rights, dates from 1914 – that is, five years after the Copyright Act
which established a fixed royalty on records. The organization took off
three years later, when it secured an appeal court ruling in their favour
against the non-payment of royalties by hotel bands. A year later they won

a ruling against moving picture exhibitors and began to organize licensing schemes to collect the dues. By the mid 1920s, as radio performance rights began to assume importance, the radio stations fell into line without contest – not willingly, however, and in 1940, perceiving a shift in popular tastes away from the mainstream repertoire represented by the composers and publishers of ASCAP, the radio stations set up a rival organization, which they called BMI (Broadcast Music Incorporated), and then announced a boycott of ASCAP music.

The ASCAP was incensed. A full-page advertisement in *Billboard* in September 1940 suggested that bandleaders and the Federal Communications Commission might both have something to say about the attempt by the radio stations 'to monopolise the air with music of the chain-organised, chain controlled BMI'.

> We believe that the chains might just as well take away musicians' instruments as take away their music.
>
> Boycott or no boycott, the public will still want to hear its favourite tunes, by its favourite writers, played by its favourite bands ... If the public cannot get the music it wants from the chains, it will get it from the individual stations ... many [of which] have signed with ASCAP.
>
> It will get it from sheet music and records. It will get it from the bands in hotels, ballrooms, nightclubs, dance halls and theaters.
>
> Music gets around. So does the public.[17]

Some of this was true and some of it was wishful thinking. It is absolutely true that music, and the public, get around, boycott or no boycott; and that the ASCAP, although it comprised only about one thousand members, had strong ties with Broadway and Hollywood and was immensely powerful. But the musicians to whom they appealed for their loyalty were mostly as pragmatic as they were adaptable, and sensed their own opportunity in the dispute between the ASCAP and the radio chains. For one thing, the ASCAP collected royalties for live performances on the radio, but BMI promised to collect for recorded performances as well, an obvious benefit for performers of the kind of repertoire that existed on the margins – jazz, blues, country and Latin American music – which they had been recording for years for little or no money. In 1942, with nothing more to lose, the AFM announced a recording ban against the major record companies, which lasted, remarkably, for two years and ended in victory. In effect it decided to play the networks off against the record industry with the demand that record companies pay musicians a royalty in compensation for lost revenues. The majors resisted, while small independent companies, without backlists or vested interests, were happy to sign. In fact, the situation was a boon for independent record labels. As one writer puts it, 'The recording ban enabled petty capital to re-enter the world of recording', and the AFM licensed 350 independent companies before the ban was over, although most of them folded once the ban did. But profits could be enormous. 'A hit like "Cement Mixer", by Slim Galliard, cost $500 to produce, and grossed $300,000, a quarter of it profit.'[18] Once again we are reminded of the potential super-profits to be made in the record business.

The majors resisted by stockpiling new recordings in the months before the ban started; by re-issuing old hits; and, since vocalists were organized by a different union, by recording solo singers with choral backings. The ban also redounded to the benefit of music not subject to copyright, which produced a vogue for 'swinging the classics'. But these were short-term measures, and by the end of 1944 the majors had conceded – although the story was not to end there.

The 1930s, in sum, was a complex period. To begin with, the Depression produced a major regrouping of forces within the US music industry, which affected all its branches. Publishing, the entertainment circuits and the agencies that served them, record companies, broadcasting and cinema – all of them moved in the direction of increasing merger and monopolization, tempered now and then by the effects of the anti-trust laws and competition from Europe.

The Depression thus oiled a process which began in the 1920s, when the emergence of radio and the talkies brought a crisis on the record business. In the restructuring of the 1930s, companies regrouped around the electrical connections between different sound technologies, and then began to re-organize as an integral part of a wider entertainment industry. The process affected the music of those musicians who remained in work. Record companies either suffered mergers and take-overs or they went out of business; the trend was set by RCA's acquisition of Victor in 1929, and led to the acquisition of Columbia by CBS in 1938. This time Columbia changed hands for $700,000, and brought the new idols of big band music and swing under contract, like Duke Ellington, Count Basie and Benny Goodman.

Again, the crisis was not limited to America. In Britain, the gramophone industry was prevented from entering radio by the creation of the BBC as the state-sanctioned monopoly broadcaster. The English Columbia company merged with Pathé in 1928, and then with The Gramophone Company in 1931 to create EMI. In Germany, Deutsche Gramophon merged with Telefunken in 1937 and was then bought up by Siemens in 1941.

In the process, the world's major music companies and the corporations to which they were linked not only rationalized the industry but divided the world market into distinct spheres of interest and control. RCA dominated the entire American market, both north and south; Decca and EMI controlled not only the British market but that of the entire British Empire; in France, a single company, Pathé–Marconi, enjoyed unrestricted access to French and French colonial markets, while the Dutch company Philips dominated the markets of north and central Europe.

Above all, what the sectoral battles of the industry in the 1930s clearly signal is the overall transformation of the mode of production of music. Recording and broadcasting are not merely techniques of reproduction but, like Tin Pan Alley, tend to the industrialization of musical production itself. These developments therefore only exacerbated the control that music impresarios habitually exert over the musicians to whom they give employ, usually by the indirect method of determining the conditions of that employment and who gets paid for doing what. With industrialization the process extended the standardization of commercial music production initiated by Tin Pan Alley, enlarging the stereotypical use of musical formulae with a proven success rate, interlarded for the sake of variety with a token dose of novelty. The aim of flooding the market with standard products is to control it, to insure the producer against the whims of taste, or at least to cushion these risks; the result is also to induce the standardization of audience response, and thus of consumption.

According to Adorno, who observed the process from the vantage point of Berlin and then America, standardization is the converse of the fetishization of the musical surface, a process in which the consumer's attention is diverted to incidental features ranging from the performer's personality to catchy phrases and special instrumental effects. It also attaches to the sonic object: the sound of the crooning voice or, another electrical innovation of the 1930s, the electric guitar. This is a process that goes on in art music as much as mass entertainment, as the case of Toscanini clearly shows (of which more later). And behind it lies the suggestion of a crucial ideological function, a service rendered by the stereotypes and fetishes of musical consumption to the social conditioning of the consumer which, not by accident, is the fundamental aim of advertising. Indeed, in the same way that radio created the theme tune, it was in the 1930s that advertising created a new musical genre of its very own – the jingle – in which music as a fetish object achieves its purest form.

But music is not, after all, a unidimensional object, and these developments have had a tendency to produce effects that were not envisaged, giving rise to new musical styles, new forms and languages, which the music industry thinks of in terms of fads and fashions but after which it is forced to chase. Fashion, however, is not simply a fabrication of the market; the fashion market is a corruption of human appetites and desires, and music shares in its trends because it is an object of pleasure and expression, an embodiment of the sentiments of a community. The record industry learned to prey upon the vanguards of popular music, diluting their creative independence, destroying their sense of judgement, taming their instincts, until a band gets stuck into its groove and another rises to replace it. The business of commercial music promotion is to keep the system geared up to these periodic injections of vital juices, plugging into the latest trend in order to take it over and plug it.

It was with the rise of the jukebox that the promotional apparatus of the post-war record industry first began to take shape. The competition grew so intense that *Variety* started publishing popularity charts in the late 1930s, and the record companies began to cook the figures to try to gain advantage. It was common knowledge that the business was not quite respectable. The machine and its music carried low-life connotations: the derivation of the term is the creole (Gullah) word 'juke', as in 'juke house' for brothel. As for the music, the jukebox particularly stimulated 'race' and 'hillbilly' recordings for the black and white markets respectively; and the record companies found distinct advantages in using jazz musicians to help them to cut the costs of production.

Indeed the recovery of the late 1930s was well served by the jazz musician's adaptability to the studio, which translated into modest production economics. The bands were small and low-paid; their facility for improvisation and creating new melodic lines over familiar harmonic structures, helped to avoid copyright payments. Moreover the musicians were in direct touch with the audience and knew what they liked. The result was to succour a new musical sensibility whose dissemination after the war would help to transform popular music completely.

Jazz was to thrive on the confusion of the war years. The popularity of swing with white audiences provided many musicians with relatively secure means of economic support, where a new generation of musicians learnt their skills. Moving between the big swing dance bands and informal after-hours jam sessions, a new style began to crystallize in the early 1940s, played by small informal ensembles which again were easy to bring into the studio. The jam session originated as a semi-private and informal site for the self-expression of the professional dance-band musician, where small audiences of cognoscenti appreciated the technical skill and creativity that the big dance bands restricted and regimented. The clubs where bebop took root were typically run by musicians, who hired a small rhythm section and invited celebrity players to 'sit in' (in return for food and drinks on the house). Here experiment was not only permitted but expected, and in practice provided the means of screening out those without the necessary technical competence: fast tempi, awkward key signatures and difficult chord sequences discouraged them from participating. Some of the musicians also spoke of a musical idiom that white musicians would be incapable of imitating. The key date in recording history is 1944, when Charlie Parker made his first small-group sides for Savoy. These recordings have acquired a documentary status. Paradoxically and ironically, the record becomes the work, the act of improvised performance caught on the wing. Because each take is a slightly different and therefore unique realization of the number, the record – even in the case of bebop, which made a cult of spontaneity – acquires respect as an art object in itself. As Eisenberg puts it, Charlie Parker's alternate takes for Savoy have come to be treasured for their endless invention, in much the same way as a series of studies by Picasso.

One more development of this period should be mentioned which, although it will take longer to bear fruit, will also turn out to have a major influence on popular musical taste. In the colonial world of the 1930s, where the spread of records and radio went hand in hand, the age of electrical reproduction brought the first commercial recordings of indigenous popular music. Radio stations were set up by either private enterprise or the colonial powers, and the first commercial records of indigenous music followed. Or, the other way round, a recording studio was set up and then a radio station. The pattern varied in different countries. Nairobi, for example, saw the first recording sessions at the turn of the 1920s, a year after the introduction of radio, with four European companies competing against each other: The Gramophone Company and Columbia from Britain, the French Pathé and the German Odeon. The symbiosis between the radio and records here took on its own dynamic, in a curious example of the effects of unequal technical development. Where unequal development is usually thought to mean that underdeveloped countries are always technically behind the centres of advanced technology in the developed world, in this case a more advanced technology, radio, is complemented by another, the gramophone, but in an older version. And the old wind-up gramophone playing electrical recordings extended beyond the domain of radio, which was limited to the reach of electricity. In this way the seeds were sown for a process that, three decades on, after the appearance of transistor radios and cassette players, would have far-reaching effects on traditional musics.

These foreign-based companies recorded indiscriminately, mixing traditional songs and modern dance music, Christian mission hymns and Islamic chants, issuing the local music and the imported alongside each other. As a result, an unprecedented range of music became available to, say, a middle-class African household, as the list of records that the writer Wole Soyinka remembered from his childhood indicates (he was born in 1932):

> The voices of Denge, Ayinde Bakare, Ambrose Campbell; a voice which was so deep that I believed it could only have been produced by a special trick of His Master's Voice, but which father assured me belonged to a black man called Paul Robeson ... Christmas carols, the songs of Marion Anderson; oddities such as a record in which a man did nothing but laugh throughout, and the one concession to a massed choir of European voices – the Hallelujah Chorus.[19]

It was entirely European record companies that ran this trade, through their local subsidiaries. Local musicians were hopelessly exploited. They were paid by the session, royalties were virtually unheard of, and there was no such thing as protection of copyright. In Africa a good deal of music was recorded, both traditional and urban, but it was sent to Europe for pressing, the discs then being exported back in a lucrative double trade which guaranteed handsome profits.

But the gramophone also brought its own benefits. Unlike radio, what it played was under the control of the operator, and its social role developed accordingly. In the Arab world, for example, where Western musicologists at the Cairo Arab Music Conference of 1932, including Bartók and Hindemith, warned their Arab colleagues of the dangers of the Westernization of Arab music, it became not only a domestic luxury but also a feature of café life, in circumstances where it was able to fulfill a powerful new cultural role. In one of the first fusions of a local music with the modern recording media, records allowed the wider diffusion of a new form, the *dwar*, based on a traditional elite style and exemplified by the Egyptian singer Sayyid Darwich. The *dwar*, in one account, united a divided Arab world from Morocco to Iraq to become, through the gramophone, 'the musical model and melodic reference of the era'.[20] We have seen this capacity of the gramophone before, and we will again, although it was only in the 1980s that the creative vigour of Third World musicians in the face of the record began to hit home back where recording came from.

6

Of LPs, EPs, DJs and Payola

Post-war reconstruction in the developed world rapidly picked up where the 1930s left off. Consumer expansion began with the re-introduction of television, the development of the LP microgroove record and the re-launch of magnetic recording. Like radio at the end of the First World War, the rapid spread of television in the late 1940s and early 1950s came from the reconversion to consumer electronics of the huge productive capacity in electronics which had been developed to fight the war. These developments would then be extended by the introduction of the transistor and the integrated circuit, which led to hand-held transistor radios and the audio cassette. In the course of this process, each sector in the entertainment industry became more and more involved in competitive symbiosis with every other sector – each competed with the others which at the same time were linked to its own market.

Taking them one by one, the LP, which in part was the record industry's fight-back against television in the same way that the sound movie had been cinema's response to radio, had been on the cards since the 1930s, when RCA had first introduced it for professional purposes, although it had hung back from launching it as a consumer format. The post-war development of the tape recorder was a by-product of military victory, when entrepreneurs in the United States pounced upon German patents which victory made available as part of the spoils. Transistor technology, for which the R&D was promoted by the space agencies' need for miniaturization, benefited all branches of electronic technology: it was not only more reliable but also cheaper and easier to mass-produce than valve-based systems, leading to both a fall in price and increase in ease of use.

It also required less power, and the appearance of car radios and battery-operated radios which could be carried around anywhere ensured that radio broadcasting more than defended its market. Indeed in Third World countries it was only in the 1950s and 1960s that radio became the principal medium of mass diffusion, followed by the rise of the cassette in the 1970s. The transistor also helped the worldwide growth of computer technology, since the computer chip represents the miniaturization of the transistor.

One factor behind the development of the LP was the search for an alternative material to shellac when supplies of the resin were seriously reduced during the war – in America at one stage, purchasers were required to return old discs when they bought new ones. The idea of using plastic was not a new one. Edison and his assistant Jonas Aylesworth had tried coating cylinders with plastic around 1909. The material they came up with was remarkably similar to a substance invented at the same time by a Dutch-born American chemist, Leo Baekeland, which he patented in 1909 under the trade name Bakelite, and was then manufactured by Union Carbide and Carbon. The first of the thermo-plastics, the material was originally too brittle for the recording surface but perfect for housing electrical components, and the radio industry put it to use for valve sockets, control knobs, and the cabinet of the radio set itself. RCA used metal, coated in a thermo-plastic lacquer, for its long-play discs in the 1930s, when a new generation of thermo-plastics appeared, but it was the Japanese blockade of Malaya that finally prompted the engineers at a new research laboratory set up by CBS in 1944 to try making the whole disc out of one of the new plastics. The result improved considerably on the long-play transcription discs of ten years earlier. Vinyl enabled the size of the groove to be dramatically reduced, with a reduction in surface noise coming from an improved signal-to-noise ratio and at the same time an enhancement in the recorded signal, thus allowing more music to be recorded on a disc the same size as before but revolving more slowly and producing a better sound. The 33⅓ r.p.m. microgroove LP was launched by Columbia in the United States in 1948, the seven-inch 45 r.p.m. a year later by RCA Victor.

In the classical market the LP was a rapid success. In a very short time, wrote Alejo Carpentier in 1951, the idea of changing the record every three or four minutes, and continuing to suffer the consequent interruptions, became insupportable. An acute observer of the musical trends of his day, which in the 1950s he chronicled in a column in the Venezuelan newspaper *El Nacional*, Carpentier makes an impeccable witness, a musically educated novelist, friend and collaborator of composers, at home on both sides of the Atlantic, who always retained a Latin American perspective. He is critical of the record companies even then for the overproduction of a narrow repertoire of favourites and their neglect of some of the most important scores of both past and present. He is suspicious too of the record collector, the aficionado who has every good version released of the four symphonies of Brahms under different conductors: but has never sat down quietly to listen to the third or fourth, because the idea that Barbirolli's Third might be inferior to Munch's distresses him, or that Munch's Fourth might be superior to de Sabata's, while to aggravate his uneasiness there are still the Fourth by Toscanini and Bruno Walter, not counting others recently recorded so magnificently in Berlin or Vienna, and which – he has just been advised by telephone – have just arrived in Caracas...[1]

He also distrusts certain psychological effects on the listener. It is logical, he writes in 1954, for the music lover to want to upgrade his equipment to get the best reproduction possible, and the latest apparatus allows the listener to modify the reproduction in accordance with factors like room size and its resonance, distance between speaker and listener, even the character of the music. 'But this possibility of control, which often reveals great musicality on the part of the owner of the apparatus, is a double-edged sword leading to serious errors of judgement. Especially when it encourages a type of hearing very different from that of the concert hall.' With its power of logarithmic amplification of sound, the 'high fidelity' apparatus accustoms some aficionados to a much higher volume level than the conductor intended, let alone the composer. Some, after listening to records at arbitrary sound levels, which are too high and over-emphasize either high or low frequencies, are then disconcerted when they hear a live performance. They even think that the concert hall has poor acoustics, when in reality this, and not that of the loudspeaker, is the sonority imagined by the composer. Excessive amplification distorts the music by imparting undue vigour and inappropriate accentuation to music that is intended to be much more discreet, but the listener who succumbs is doing nothing more than the engineer who has already discovered the surface attraction of a sharper, more brilliant sound.[2]

Nevertheless, Carpentier also celebrates the worldwide diffusion of music through recording, which conquers cultural isolation and artistic backwardness and accelerates musical life. Who in seventeenth-century Paris, he asks, knew about Buxtehude? Was Lully known in Germany, except to a few composers who had travelled? Even Bach was generally unknown before Mendelssohn introduced his work to the European concert halls in 1830; Mussorgsky's *Boris Godunov* had to wait thirty-four years before it was first heard in the West, in Paris in 1908; Debussy was unheard in the Americas before he was close to death. And in the mid 1950s, we learn, there are still important works by Stravinsky, including *The Rite of Spring*, that remain unperformed in most Latin American capitals. Nevertheless, says Carpentier, Debussy, Ravel, Stravinsky and others 'have become popular among us thanks to the marvels of the disc'. In other words, recording not only conquers geographical space but bridges the distance of years which previously kept certain works from finding their audiences. For example, where Schoenberg's *Five Pieces for Orchestra*, written before the First World War, suffered long neglect on account of the violent reactions provoked at its premiere, in 1955 his opera *Moses and Aron* reached a worldwide audience although it received only one short run of performances in a single German opera house.

It is not a question of numbers, which in comparison to pop music are very small. Carpentier is speaking of changes in cultural relations: not only between composer and public, but also between the metropolis and the periphery of cultural empires. Recording and its diffusion clearly have the power of cultural integration. Perhaps, with greater access to cultural goods, the periphery may begin to feel less peripheral? But this also depends on whether the response that the process stimulates is heard in the metropolis. This takes much longer to happen and, when it does, assumes a wholly unexpected form.

The introduction of the LP created problems in the recording studio. The LP was developed as a format for distribution, not recording, which at first still required a cutter to inscribe a groove into a master disc revolving at 78 r.p.m., with a maximum length of four minutes or so (depending on the kind of music, since louder music made wider grooves and reduced the time). An alternative technique was available but had never been adopted by the record industry – the optical sound systems developed for the cinema. But suitable versions of these systems, which offered high recording quality and even the possibility of editing, were still at an experimental stage and therefore scarce. John Culshaw, a record producer with Decca in London (later responsible for the first complete recording of Wagner's *Ring* cycle), recounted how Decca's first LPs were made: by stringing together a series of 78 r.p.m. masters while re-recording onto a cutter revolving at 33⅓.

> It was a nightmare ... I stood there with a score and began a countdown during the last thirty seconds of a side and then shouted 'Drop!', at which point one engineer would fade out the side that had just ended while another, with luck, would lower the pickup on the beginning of the next side. If anything went even slightly wrong there was nothing to do but go back to the beginning, and as every LP has to be cut at least twice in case of an accident during processing at the factory it was a tedious and frustrating business.[3]

In short, there was now an urgent need for a new medium for mastering long takes at a quality equal to the microgroove. Informed opinion knew that such a system was in the offing, but it was not the photographic system used by cinema – it was magnetic.

The first magnetic recorder was devised by the Danish inventor Valdemar Poulsen as early as 1898, when he was an engineer at the Copenhagen Telephone Company. Originally using wire as a recording medium (like several other prototypes as late as the 1940s), the telegraphone which he marketed through his own company five years later employed a magnetized disc of steel, although it was small and light enough to be sent through the post; the main limitation was the lack of amplification and the company went out of business. The first tape system was demonstrated in Germany by one Fritz Pfleumer in the late 1920s using paper coated with metallic oxide; it was launched commercially at the German Radio Exhibition in 1934 by AEG, who made the recorder, and BASF (a subsidiary of the electrical giant Siemens), which produced a plastic recording tape. The idea of a plastic base coated with magnetic oxide was modelled on the film strip with its photographic emulsion, but the technology was crude, the frequency response limited and the distortion considerable. The machine was marketed, like Poulsen's telegraphone and the early phonograph, as an office machine, this time brand-named the Magnetophone.

In Britain, around the same time, the BBC tried out a recorder developed
by a certain Kurt Stille and funded by Marconi, which employed a polished
tungsten steel strip as the carrier. The fidelity of the recording was better
but the machine was considered so dangerous it was housed in a separate
room from the operator.

In the United States during the Second World War, the Navy and the
Air Corps funded the development and production of a magnetic wire
recorder developed by a third inventor, Marvin Camras, who worked in
an academic research institute in Illinois. The machines were built 'right
there on the school premises, using students for labour'.[4] During the D-
Day invasion, recorders like these were used to play battle sounds, amplified by thousands of watts, at locations where the invasion was not taking
place in order to mislead the Germans. (Forty-four years later the US
Marines blasted rock music at troops loyal to General Noriega when they
invaded Panama in order to topple him.) After the war, using German
patents, an improved machine was re-launched in the United States, using
tape produced by 3M and machines made by a small Californian company
called Ampex. Ampex company president A.M. Poniatoff was one of the
American troops who had discovered the German magnetic tape recorders
when the Allies captured Radio Luxembourg in 1944.

That Ampex set up shop in California was no accident. The concentration of the entertainments industry in Los Angeles provided the best
point of entry, and tape recording found its way into professional music
production from the moment Bing Crosby first used it in 1947 to record
his network shows. Newsweek reported his delight a few months later.
The crooner not only preferred the reproduction of his voice on tape
over that of discs, but he put his money where his mouth was and started
marketing Ampex machines. Radio producers quickly discovered the ease
with which tape could be spliced and edited, and American broadcasters
and record companies began to abandon discs as a mastering medium. In
the film studios, magnetic coating replaced photographic emulsion as the
medium of recording and editing, and the artistry of the film soundtrack
advanced by leaps and bounds. Movie studios spoke of the benefits of
being able to monitor the recording while shooting and thus reduce the
number of retakes due to sound defects. Mixing and dubbing too were
hugely facilitated, and subsequently, combined with a wide screen and
then colour, allowed the Hollywood majors to fight back effectively against

competition from television. Meawhile, Ampex went on to introduce the first videotape recorders in 1956. (Camras worked on both developments, illustrating the close relationship developed in the United States between industry and campus research.)

In the classical record sector, the initial impact of the tape recorder included a direct challenge to the big monopolies on their own ground. Carpentier noted that while the majors were busy transcribing old recordings and re-issuing them, a number of smaller companies were exploring new repertoire. As Roland Gelatt explains:

> For an investment of a few thousand dollars one could buy a first-class tape-recorder, take it to Europe (where musicians were plentiful and low-salaried), and record great amounts of music; one could then bring the tapes back to America and have the 'custom record department' of either Columbia or RCA transfer them – at a reasonable fee – to microgroove records. One not only could, one did. Between August 1949 and August 1954 the number of companies in America publishing LP recordings increased from eleven to almost two hundred.[5]

Gelatt is misleading in only one respect: most of these independents were not interested in classical music. The minority markets they supplied were popular, and their primary format was originally and for some time not the LP but the seven-inch 45.

In many ways the rise of a new generation of independents was only a repetition of what had happened in the 1920s, when small, often local record companies had flourished by serving minority buyers in regional markets, like the American 'race labels' which promoted jazz and blues. These labels were wiped out by the Depression, only to be replaced by a new generation which sprung up in the 1940s, when the response of the majors to the shortage of shellac was to cut back on minority markets and concentrate on mainstream artists. Most of the companies that stepped in to fill the vacuum collapsed when the majors reasserted their clout after the war, but this time there was no contraction in the market they supplied. On the contrary, the end of the war saw a boom in sales. In 1946 most people in the business, say the industry historians Russell and David Sanjek, 'believed that the released flood of pent-up post-war demand would improve conditions, but nobody was ready for the doubling of sales that took place, to $89 million and 350 million records'. All but fifty million of these were released by Columbia, Decca, Victor and Capitol. Thirty-two pressing plants were operating, supplying the additional fifty million records sold by the independents.[6] A year later, sales exceeded the industry's previous best in 1921, although they subsequently fell back again.

The fact that 90 per cent or more of the output that resulted was played and sold for no more than a few weeks and then effectively disappeared does not negate the impact of this musical explosion. In the first place, the market was geared to instant success. As one writer puts it, no one cared about longevity. 'It didn't have to last. It probably wouldn't. All it had to do was sell.'[7] This was not just a mark of commercial philistinism but also a characteristic of the living popular culture from which the music came, which held no store by permanently fixed versions of anything. Hence, more important and striking is the link that appears between independent record producers and new currents of popular musical expression, which suggests that the growth of the market is not a purely passive affair.

It is part of the pattern that when independents are successful, they succumb to the majors, which are eager to acquire their artists (for they operate on the principle that if they cannot buy the singer then they buy the company for which he or she sings). The process, which has been repeated many times, often begins with a distribution agreement, which may even run for several years before the smaller label loses the remains of its erstwhile independence. This leaves spaces to be filled by the next generation of indies, for what the majors cannot acquire is what a later decade will call street credibility. The result is that successive generations of independent labels are associated with successive musical styles, and the changing styles with successive generations of artists. These styles have a lineage, a genealogy, and the history of the independent labels is often the history of pop music itself. For example, in the 1940s, labels like Apollo, King and Specialty featured a new generation of singers such as Aretha Franklin performing a new style known as gospel, which has been called 'the spiritual with a jazz rhythm and inflected by the blues'. In the 1960s, the growth of alternative rock and black music was again led by new labels like Motown and A&M. The souped-up strain of black gospel that put Motown on the map is called soul.

This pattern would seem less true of companies that busy themselves with the classical market, yet here too independent producers are sensitive

99

to changing taste, are frequently linked with new recorded repertoire and, in the same way as the pop independents, are gradually absorbed by the majors. Carpentier observed the phenomenon in the middle 1950s, when he remarked that it was often left to small companies to record big works that were rarely performed because of their special demands or character. In the 1980s, when the compact disc appeared, something similar happened as a new generation of independents came into being to cater for what were now called 'niche markets', ranging all the way from early medieval to Californian New Age.

The truth is that the classic conditions described by Rosa Luxemburg in her study of *The Accumulation of Capital* also operate in the domain of cultural production, and the majors need the independents in the same way that industrial capital needs the small producers that play the role of pioneers towards new markets. Moreover another economic law operates here as well, namely the relative ease with which small operators can take advantage of expensive new technologies whose research and development has been borne by the market leaders. But music has another dimension too, and manages in this way to loosen its subordination to the market and claim the space for original currents of expression. The result is seen especially in the explosion of new forms of popular music in the 1950s, beginning in America, quickly taken up in Britain, and then rapidly conquering the world.

The majors, which aimed their product at white markets, at first retained their dominance over the American market. Of 163 records selling over a million copies each between 1946 and 1952, all but five were recorded by one of six companies. Three dated back to before the war and were based in New York: Columbia and Victor, which had their origins in pre-electrical days, and Decca, which dated from 1932, when it was set up as the American branch of the British Decca company. The other three were newcomers. Two were located in Los Angeles: Capitol, the first West Coast major, established in 1941, and the label set up by MGM in 1946, which fell in with EMI for worldwide distribution of Hollywood stars and sound-track music. The third, Mercury, dating from the same year, was Chicago-based. Of the newcomers, Capitol was the most aggressive: it is said to be the first record company regularly to service disc jockeys with free releases.

Los Angeles, with its growing black population, was also one of the centres for the new indies, the location of labels like Specialty, Aladdin,

Modern, Swingtime and Imperial, although much of the music they drew upon came from the fertile musical sources of New Orleans and Memphis. But they were not unique. Spread out across the country, says Charlie Gillett in his classic history of rock,

> similar types of record companies were established from humble beginnings in garages, store-rooms and basements, with early distribution carried out by the owners from the trunks of their cars. King, in Cincinnati; Peacock, in Houston; Chess, in Chicago; Savoy, in Newark, New Jersey; and Atlantic, in New York, were all founded between 1940 and 1950, a decade in which as many blacks (one and a quarter million) left the South as had done so in the previous thirty years.[8]

This huge migration created new markets with which the majors were not in touch, and in these circumstances a new pattern of operation emerged, at first very much hand-to-mouth. Jerry Wexler, who went from *Billboard* journalist to record producer at Atlantic, describes this kind of operation neatly:

> There was a kind of record man ... who did the whole thing ... he had to find an artist, find a song, con the artist into coming into his studio, coax him into singing the song, pull the record out of him, press the record; then take that record and go to the disc jockeys and con them into putting it on the radio, then go to the distributors and beg them to take a box of twenty-five and try it out.[9]

Atlantic has been regarded by many commentators as the exemplification of the new independents; it was set up in 1947 by a pair of jazz enthusiasts, one of whom, Ahmet Ertegun, was the son of the Turkish ambassador in Washington; the other, Herb Ambramson, was a New Yorker with minimal experience as a record producer with National Records. But it was not entirely typical; for one thing, Atlantic operated nationally, not locally, originally building up distribution by making reciprocal arrangements with other independents in different parts of the country. But they also turned to the American South as a hunting ground, where they undertook what Ertegun called 'ethnomusicological expeditions' to discover new artists and new repertoire.[10] The results converted them into the most important rhythm and blues label in the 1950s, sporting artists like Ray Charles, Joe Turner, Clyde McPhatter and others.

Rhythm and blues was a new term for race music adopted by the trade paper *Billboard* in 1949 in an attempt to remove prejudicial connotations, in much the same way that what used to be called 'hillbilly' was then similarly renamed 'country and western' in an attempt to update its image. However, in the words of a *Billboard* journalist of a later generation, the paper was not setting a trend 'but responding to a phrase and a feeling the independent labels had already made part of the vocabulary'.[11]

The majors now developed the tactic of using their own white artists to 'cover' black records: that is, when an independent scored a hit, one of the majors or its subsidiary labels would produce its own version and reap the benefits. Under American copyright law and the system of compulsory licensing, this siphoned off potential sales from the black version, although whoever owned the musical copyright still got their money. The hardest hit in these circumstances was usually the original singer, who only got royalties on their own record. The independent labels could set up their own publishing companies and wherever possible secure the copyright on any song they recorded, thus reaping the advantage when songs were covered by other artists on other labels and proved successful. They readily attracted new black singers and their agents, who found them much more approachable than the majors, with A&R men and musical directors who were familiar with the type of music. Most of the companies, pleading poverty, exploited songwriters ruthlessly, and composers were often forced to sell their copyright for a small lump sum or even sign it away for the 'privilege' of recording. In this connection, Atlantic has also been singled out, by writers both black and white, for the honesty and fairness of its treatment of recording artists. Although offering notoriously low advances, it paid royalties and was loyal. But it too lost songs and artists to the majors, and ended up being taken over in 1967 by Warners.

In these circumstances it even made sense for independents, black as well as white, to encourage white cover versions. In the case of a successful cover artist like Elvis Presley the earnings could be phenomenal. 'Hound Dog', for example, was originally issued in a version by Willie Mae ('Big Mama') Thornton on Peacock in 1953, when the song was credited to Johnny Otis. When it was recorded again by Elvis Presley for RCA in 1956, it was ascribed to Jerry Leiber and Mike Stoller, the freelance producers who wrote a whole string of Presley hits. The authorship of this song was twice subject to court hearings: first Leiber and Stoller went to court accusing Otis of stealing it from them, and then, when Presley covered it, Otis countersued. But Otis was not the composer either. He was a West Coast bandleader with the knack of finding good musicians and singers, and a flair for packaging them, an operation that included buying up everything outright. He 'discovered' Willie Mae Thornton at an audition in Houston and, according to her own account, for a single payment of $500 she recorded and sold her rights in a song that three years later sold two million copies in a few weeks.[12] But these practices were common and widespread, and not only in the litigious business culture of the United States. The plight of the original composer of a popular hit who has been robbed of his royalties is the subject of feature films hailing from Brazil (*Rio Zona Norte*, directed by Nelson Pereira dos Santos and starring Grande Otelo, made in 1957) and Jamaica (*The Harder They Come*, 1972, starring Jimmy Cliff and directed by Perry Henzell).

Tape recording shook up recording technique on both the classical and popular sides of the business, but differently, and in stages. (I shall examine the effects on classical music in the next chapter.) By the early 1950s most recording studios in the United States were using tape for the same reasons as broadcast studios, as an improved mastering medium with added advantages (sometimes it was the same studio, hired out by a local radio station to an out-of-town record producer). The equipment was not expensive and tape was re-usable. They included small set-ups in regional cities, like Sam Philips' Recording Service in Memphis, Tennessee, the studio of Sun Records where in 1953 Elvis Presley cut his first discs which popular commentators are wont to call the birthplace of rock 'n' roll. Philips had a distinctive style. According to one rock writer he was one of the first to go for a heavy echo effect, but the overall sound was crisp, clean and full of life. According to another, the 'live' quality was mainly the result of microphone placement. With the musicians lined up in front of the microphones the same way they lined up on stage, the microphones picked up sound from adjacent instruments as well as a measure of ambient sound. The sound went through a mixer where reverberation was added and recorded straight onto a monaural tape recorder (with a conventional disc cutter as a back-up).

The redesign of the control room also began to leave its mark, by redefining certain jobs. As disc cutting could now be removed from the studio to the record factory, the recording engineer was freed to concentrate more on the signal coming from the microphones rather than the delicate task of putting it down on the disc. To help the engineer, a new generation of small specialist electronics companies grew up to supply a proliferation of equipment to monitor and control the signal. In the pop music studio at least, any vestiges of the old documentary approach to recording disappeared, and engineers developed a technique that could be called either contrived or creative, depending on preference. Engineers appeared who became associated with a particular type of sound exploited by a particular label, like Atlantic's Tom Dowd, responsible for the special clarity of the label's sound.

The Atlantic sound contrasted with what was called the RCA mix, the effect of using just one or two microphones for the orchestral accompaniment, which was pushed into the background behind a well-focused voice. In the sonority that engineers like Dowd gave to R&B, each instrument can be heard clearly and, according to one account, 'the level doesn't change during the instrumental solos, as it did on many of the more casually recorded records of the time'.[13] According to the testimony of Jerry Wexler, it needed fine acoustic discrimination, and he described Dowd as one of his teachers. His colourful account is revealing on several points:

> Our gig was to get the music played right and righteous in the studio. Tom's job was to capture it on tape. It was up to him to find a true mix of timbres, bass, treble and midrange; to load as much volume as possible without distortion. Tom pushed those pots [the volume controls] like a painter sorting colours. He turned microphone placement into an art. Most of all, in those days of mono, he was responsible for catching the right mix on the fly. There was no 'We'll fix it in the mix.' Single tracking was get-it-or-gone.
>
> Tom also knew the music. He actually taught me how to count bars...[14]

Remixing there was not – the technology was still a few years away – but tape editing meant that it was no longer necessary to select between the best of several alternative takes of a complete item, since a 'perfect' version could be assembled from several imperfect ones. The technique at first affected the organization of the recording session mainly by reducing recording time (later, studio time increased again as the process became more complicated), and by promoting the role of the producer, who was not only responsible for paying the bills and organizing the session efficiently but also for supervising the post-production stage, which now became more important. Wexler quotes Dowd himself on the subject: 'The early Atlantic sessions ... had me experimenting like a madman. I had no choice. Jerry [Wexler] and Ahmet [Ertegun] were sticklers for a clean, crisp sound, and I was determined to get it.'[15]

In fact there are no hard and fast lines of demarcation between the jobs of producer, engineer and the traditional A&R man, but different combinations of a range of skills, and different styles and regimes of operation according to circumstance. The skills are variously musical, technical and organizational, the circumstances principally economic. These have altered with the evolution of the record industry, but in every period several different levels of activity co-exist, and with them various types of producer: the entrepreneurial, the corporate and the independent, the jack-of-all-trades and, last to emerge, the artistic. Radio DJ and record producer Charlie Gillett argued in 1977, addressing a New York symposium on the centenary of the phonograph, that 'the artist on a record can very well be the producer, not the performer'.[16] In fact his account reveals the process of producing a successful record to have not one but multiple authors, not only working as a team but sometimes achieving results in spite of each other. (The producer as creator, however, re-emerged later, when the process of musical production became computerized, and a single pair of hands could produce sounds from electronic instruments, record them, mix them, produce the final master track, and then issue the results on their own label.)

In the early days, men like Gaisberg were jacks-of-all-trades. The restructuring of the industry in the 1930s turned the role into the corporate Artist and Repertory Man (they were always men), who ran the big stars for the majors. Less of a talent scout (he would have scouts working under him), he picked the songs and the arrangements and supervised the recording sessions. He was a 'fixer with a salary'. 'All he had to do', says Gelatt, 'was to bring together the various components – a song written for a movie, an orchestra, an arrangement by Nelson Riddle, and a singer' – his example is Frank Sinatra singing 'Three Coins in a Fountain' on Capital in the mid 1950s, produced by one Voyle Gilmore. 'I don't know how much such a producer thought about the audience; if he did think about it, it would have been in a rather cynical way ("They'll lap this one up!").'[17]

In comparison, the first generation of independents, like Wexler and Ertegun, were 'Renaissance men' who did a little bit of everything on the basis of very strong musical instincts. These are Gillett's second type of record producer, who thereby emulate the jack-of-all-trades tradition of their grandfathers' generation. As well as talent scouting they could engineer the take and, if necessary, sing in the chorus, even turn their hand to songwriting, although they rarely had any degree of musical training. Hence they favoured arrangers who wrote their own material and rehearsed their own musicians, like Jessie Stone at Atlantic, who was equally responsible for the characteristic Atlantic sound. A seasoned show-biz veteran whose career went back to Kansas City in the 1920s, Stone contributed the rocking rhythmic blues-like bass line. If a white-owned company like Atlantic was indeed sensitive to shifts in black musical tastes, says Nelson George, it was because of the contribution of their black musical directors. Similarly,

> Leonard Chess of Chess Records could claim he knew everything about the blues, but it was bassist Willie Dixon whose musical judgements would be crucial to the recordings of Chuck Berry, Bo Diddley, and Muddy Waters. At Duke-Peacock … it was trombonist and house-arranger Joe Scott who gave [Don Robey's] music its haunting pathos. At King Records in Cincinnati … arranger Henry Glover was critical to actually making the music happen in the studio.[18]

Where the songs came from, as we have already seen, was another matter. As Gillett puts it,

> For a long time, many of us thought that Dave Bartholomew was a fantastic songwriter: often, on the charts of the top hits, there would be 'Lennon and McCartney' on top and 'Domino and Bartholomew' just below them. But actually, Domino and Bartholomew were just buying songs from all kinds of unknown people in New Orleans. Nevertheless, the songs they bought were good. A man at King Records in Cincinnati named Henry Glover … did a similar sort of thing.[19]

Dave Bartholomew, he adds, did 'invaluable' work as producer for Fats Domino.

When the songwriter, instead of selling their song to a Dave Bartholomew, set out to become their own producer, you get Gillett's third type of producer. The models are Leiber and Stoller. It was partly their litigious experience with 'Hound Dog' that induced them to set up their own record and publishing companies, which brought them to the notice of Atlantic. According to Stoller, talking to Gillett, the resulting deal, whereby they went to work as producers for Atlantic without giving up their right to work for other labels, might have been 'the first independent producer contract ever made', and a step towards the restructuring of the record business.[20] This is the artistic kind of producer – they write their own material, choose the artists and direct the whole operation; like many a film director.

How creative they are is another matter. By the end of the 1950s there was a whole generation of producers adept at manufacturing performers as well as records, in a process that made recording technology more important than musicality. As an American journalist put it in 1959:

> Recording techniques have become so ingenious that almost anyone can seem to be a singer. A small, flat voice can be souped up by emphasising the low frequencies and piping the result through an echo chamber. A slight speeding up of the recording tape can bring a brighter, happier sound to a naturally drab singer or clean the weariness out of a tired voice ... The gadgetry dam really burst after Elvis Presley's recorded voice was so doctored up with echoes that he sounded as though he were going to shake apart.[21]

These practices have of course continued. A writer in 1992 says that 'Madonna's voice is often made to sound higher and lighter (and therefore younger) ... by the simple method of increasing the tape replay speed'.[22]

But we shall return to the question of the producer in a later chapter, when we consider the figure of George Martin and the rise of the studio album, which represents a new kind of musical genre and hence a new set of production values.

In many accounts, the rise of the independents is closely linked with the disc jockey, with the explosion in the mid 1950s of a new musical genre called rock 'n' roll, and a new style of radio station called Top 40, which played the hits of the day in rotation. Top 40 was devised in 1953 by a commercial station operator called Todd Storz, although the first 'hit parade' programmes go back to the mid 1930s. The term 'disc jockey' was coined by *Variety* in 1937 to describe the announcers who interspersed their comments between the records – although in a sense, says Erik Barnouw in his history of American broadcasting, the figure goes back to Reginald Fessenden playing records on his Christmas Eve broadcast in 1906.[23]

The role of the disc jockey is a central one in the culture generated by pop music since the 1950s, and associated as much with dance halls and clubs as with radio. A typically masculine role, the quintessential DJ is a kind of performer on the turntable to the accompaniment of his own speech; the performance is often as ear-catching as the records. But the cultural role of the DJ has never been limited to the job description. The classic DJ is an activist who animates people, a promoter of records and of bands; some became managers or record producers or vocal performers.

The history of deejaying has yet to be written, but it clearly reveals a succession of styles in the presentation of records on air which among other things reflect changing concepts of the radio audience. In the 1920s there was little notion that audiences consisted of anything other than large numbers. In the 1930s, the first audience researchers discovered that different kinds of people listen at different times of day, and programme schedules were devised accordingly; with soaps in the afternoon, for example, when housewives were the largest segment of the audience, or swing in the evening. Since then, audience measurement techniques developed by companies like Nielsen have profiled listeners and viewers in ever greater detail, providing vital information for advertisers and programme producers along with the ratings. The process, however, hides a fundamental problem about radio: not who are the people that the announcer addresses unseen through the microphone, but how to address them?

The earliest model for the announcer was that of master of ceremonies, which assumes that the listening audience is basically the same as it would be if it were present, to be addressed accordingly. One model for record programme presenters in the 1930s, therefore, was that of the ballroom emcee, whose style in America was rather more informal than in Britain. At the BBC, Reith had issued a famous directive in 1925 that announcers were to wear dinner jackets in the evenings; he also rejected what was called 'highly individualized announcing in the American style' and told his station directors that announcers should be 'men of culture, experience and knowledge' – and anonymous.[24] This was in line with his high concept of the duty of radio in the service of the nation but did not answer the announcer–presenter's real problem, which is one of intonation. Intonation is produced in the act of dialogue; it is the tone of voice in which a speaker addresses the person to whom they are talking in accordance with the situation in which they find themselves. What happens when the human person is replaced by a microphone, and the situation is reduced to a studio?

By the mid 1930s the BBC had become sufficiently worried about the wayward intonation of their announcers that they co-opted linguists to help them. According to one of them the real problem was not establishing a standard pronunciation suitable for communicating with all parts of the English-speaking world, but how to create a new form of public speech to be heard not in public spaces but in the intimacy of the home.[25] The question was not considered parochial, but of great concern to the body politic, since radio constituted an unprecedented means of political communication. In America, the presidential 'fireside chats' initiated by Franklin D. Roosevelt on taking office in 1933, contrasted strikingly with the broadcasts of Hitler and Mussolini, who were heard in public appearances with a background of hysterical crowds. Roosevelt was the voice of power disguised as that of a friend or neighbour. The radio men who crewed these broadcasts, says Barnouw, spoke of him admiringly as 'a real pro'. According to a member of his Cabinet, watching, he seemed totally unaware of those around him: he seemed to be trying to picture in his mind the people to whom he was talking, 'as though he were actually sitting on the front porch or in the parlour with them'. Or in the less friendly words of John Dos Passos, 'There is a man leaning across his desk speaking clearly and cordially to youandme ... leaning towards youandme across his desk ... so that youandme shall completely understand...'[26] Those who understood the political effects of radio were quite aware of what was at issue. In the words of the BBC's Head of Talks in the same year, Hilda Matheson, it was the need of every dictatorship, 'left or right or neither', to secure 'at least an acquiescent public'.[27] A year later, Joseph Goebbels began to advocate a *volkstümlich* (popular) approach, encouraging announcers to use more casual forms of speech: 'The announcer must never be impersonal. The radio speaker must sound like the listener's best friend.'[28]

The question is, to whom does the voice really belong. Recording and radio transmission are responsible for a fatal shift in the natural order, which separates voice and body. Consider what happens to the singer's voice, for instance, when it parts company with the singer. For several years, Barnouw mentions, a warning was carried on the records made by top network radio performers like Bing Crosby: 'Not licensed for public broadcast.' The purpose was to prevent records undermining their network contracts, and they backed up the warning with law suits. But in 1940, in a case involving Paul Whiteman, the courts ruled that broadcasters were free to broadcast any record they had purchased, effectively confirming what was already the case, that the singer who records their voice loses control over it.

The ruling put the disc jockeys on a secure legal footing, and their numbers began to mushroom. For local stations it was a boon, for this kind of programme required a minimum of investment. The 'talent' consisted of a disc jockey who was paid by commission on the sponsorship and advertising that the programme atttracted. But if he who pays the piper calls the tune, then the rise of the American disc jockey to a new prominence in the 1940s is based on a fatal link with advertising. For the DJ developed his talents accordingly. Since he was paid on commission, he went out searching for new business, and helped to sell the programme by appearing at department stores and supermarkets. He thus became adept at different kinds of vocal camouflage. In part he sold the station, which became identified with his voice. In part he was selling the sponsors. Because radio is an aural showcase, in part he sold records. And in part he was selling himself. The programmes were clearly popular – in 1941, Martin Block's 'Make Believe Ballroom' received 12,000 letters a month, and one of the sponsors, a bakery firm, reported a sales increase of more than 430,000 doughnuts per week.[29]

Programmes that sold doughnuts created hits when it came to records. Record companies began to change their attitude, and disc jockeys 'began to be wooed and cultivated, and became the chief promotion channel for the reviving ... record industry'.[30] By the time the war ended, the disc jockey was the economic basis of the local radio station. A writer might be needed for announcements and promotional copy perhaps, but commercials were often ad-libbed by the DJ and news was taken from one of the agency ticker-tape machines, all of which now provided material specially written for what was called a 'rip-and-read' operation. The station's main staff were engineers and salespeople. It hardly even needed a studio.

The DJ had to switch between announcing records and presenting commercials, station identifications, and news bulletins. Each of these functions required and developed its own characteristic accents of delivery; a repertoire of stylized speech at which the DJ becomes adroit. Linguistic analysis has shown how news, commercials and the disc jockey's patter and intros are each delivered in a different kind of rhythm, and with the accent on different types of words – often words that are not usually accented in normal conversational speech at all, like prepositions. The news, in its bid to be impersonal, is delivered in short, clear and well-accented phrases which end up failing to differentiate what is actually new and important in the information. Commercials, insisting on the personal appeal of direct second-person address, end up imposing a peculiar lilt of their own ('*you* can save – *one* hundred dollars – on *any* used car – on dis*play*'). The disc jockey performing his primary function is allowed to speak in the first person, and also addresses the listener as 'you', but he has two basic modes of delivery: long stretches of rapid speech, which then contrast with the slower and more deliberate way in which the record is announced. All these are modes of delivery that depart in various critical ways from the natural rhythms of spoken language.[31] And as the role of the DJ becomes more individualistic, the privilege of first-person speech produces the phenomenon of the 'personality deejay'. At its most highly developed, the patter becomes a vocalized interior monologue, which spins off what is going round inside the DJ's head.

The emergence at the end of the 1940s of a new breed of local stations aimed at black audiences produced a notable phenomenon. The new black DJs were not originally identified as black on the air, as if voice had no colour. Among the few voices that did was that of Al Benson, who was derided, says Nelson George, as 'just the sort of character any self-respecting upwardly mobile black would view as a discredit to the race'. But the lessons he taught, about the appeal and profitability of his 'black everyman's style', were adopted all over the country and the era of the 'personality deejay' arrived. As with the indie record labels devoted to R&B, 'the overwhelming majority of black-oriented stations were white-owned ...

but the deejays, not the owners, defined the stations and made them profitable'.[32] When Storz came up with the Top 40 format he was extremely wary of the personality DJ. The disc jockey, he thought, was not representative of the public: 'Because he is usually above the audience mentally and financially, and lives with popular music, his own preferences are a dangerous guide.'[33] But that of course is precisely the point. The DJ was a trend-setter, and this led to conflicts with his role as the paid voice of the station. New types of radio station format would be needed – in America they developed with the spread of FM broadcasting – which gave the personality DJ his head.

Another notable phenomenon appeared – what Norman Mailer in 1957 was to dub 'The White Negro', a new white social outlaw wandering the landscape, a 'hipster', a 'philosophical psychopath', whose primary inspiration was the sexuality and music of the Afro-American.[34] In the same way and at the same time that white cover artists appeared, like Elvis Presley, whose style and manner came from black performance traditions, white disc jockeys emerged who not only played black music but also modelled themselves on their black counterparts. Of these, the most famous was Alan Freed, first because his name became linked with the words 'rock 'n' roll', which he adopted in the title of his radio programmes, second because of his subsequent conviction in the scandal of Payola, or pay-for-play, at the end of the 1950s.

In terms of market penetration, the midwife of pop music was the 45 r.p.m. single, mass-produced and cheap. It was cheap enough that, in order to cope with the unpredictability of a hit, a practice developed which consisted in minting large editions and either pulping the misses or selling them off in bulk to the cut-price market. The situation became increasingly problematic for the major record companies because, on the one hand, the rise of independent studios meant that they had lost their grip over what was recorded, while on the other, DJs took away their command over what was sold. In 1954, independents produced twenty-two out of the top thirty R&B numbers; in 1956, when rock 'n' roll started dominating the white charts, ten of the top nineteen, and in 1957, twenty-nine of the top forty-three tunes came from independents. The majors reacted by instead redoubling their efforts to get their records into the charts – by whatever means necessary. In record industry lore, the golden principles of the pop business were simple: there was enormous money to be made from a hit, no money without one; most artists on your roster lost money, but a handful of stars compensated for all the losses – the problem was knowing who was going to be the next star. Hits were made by Top 40 radio, and it was axiomatic that for each single in the Top 10, you could sell a million albums. To get your record played on air was not a matter of mass sales promotion, but of 'persuading' a relatively small number of key disc jockeys who could be targeted individually if you had the right apparatus for doing so. Disc jockeys being individualists, corporate promotion was less effective than stroking their egos individually. Accordingly the record companies turned to 'independent promoters' to 'lobby' on behalf of the records entrusted to them, and in this way promotion came to cost millions. At CBS, for example, the bill grew from a tiny line item to the company's biggest expense after salaries. A large part of it was payola.

According to the Sanjeks in their book on the American popular music business, no one knew exactly how many disc jockeys there were. The best estimates were around 2,000 (attendance at the first Pop Music Disc Jockey Festival promoted by Storz in 1958 was 1,700), but 'smart record-company promotion men concentrated on about 100 "real song-breakers"'. *Variety* reported in 1952 that no more than 100 disc jockeys really controlled the popular music business. 'Without their concentrated action, no song could become a major song and no artist could remain a major artist, nor could a new name be made.'[35]

The scandal that brought down Alan Freed came about partly as the result of the persistence of the feud between the two agencies that licensed copyright: ASCAP, representing the old school of publishers, and the radio chains' agency, BMI. The growth of rock 'n' roll favoured the latter, and was beginning to invade Hollywood with films like the 1956 teenage movie *Blackboard Jungle*. Indeed the hit song from this film, 'Rock Around the Clock' performed by Bill Haley, is frequently cited as the first time that rock 'n' roll fully broke into the teenager market, although others cite the success of Alan Freed's radio shows over the preceding three years. The first indications of trouble date from 1955, when subpoenas were served in New York on the Big Four and some smaller companies, connected with an investigation by the Justice Department into the shipment

of free records to radio stations, unfair dealings with independent distributors, discriminatory LP pricing practices and price cutting, although nothing came of this probe. A year later, a Congress sub-committee, scrutinizing
network radio and television practices, heard accusations by ASCAP members that the BMI controlled the popular songs heard over the air and on
records. Witnesses charged that BMI was 'responsible for rock and roll and
other musical monstrosities which are muddying up the airwaves', and the
singer Frank Sinatra sent a telegram to be read into the record, claiming
that his record company denied him the right to choose his own material,
and that he had been forced to sing 'inferior songs' from the BMI camp.[36]

Another government hearing in 1958, this one examining communications, gave ASCAP another chance. This time one witness, a Beverly
Hills lawyer, claimed that BMI was paying disc jockeys to play certain
discs, adding that this was 'practically the only way that a song can be
exposed'.[37] Author Vance Packard complained that, along with BMI,
'conniving disc jockeys' had foisted 'cheap music' on teenagers. Finally, a
third Washington sub-committee, this time on legislative oversight, inves-
tigating the scandal of rigged game shows on television like 'The $64,000
Question', was persuaded to take up the rigging of the record charts.

One of the witnesses on this occasion, the music editor of *Billboard*,
made a comprehensive statement on the history of payola in which he
said that the practice was rampant long before the era of the disc jockey
or even the expansion of the record business. Others spoke of vaudeville
performers of old who had been open to persuasive gifts to feature new
songs, or band leaders who were open to bribes from song pluggers.
Another noted that in the big-band era, a record company 'paid for band
arrangements, picked up many a "tab" and in return got its song played a
lot on tour'.[38] But several disc jockeys giving evidence satisfied the bias of
the politicians by revealing links between payola and rock; one of them
admitted that, like most jockeys, he would not take the time to listen to
new rock records unless someone gave him 'a gratuity'. The committee
also conducted their own survey which revealed that over a quarter of a
million dollars had been paid by record companies to 207 people, mostly
jockeys, in 42 cities, a practice that in many states was not in fact illegal.

One result was a bill passed by Congress which made payola a federal
offence, with the radio stations to be held responsible for any employee
who accepted such gifts. It is questionable whether it had much long-

term effect, but in the short term, Alan Freed became a scapegoat when in 1960 he went down for taking bribes to play records on the New York station WINS. At the same time, fresh charges issued by the Federal Trade Commission against various record manufacturers and their distributors for paying disc jockeys for favours, were dropped. The episode symbolizes the response of authority to the fearsome threat of revolt against the body politic unleashed by the record industry in spite of itself in the form of rock 'n' roll. But convicting disc jockeys for taking bribes and dropping charges against the givers is no way to stamp out the practice, and another trial in New York in 1987 revealed that in more recent years, payola became a sphere of the Mafia.

7

The Microphone and Interpretation

In 1926, H.H. Stuckenschmidt, a young German composer with a growing reputation as a critic, published an article under the title 'Praise of the Gramophone', celebrating its dissemination of music from jazz to Stravinsky (who had just recorded his own *Serenade*), predicting that future generations 'will understand better than us the real sense and purpose of the machine, and treat technology as an ideal means of simplifying human existence rather than as an object of breathless adoration'.[1] Even Adorno, the most stringent critic of the culture industry, found this circumstance hopeful. In principle, he says in his *Introduction to the Sociology of Music*, the medium of recording makes all of musical literature available. True, the recorded repertoire 'mirrors the official life of music in its most conventional form', and records become fetish objects. Nevertheless the 'potential abolition of educational privilege in music should socially outweigh the disadvantages which hoarding records as a hobby of an audience of consumers involves under present conditions'.[2]

Kurt Weill was quite sober in his evaluation of the realities when he said that radio demanded the clarification of sonority, and scored his *Berliner Requiem* of 1928 – commissioned by Frankfurt Radio – accordingly, employing stark textures which admirably manoeuvred the technical limitations of the day. The same year Schoenberg observed something similar when he remarked that radio and the gramophone 'are evolving such clear sonorities that one will be able to write much less heavily instrumented pieces for them'.[3] Bartók demonstrated such a solution a few years later when he wrote *Contrasts*, a trio for clarinet, violin and piano, to a commission by Benny Goodman for a work to fit on a couple of 78s.

For his part, Stravinsky considered the gramophone as both the ideal means of documenting composers' own interpretation of their music and a welcome supplement to their income. Indeed he left a huge phonographic legacy covering virtually his entire output as a composer, which due to his early fame and long life stretches from the early days of the recording process down to the era of the stereo LP. Nevertheless, he had no illusions about its overall effects. Today, he says in his autobiography, published in 1935,

> anyone, living no matter where, has only to turn a knob or put on a record to hear what he likes. Indeed, it is in just this incredible facility, this lack of necessity for any effort, that the evil of this so-called progress lies ... For one can listen without hearing, just as one can look without seeing. The absence of active effort and the liking acquired for this facility make for laziness ... Listeners fall into a kind of torpor.[4]

In this regard, Stravinsky and Schoenberg, while musically at odds with each other, were effectively in agreement. In an essay dating from 1933, Schoenberg held out the hope that repeated radio performances might help to educate the public for modern music, but three years earlier he replied to a questionnaire about radio: 'Quite certainly the radio is a foe! – and so are the gramophone and sound-film' – because they only made for a 'boundless surfeit of music. Here, perhaps the frightful expression "consumption of music" really does apply after all. For perhaps this continuous tinkle, regardless of whether anyone wants to hear it or not, whether anyone can take it in, whether anyone can use it, will lead to a state where all music has been consumed, worn out.'[5]

Adorno agreed about these effects on the consumption of music, and insisted on the negative aspect of music's adaptation to reproduction. In the early days, he noted, the effects of compressed dynamics, distorted colours and flattened textures altered the proper sound of music. The power of a symphony orchestra depends in part on its sheer volume. Monaural living-room reproduction was a long way from the enveloping experience of true symphonic space. The gramophone and radio reduced it to the capabilities of a single loudspeaker (until stereo made it two), and handed control of the volume over to the listener. In this situation, he said, music develops a liability to decompose. It becomes a stream of highlights: striking melodic intervals and turns of phrase, unsettling modulations, special instrumental effects, intentional or unintentional quirks of interpretation. In this way individual and often accidental features of the music become fetishized.

The same process was described by a contributor to a centenary conference on the phonograph and musical life at Brooklyn College in New York in 1977, the critic David Hamilton. The listener may become fascinated by some technical aspect or a particular timbre. 'I have this kind of fixation on the sound of Rosa Ponselle's voice and on Tito Schipa's lambent, loving pronunciation of the Italian language; on the chiaroscuro that Rachmaninov brings to passage-work, on the sheer aplomb of Dennis Brain's playing of the French horn...' In such cases, he says, we are not merely focusing on the performance rather than the work; we are intent on a particular characteristic which is usually not even musically essential to the piece.[6]

This, for Adorno, is only symptomatic of a larger process in the industrialized culture of the twentieth century, in which certain regressive tendencies became manifest. Music on the radio, for example, becomes a potpourri, a continuous atomized medley which leaves the impression of a kind of collage. But people who listen atomistically dissociate what they hear; they can only become fixated on the fragments. The end result of this 'avalanche of fetishism' takes it out on both the music and the personalities who perform it. On the one hand, 'there exists today a tendency to listen to Beethoven's Fifth Symphony as if it were a set of quotations from Beethoven's Fifth'.[7] On the other, there is the cult worship of certain conductors and soloists, like Toscanini, with his much-touted objectivity and textual fidelity. With Toscanini, says Adorno, quoting with approval his teacher Steuerman's description of Toscanini's approach as 'the barbarism of perfection', there is 'iron discipline. But precisely iron. The new fetish is the flawlessly functioning, metallically brilliant apparatus as such, in which all the cogwheels mesh so perfectly that not the slightest hole remains open for the meaning of the whole ... The performance sounds like its own phonograph record.'[8] If it does not, then the concert-hall listener is discomfited. The reason that this streamlined performance comes to replace interpretation and its elements of spontaneity is precisely to ensure that the concert performance shall indeed be a copy of the record, and the concert-goer will not be disappointed.[9]

But from a musicianly point of view this is monstrous. The American composer Roger Sessions spoke in his Harvard lectures of 1969 of the day he hurled a record of a favourite piece of Debussy across the room in anger. 'What infuriated me was my fully developed awareness of having heard exactly the same sounds, the same nuances, both of tempo and dynamics, the same accents, down to the minutest detail, so many times that I knew exactly – and I emphasise *exactly*, to the last instant – what was coming next.'[10] Hamilton interprets this as the final loss of aura, to use Walter Benjamin's word, which is inevitably produced by mechanical reproduction in the act of separating the music from the physical act of performance, 'its presence in time and space, its unique existence at the place where it happens to be'. Benjamin's definition of aura is 'that which withers in the age of mechanical reproduction'. This verb, says Hamilton, is an accurate one, because the spontaneity of the live performance 'doesn't vanish automatically the minute the recording is made; it is obviously present the first time someone – anyone – hears it'. But with repeated hearings its loss is inescapable.

This suggests a psychological process, in which, by stages, the function of memory is significantly altered. The fact that Hamilton, like Adorno, speaks from the position of what Adorno called 'the expert listener', who looks down on the use of music for mere entertainment as a lower form of life, does not invalidate his basic perception of what is going on here: 'I don't doubt', says Hamilton, 'that for some listeners (and perhaps occasionally for all of us), the unchanging aspect of recordings can be pleasing and reassuring; they can act as aural security blankets, particularly if they have extra-musical associations.' This not only plays a major role in popular music but explains the rise of a new category in the catalogues, much reinforced by recycling, namely, nostalgia: 'life may be getting worse, but the old records, at least, stay the same'.[11]

For Adorno, however, the concept of musical fetishism cannot be psychologically derived. He means that it cannot be explained away, but follows from the domination of all contemporary musical life by the commodity form. If this produces irrational fixations in the listener – or the performer – upon aspects of technique or notions of authenticity, then such effects are traceable to the fetish character of the commodity as perceived by Marx: the veneration accorded to the manufactured product which disguises the social relations of the labour expended to produce it. Music, with all its attributes of the sublime and the ethereal, is not only commodified in the form of the record but also disembodied by dissolving it into the air-waves and passing it through a loudspeaker. How easily it becomes in the process merely an advertisement for commodities the consumer must acquire in order to be able to hear it. In this *quid pro quo* it is doubly reified, and the fatal attraction of its surface features is only the converse of this condition.[12]

This situation takes its toll on the practice of interpretation and the style of performance – it would be surprising if it did not. The evidence preserved on record is unequivocal: since the beginning of our century performance style has changed decisively, and with it, attitudes towards musical tradition and history. In the words of Glenn Gould, a pianist wedded to the record, 'Recordings deal with concepts through which the past is re-evaluated.'[13]

Recording produces an entirely novel state of affairs in the history of music, in which the evolution of interpretation ceases to disappear into an irretrievable past but remains available on the shelves of the record library (whence it re-emerges in the shape of vintage recordings to be lovingly played and discussed in radio programmes). In many early recordings it is still possible to hear a Romantic style of performance which did not survive the two world wars. Compare the leading string quartets recorded before and after the Second World War. In post-war recordings by the Amadeus, the Juilliard or the Italian Quartets, for instance, you no longer hear the portamento and rubato – the elastic treatment of pitch and tempo – employed as late as the 1930s by the Busch Quartet in their celebrated Beethoven recordings, which by then had been largely banished from orchestral performance. In short, a whole series of performer's prerogatives have virtually disappeared, and musicians are now apparently less self-indulgent. The question is why. Could it really be the effect of technical reproduction itself? Or did the technology of records and broadcasting perhaps accelerate a process already unfolding, a tendency with other causes? It is difficult to answer this question. If recording for the first time allowed musicians to hear themselves as others do, and to make new comparisons, nonetheless the evidence is not entirely unequivocal.

The career of Toscanini provides an object lesson. In his novel study *Understanding Toscanini*, subtitled *How He Became an American Culture-God and Helped Create a New Audience for Old Music*, the North American music critic Joseph Horowitz shows how radio led the record industry in making Toscanini a household name in the United States, much as television later did for Leonard Bernstein. The handsome old Italian became tied in with NBC as conductor of their showcase orchestra from 1937 to 1954; a valuable property in the commercial empire which, through common ownership by RCA, linked the country's largest radio network (in 1938, more than 140 stations covering 88 per cent of the population) with the country's largest record manufacturer, Victor. NBC, we learn, paid a good price to steal him from CBS, but the money was well spent. The record industry had slumped badly during the Depression. As it began to recover, music on the radio, far from undermining the phonograph, stimulated record sales. RCA–Victor's sales, says Horowitz, 'rose 600 percent between 1933 and 1938 – with symphonic, not popular, releases leading the way'.[14] Toscanini's marketability became truly huge: at his retirement in 1954, RCA had sold twenty million copies of his records to a value of $33m; four years later, when they launched a new record club and offered bargain-price sets of Toscanini conducting the Beethoven symphonies, 340,000 customers signed up in the space of three months. Today such items can be digitally remastered and marketed on compact disc, and still the shekels flow in.

Horowitz follows Adorno in regarding the streamlined and machine-like orchestral style of the age of the long-playing record as part of the Toscanini legacy, a consequence of his elevation, above all in the United States, to the status of a musical deity. But he also shows it as the unintended effect of a process driven by its own dynamic. The signs were already there in the days of acoustic recording. Compare Toscanini's 1921 recording of Beethoven's Fifth with the Nikisch version of 1913, says Horowitz. Unlike Toscanini, 'Nikisch relishes all of the finale's "traditional" rubatos and tempo changes, and others besides.' As a result, the pulse in Nikisch is flexible throughout, while in Toscanini it is more uniform. 'Where Toscanini's phrasings are terse, Nikisch's are elongated. Where Toscanini's massed chords are staccato, Nikisch's are "rolled",' and his violins slide more than Toscanini's do.[15] If Toscanini acquired as a result the reputation of a modernist, with a 'simple, natural and honest' style which liberated music from histrionics, this modernism was only skin deep. When the Italian maestro took La Scala to Berlin in 1929, for instance, Hans

Curjel, dramaturg at the controversial Kroll Opera, described the produc-
tions in a letter to Kurt Weill as 'musically beyond description, scenically
ridiculous'.[16] As Horowitz puts it, 'Toscanini, who once threatened to desert
Salzburg unless Falstaff was shown drying himself in the sun outside the
Garter Inn, as Verdi prescribed, rather than in bed under a pile of blankets,
was less concerned with espousing new aesthetics than with disciplining
errant Italian musicians.'[17]

When it came to the studio, Toscanini disliked the process of recording
and had no real understanding of its techniques. According to his record
producer at RCA, he was impatient with the medium, refusing to understand its possibilities and limitations. 'He will not, by so much as one
decibel, modify his dynamics ... nor will he redress orchestral balance in
relation to the conditions under which recorded music is normally reproduced.'[18] Ironically, it was precisely because the technology was still acoustically limited, tending to blur and thicken the orchestral texture, that the
incisive, relatively lean sound that Toscanini drew from his orchestra proved
particularly adaptable to technical reproduction. Indeed despite Toscanini's
distrust of recording, the process of modernization in his recordings is
progressive; it parallels the development of the record industry, and in the
end becomes completely self-consuming. His 1951 recording of Beethoven's
Seventh, says Horowitz, 'brings the change into focus: it is faster, tighter,
stiffer than his Sevenths of 1936 and 1939'; his beat is more rigid, the
playing of the orchestra becomes coarse, nuances of tone and articulation
narrow in range and diminish in number. But already in 1937, John
Barbirolli (Toscanini's successor as conductor of the New York Philharmonic) had felt an increased preoccupation with energy and drive in
Toscanini's performances in London with the BBC Symphony Orchestra,
combined with less attention to polish, and 'an almost complete lack of
serenity'; as if, he said, he had to prove he was still young.[19]

If Toscanini ends up more idolized than he deserved, another object lesson
is Stravinsky as conductor of his own works, which seems to reveal a
different process. There are several works that he recorded two, three or
four times, mainly to keep pace with developments in recording technique,
but according to the American music critic Samuel Lipman, the earlier
recordings invariably represent the better, more exciting and convincing

performances.[20] Especially revealing is the case of *The Rite of Spring*, which he recorded three times. The last, dating from 1960 and made in Los Angeles, uses a pick-up band under the name of the Columbia Symphony Orchestra; Lipman calls it 'tonally lush, rhythmically flaccid', correct in detail more by virtue of the tape-splicer's art than the discipline acquired through performance. This is a stereo version intended to supercede the second recording of twenty years earlier, made with a regular orchestra, the New York Philharmonic, first put out on 78s and then re-issued in 1949 as one of the first LPs. Given the old recording methods – the only way to correct mistakes was to re-record an entire four-minute 78 r.p.m. side – the performance (says Lipman) is a creditable one. But it cannot compare with the first recording, made in Paris in 1928, 'a scant fifteen years after the *Rite*'s scandalous premiere', which enshrines a performance quite different from what is generally heard nowadays. The playing on these old records is 'without that quality of trembling emotion so fashionable on today's concert platforms'. Not only does this recording give us Stravinsky as a conductor with reserves of youthful energy as yet undiminished by age: 'here can be heard an orchestra faced with a modernist adventure rather than with just another performance of a repertory piece ... Here can be heard as well the transparent sound in which the French musicians of the time were trained, that must have been in Stravinsky's ears when he wrote the *Rite*.... The result is a rendition as dry in sound as the 1960 recording is lush.' The opening bassoon solo, for example, suggests the cold spring of Russian experience, not, like nowadays, the quasi-tropical foliage of southern California; and the famous barbaric chords near the beginning 'do not seem the piquant exercises in mild dissonance they are in today's performances; the French musicians of an earlier day ... heard them as willful impositions of dissonant sound rather than as logical constructions'.

Lipman's nostalgia for these early and unsentimental renderings invites comparison with the nostalgia of the early music movement for the unemotional rendering of past music. Questions of performance style naturally attract the attention of early-music scholars. For instance, according to the Berkeley music professor Richard Taruskin, the style nowadays preferred for early music is less the result of historical scholarship than contemporary musical taste, which has definitely changed. We have a better idea, he says, of what music sounded like in Tchaikovsky's day than we shall ever have of what it sounded like in Bach's, yet no one plays Tchaikovsky like the Elman Quartet any more, recorded circa 1918, with all their scoops and slides.[21] Here again Stravinsky's example is significant. Taruskin compares his recording, partnered by his son Soulima, of Mozart's Fugue in C minor (K426) for two pianos, with the same composer's Sonata for two pianos in D major (K448) as recorded by Bela Bartók and his wife Ditta. Bartók is no less of a modernist than Stravinsky, but the Hungarians' performance is very much more 'in style', full of tiny, unnotated 'and hence (in Stravinskian terms) criminal and treacherous' crescendos, diminuendos, accelerandos and ritardandos, 'and that most heinous of "sins" and "follies",' the tendency to speed up in a crescendo and slow down in a diminuendo.[22] Stravinsky, however, is 'execution, pure and simple. You could not hope to find a drier, harder – in a word, more geometrical – performance of any music.'

To test out what is happening here Taruskin has investigated the record libraries, and the findings he comes up with are striking. For example, he studied a series of recordings of Bach's Fifth *Brandenburg Concerto* made over a fifty-year period from 1935 to 1985. Listen, he says, to Furtwängler's version, dating from 1950, with a full string orchestra and Furtwängler himself banging out 'hamfisted' continuo chords on a piano at full blast – this was already anachronistic when it was recorded. 'By comparison, *any* performance we may hear today will seem virtually weightless…'[23] (except perhaps for Furtwängler's successor Karajan). The band is nowadays much smaller, the texture is clearer, the music much more buoyant. Overall, he says, these recordings show a transition from a 'vitalist' style of performance – late romantic, emotionally intense, with continual wide fluctuations of dynamic intensity and tempo – to a 'geometrical' one; by this he means not only more angular and precise, but also increasingly inelastic in terms of dynamics and, as a general rule, notably faster. Where Furtwängler, for example, has a metronome speed of crochet 72, recent recordings like those of Christopher Hogwood or Collegium Aureum – the latter heavily touted as one of the first on 'original instruments' – move along at a nimble crochet ninety-something.

There is a consistent trend here. Take the Beethoven symphonies recently recorded on period instruments under the direction of Christopher Hogwood. According to another writer in the same volume as Taruskin, 'There are differences, but in questions like what is a phrase, what does tempo mean, where is the symphony going, Hogwood is much closer to

Karajan than he is to, say, Artur Nikisch, who was born in 1855 and recorded Beethoven's Fifth in 1913.'[24] Karajan's weighty recordings have plenty of colour and dynamics, yet they are also 'geometrical', and the range of feeling is curtailed. Not only that: Taruskin reports an investigation by another early-music enthusiast comparing recordings of a wide repertory of pieces from plainchant to Schubert. In each case a recording from the 1950s or 1960s was compared with a later and supposedly 'authentistic' performance. In every instance, the stylistic contrast between the earlier and the later was essentially the same. The earlier recording showed 'greater variation of dynamics, speed and timbre', it was more 'emotional' and 'personal'. The authenticist performance was 'characterised by relatively uniform tempo and dynamics, a "clean" sound and at least an attempt to avoid interpretive gestures beyond those notated or documented as part of period performance practice'. These findings, says Taruskin, can be extended. If you compare recordings of the 1920s and 1930s with those of the 1950s and 1960s, the results would be substantially the same, as they would also be if you compared early 'electrics' with turn-of-the-century acoustic discs. In short, 'modern performance gets moderner and moderner, as Alice might say'.[25]

Taruskin's conclusion is that the 'geometrical' style of performance does not originate in historical research or aspirations to historical authenticity: it is a general characteristic of streamlined twentieth-century performance practice typical of both conventional forces and the early-music movement. What we find is a shift in emphasis from the expressive to the more formal and abstract properties of music. This, in the view of the German music critic Jürgen Kesting, is connected with the effect of recording on music's relationship to time. If the gramophone was responsible for changing our hearing, then it also deadens the musical sense of time and changes musical aesthetics in the process. In live performance, the ticking of the clock is negated by the pulse of the music and time becomes plastic, suspended between the notes, which constantly alter their tempo and rate of acceleration. This sense of suspended time is not present when music is reproduced mechanically. It continues, in this canned form, to act upon the human autonomic system, as all music does: it quickens and slows our pulse and our breathing. But in becoming disembodied, the loss of physical presence removes it from the domain of living time. It still affects our temporal experience – it helps to fill it – but without the human contact of live performance, the vital element of communion with the musician and the constant play of suprise that this brings. Conversely, this is why a rubato or fermata or other nuance which might move us in performance can become problematical, even disturbing, on record, and the typical rubato found on older recordings is replaced by performances that are metrically strict and accord with what Stravinsky in his musical poetics called the 'chronos of the present day'.[26]

Of course once again there are counter-examples to consider. The early music movement has also revealed a certain trend in the opposite direction, in other words, the return of the repressed freedom of inflection, articulation and timbre so deeply embedded in *musica practica* but rendered inarticulate by the advance of notation. In the words of a recent survey of the recorded repertoire by an Anglo-American musicologist, the early 'early music' movement cultivated 'a light, clear, transparent singing style and a quiet, introverted manner of presentation' which contrasted sharply with the dominant style of the concert platform, with its tendency towards bombast and histrionics.[27] Then along came a new generation, which challenged the overall conception of the sound of early music by preferring a harsher vocal quality; and after that, some performers adopted an ethnomusicological approach. Following Bartók's lead, they looked to other cultures to find living traditions of comparable types of music. They took to using highly colourful ensembles of instruments, borrowing the forms of attack from the music of North Africa and the Middle East, and exploring techniques for improvising accompaniments, interludes, even rudimentary counterpoint. At this point the music began to make contact with wider audiences. By the 1960s there were even rock groups playing a similar kind of modern folk music, like the Breton nationalist Alain Stivell, or the English folk-rock groups Gryphon and the Albion Band.

The question is whether the progressive modernization of performance is a product of the technological development of the recording process itself. If we follow Benjamin, the answer would have to be yes. When Benjamin observes that the movie image is the end product of complex procedures, and in the film studio with its panoply of equipment, 'the sight of immediate reality has become an orchid in the land of technology',[28] then we can hardly deny that sound recording can be similar, and recording studios no less alienating than film or television studios. Above all, they lack an audience, and hence the live stimulus of their feedback. It is difficult to avoid the conclusion that recording engineers have become the agents of a transformation which has depended as much on their ears as the musicians'. Or as Samuel Lipton puts it – and this is also true of the radio studio – the judgement of the producer in the control booth substitutes for that of the musician in front of the microphone.[29]

The producer has a task and plays a role: the task is to be all ears; the role is to substitute for the audience. Take the account of the EMI classical producer Suvi Raj Grubb. A recording, he says, brings out more of the inner parts than you can hear in most concert halls; in the studio you can make an inner line ride effortlessly over accompaniment that in the concert hall would often drown it out. It is the job of the producer to decide, in consultation with the conductor, how much detail the composer wanted you to hear. At the same time, 'When Yehudi Menuhin plays in the studio he is not playing to the inanimate microphone in front of him. His playing is addressed to an ideal listener capable of responding musically and emotionally to his performance – on this occasion I am that ideal, and perhaps idealized, listener.' What this role requires above all is tact. 'The artist has to have complete faith in the musical sensibility of the producer ... and the producer must have confidence in the artist.'[30] (He does not say so, but this also goes for the engineer. It is the recording engineer who operates the equipment, but engineers rank below producers. Pity the conductor who works with a producer who does not realise that his ears are not as good as his engineer's.)

Busoni complained about the strain and artificiality of recording in 1919, of the fear of inaccuracy and being conscious the whole time that every note was going to be there for eternity, which eliminated inspiration, freedom, swing or poetry from the performance. A few years later, engineers at the BBC commented on the brutal objectivity of the microphone. 'There are some who may pass muster in public places where the evidence of the ear is outweighed by the seduction of the eye, but the sensitive electric instrument's photographic reproduction of the performance shows lamentably how much is lacking in finesse, in delicacy.' As the writer who quotes this remark puts it, 'The microphone favoured none, and allowed no faking. It demanded clean, legitimate execution and beautiful tone. In short ... new standards of professional competence, of technical efficiency combined with quality of tone.'[31]

There is a critical loss in this process. Alejo Carpentier quotes the declaration of 'a famous interpreter' in 1951 that 'in the presence of an audience you play with heat, but the disc is recorded cold'. What is missing is the human contact of the live performance which produces 'a type of collective emotion' which is lost to the recording. Whether shared by two or two thousand, this is often quite enough to make the activity of performance rather more important than its delicacy or finesse, for it lies at the basis of music as a social activity. Because of this, in the right circumstances collective enthusiasm 'communicates to certain concerts the character of an artistic ceremony, a rite, which is never achieved in front of a disc revolving – still less when listening is interrupted by phone calls, conversations, children's cries, etc.' (This, of course, was written some time before the rise of the disco, where turntables themselves became the centrepiece of a para-ritual cult.) He is quite philosophical about it, however. 'The disc is to live performance what colour reproduction is to an original painting ... if we in [Latin] America want to have an idea of the work of Gauguin, Cézanne, Picasso, we have no other option...'[32]

Popular music, inspired by different cultural imperatives from the classical tradition, began responding to the microphone differently, without the same inhibitions. Vocalists discovered how to treat the microphone as an instrument in its own right, not just a passive means of capturing sound. They invented in the process a whole range of new vocal effects and techniques, even new kinds of singing; all based on the simple principle that close microphone placement brings the sound forward, suggesting, as one writer says of Bing Crosby's crooning, 'an intimate, personal relationship with fans'.[33] From crooning to rap, the repercussions on popular vocalizing have been enormous – as if simply to pick up a microphone is to undergo a personality transformation, and out of this transformation pop stars are born. The classical musician was more circumspect.

Close microphones not only clarify articulation, they tend to overclarify. And in the case of an orchestra, they all too easily carry the danger of ruining the balance, compressing dynamics and blanching colour. To record the sound of a highly disciplined symphony orchestra, the ears of whose members are all extremely acute, atuned by long practice to creating a powerful and unified sound image, playing under a conductor who knows, through equal experience, how to judge the hall and the audience and mould an interpretation – in these circumstances everything depends on the acoustic conditions and the ear of the recording engineer. The record producer John Culshaw has recounted what happened when Furtwängler came to record for Decca in London in 1948 and countermanded the company's engineers. During the war, Decca had received military funding to improve the quality of recorded sound: the RAF coastal command wanted training records to illustrate differences between the sounds of German and British submarines, which involved subtle aural distinctions. At the end of 1944 Decca put the results on the market and proceeded to register a new trademark: 'ffrr', for 'full frequency range recording'. The Decca engineers, by developing new cutters and new microphones, achieved new recording standards: the treble, says Roland Gelatt in *The Fabulous Phonograph*, was more brilliant and incisive, the bass fuller and more resonant, 'with a heightened sense of presence and room tone never before encountered on a phonograph record to such stunning effect'.[34] The claim is quite relative, of course, not like the improvement represented by electrical recording over acoustical recording. In any event, when Furtwängler came to London, the recording crew were experts in microphone placement and perfectly familiar with the hall where the recording sessions took place. On seeing the bank of microphones, says Culshaw, Furtwängler objected, insisting that a single microphone 'should be suspended over the centre of the orchestra, and that all the others – there were perhaps five – should be disconnected and removed from his sight.' When the records were released, 'the critics were bewildered by the change in the famous Decca sound: instead of the usual combination of warmth and clarity [they were] diffuse and muddy.' A pity, says the producer, as the performance was remarkable. 'Not much, however, of what I heard in the hall itself found its way on to the record, and it was the conductor's fault.'[35]

However, close miking always added to the dangers; witness the late recordings of Toscanini with the NBC Symphony. Abandoning the studio and moving into the Carnegie Hall for recordings in the early 1950s, the expectable acoustic benefits, says Joseph Horowitz, 'were minimised by engineers who crowded and rebalanced the orchestra with their microphones so that the hall could not be "heard"'.[36] In other words, the reverberation of the hall was eliminated, with the result that amplified pianissimos and forward winds are heard against a backdrop of dead space.[37]

Moreover, after 1950, RCA began to blatantly doctor its Toscanini recordings with phony resonance, boosted treble and the like. 'Without rescuing
the skewed balances and dynamics, these "enhanced" versions added fresh
falsifications of timbre and perspective.'[38]

On the other hand, there have been conductors, like Igor Markevich,
who valued recording precisely for 'allowing us to hear the music in better
conditions than in live performance'. There were certain works, he told
Carpentier in 1958, like *Les Choëphores* by Milhaud, 'in which it is practically impossible to hear certain details in a concert performance ... thanks
to the easy arrangement of the microphones, the work "gets across" just
as it sounded in the composer's head.' In live performance one group of
instruments may neutralize the sound of another, but in the recording,
'with the help of the technicians, we can rectify this problem. We can
even achieve an effect such as having a singer whispering right into a
microphone while the trumpets play fortissimo without being drowned by
them.'[39]

But these problems are not always the composer's fault. Change the
acoustics and the nature of the sound image changes too. Culshaw also
recalls what happened some years later, when he first went to record in
the new Mann Auditorium in Tel Aviv. The results were a bitter disappoint-
ment, no matter the amount of tinkering with microphones or alteration
of orchestral layout.

> One day an engineer was clambering in the area immediately above the platform
> while the orchestra was in rehearsal, and he sent a message to ask me to join him
> ... he urged me along the catwalk and there, suddenly, was the sound of the
> Israel Philharmonic. It was passing upwards instead of outwards towards the
> auditorium, and seeping through the gaps between the hollow pyramids installed
> by the acoustical experts.[40]

(The hall was subsequently modified at considerable expense, though not
as costly as the Avery Fisher Hall in New York, where they tore the
insides out and started again.)

Recording practices began to change with the introduction of magnetic
tape, which not only provided a high-quality format for the master recording but was also editable. The techniques involved, however, were

first developed not in the centres of classical recording in places like London and New York but in Hollywood, where they were already used in film sound post-production. Bing Crosby discovered that magnetic tape offered the possibility to a star performer of regaining a measure of control over his own creation. He was not mistaken, and the general adoption of tape strengthened the situation of many performers – simply by removing the tyranny of the needle and allowing a measure of selection and correction of the recorded material. But the new situation also brought a clash between musician and producer over control of the recorded sound image, and in practice most performers gave way – in the interests of their careers.

Changes in recording technology affect control-room procedure first, performance in the studio second. The 'action' moves from the floor of the studio to the control room, where the mixing and editing equipment is located. In 1965, according to *Time* magazine, the 'grand designer' of a recording 'is no longer the conductor but producer ... With a mountain of sophisticated machinery at his command, he has become a space-age sculptor of sound. His raw material is the performer, his workshop the glass-enclosed control room.'[41] But the process was still essentially a collaboration and the named artists in the recording were invited to listen to playbacks and involve themselves in the selection of material. The main difference on the studio floor from the old days was the varying length of takes and their repetition. The biggest problem for the performer was not just being deprived of an audience, but the altered status of interpretation, especially in a situation where performance becomes fragmented. As one opera singer put it, 'You have to put over emotion in bits and pieces, and all the time you feel you're singing not just for an evening but for always.'[42] In a single act the performance is removed from an audience and from time, and expression and the impression of spontaneity become the objects of technique and control.

In the classical arena, the new techniques occasioned much controversy. The pianist Glenn Gould reported that 'the great majority of present-day recordings consist of a collection of tape segments varying in duration upward from one twentieth of a second ... The antirecord lobby proclaims splicing a dishonest and dehumanising technique...'[43] Gould is an important witness in this debate, whose thoughtfulness about the recording medium contrasts utterly with the likes of Toscanini. As a highly gifted pianist who gave up 'concertizing' because (he claimed) of severe stage fright, at any earlier time this would have disqualified him from a performing career, but Gould became a dedicated recording artist with a very striking and individualist line in interpretation (and one of the finest Bach keyboard players of the century). He also began producing radio programmes for the Canadian Broadcasting Corporation – nowadays available on CD – and thought deeply about the medium of sound reproduction.

Gould argues that the experience of the listener lies at the centre of the technological debate, and the listener's experience of electronically diffused music is 'not within the public domain'. This does not mean that it is removed from the commercial circuit. He also observed that since the recording industry is directed to an audience 'which does most of its listening at home', it is not surprising if it promotes the revival of the baroque *Hausmusik* of the past. And where Carpentier had speculated in the mid 1950s that certain works – big as well as small – would live only in recorded performances and disappear from the concert hall, Gould prophesied, in the magazine *High Fidelity* in 1966, 'that the habit of concertgoing and concert giving, both as a social institution and as chief symbol of musical mercantilism' will become dormant.[44] In Britain almost twenty years later this trend has been confirmed: a review of the country's orchestras carried out jointly by the BBC and the Arts Council in 1994 found that 18 per cent of adults listened to orchestral music, either on disc or on the radio, but only 11 per cent attended concerts.[45]

But in Gould's opinion recording brought many benefits. For one thing, it frees the performer from the drudgery of routine: 'In the course of a lifetime spent in the recording studio he will necessarily encounter a wider range of repertoire than could possibly be his lot in the concert hall.' (How many musicians would like to be able to say the same!) His approach will be freed from preconceptions, as he makes each new work 'a vital part of his life for a relatively brief period' and then passes on to some other challenge. In the same spirit, Gould defends the tape-splice not only as a means of rectifying mistakes but also for giving the performer a new relationship to performance, that of editorial intervention. As an example he offers a recording session in which he made eight takes of a two-minute fugue from Bach's *Well-Tempered Clavier*, which at the time they thought included two that were note-perfect. Listening back later, Gould felt strongly that both were monotonous; but by combining the two, one of which was played in legato fashion and the other staccato, with simple splices, the result was a recorded interpretation 'far superior to anything we could at the time have done in the studio'. Of course it is also possible to play tricks with this technique. Elizabeth Schwarzkopf appended a missing high C to a tape of *Tristan and Isolde* sung by Kirsten Flagstad, and indignant purists howled her down; although whether the music actually suffers is a different question.[46]

Recording has developed conventions that contravene the acoustical limitations of the public auditorium. Today, wrote Gould in 1966, the sound the listener hears possesses characteristics that two generations ago were neither available to the profession nor wanted by the public, like analytic clarity and almost tactile proximity. We have come to expect a Brünnhilde, blessed with amplification, 'who can surmount without struggle the velvet diapason of the Wagnerian orchestra', or a searching acoustical spotlight on 'the filigreed path of a solo cello' playing against the whole orchestra in a concerto. There was also stereo.

Prerecorded stereo tapes first went on sale in 1954; equivalent records came four years later. By simply doubling the tracks, stereo followed the introduction of tape with what in this case is a certain technical inevitability, given that the idea of recording separate channels simultaneously to create a spatial effect on playback was once again far from new. According to one source, the earliest attempt at some form of binaural reproduction dates back to 1881, when experiments were conducted in Paris over telephone lines. More research took place on both sides of the Atlantic following the introduction of electrical recording, although as a commercial contender, the insecurity of the record market kept it at bay. However, an engineer at EMI, Alan Blumlein, developed a cutting technique in the early 1930s which the major record companies adopted as a standard when they finally went for stereo in 1958.

Immediately the character assumed by the stereo image aroused controversy. EMI's senior classical producer, Walter Legge, berated the philistine notions that quickly sprang up around him. His

declared principle of recording was: 'I want to make records which will sound in the public's home exactly like what they would hear in the best seat in an acoustically perfect hall.' The increased ambiance of stereo recording gave me the opportunity more completely to realize this aim than ever before. I soon came into conflict with the technical and sales departments over this. They believed that the public wanted the 'gimmick' of stereo – would like to listen to the left and right extremes which in those days left a hole (I called it a 'frozen nose' or 'ping pong listening') in the space between the loudspeakers. It took a long time for me to induce these people [to realize] that their ideas of stereo were the very opposite of what musicians and the musical public wanted.[47]

Legge achieved his position as doyen of classical record producers because of his exceptional musicality, which provided the perfect foil for a whole number of artists (not least his wife, Elizabeth Schwarzkopf). Here a third object lesson is provided by the case of Maria Callas, whose relationship with Legge (and EMI) began in 1953. If the microphone and the recording studio indeed produce a different approach to interpretation from that of the concert platform and the opera house, then what the difference consists in can be gauged by comparing the several different versions of the same operas that Callas recorded over her relatively short career, between the late 1940s and the mid 1960s. In the view of a recent biographer, Callas owes more to the gramophone record than to all her public performances, because her extraordinary artistry, says Jürgen Kesting, turned the gramophone into a theatre of the imagination which Legge's carefully produced stereo recordings enhanced.[48]

The curious part is that Callas seemed to belong to a tradition that was thought by many to be lost. It is still possible to hear in the earliest acoustic recordings of operatic arias something of the old *bel canto* style, in which singers employ a panoply of devices which since then have mostly dropped out of use: they linger on the nuances, interpolate notes and inflect the pitch with a special timbre where a note or a word asks for emphasis. By the 1930s, it was no longer possible to hear anything remotely similar on the stages of Berlin, New York, Vienna or even Milan. Ornamented singing was considered an anachronism. The transition from ornamented *bel canto* to controlled dramatic singing which began with Verdi had culminated in the rise of *verismo* and the *espressivo* style of composers like Mascagni, Leoncavallo and above all Puccini. Within a few decades, says Kesting, roughly between 1890 and 1910, the aesthetics of opera singing changed, especially to the disadvantage of the female voice. The new paradigm was that of the tenor Caruso. Over the same period as the rise of the gramophone record, the old type of female coloratura was eclipsed by a succession of singers following in Caruso's footsteps, from Beniamino Gigli and Richard Tauber to Mario del Monaco and Giuseppe di Stefano, who were courted by the cinema and, in Kesting's words, 'gave the masses ... music of the "soul" ... complete with sobs and sighs and a mixture of emphasis and vibrato which later infiltrated its way into pop music'.[49]

Maria Callas owed her supremacy in the 1950s and 1960s, despite certain imperfections in her voice, to what had become by then a rare capacity – and not only in a soprano – to employ the full range of dramatic nuances available in *bel canto* in their proper places. But there was more. When Callas arrived on the scene at the end of the 1940s, she brought to the opera stage a unique combination: a virtuoso classical technique at the service of modern sense of vocal expression. Blessed with a wide tessitura of three octaves, the range of roles she took on was unprecedented; on one famous occasion she sang Wagner and Bellini in the same week. Perhaps it was this repertoire that eventually defeated her voice, forcing her to retire from the stage at the early age of forty-two. Yet in bringing together coloratura agility and dramatic verve, she did more than give back to ornamented singing its original musical sense. She not only brought to the words she was singing the vocal acting which the old theoreticians of *bel canto* had demanded, the control of dynamics, accent, intonation, colour and articulation, in the service of the words and dramatic meaning; she also transformed these roles by projecting onto the mental confusion of the mad heroines of Bellini and Donizetti – conventionally sung by light-weight sopranos – the intense and tragic vision of Isolde.

The Callas discography spans twenty-four years, with studio recordings of sixteen complete operas including several she never sang on stage, while live recordings preserve thirty-four of her forty-seven roles. The recordings of excerpts and complete performances in Verona, Mexico City, Trieste, Lisbon, Dallas, Rome, Florence and of course Milan, were made with magnetic tape. No such chronicle of the singer's career would have been possible otherwise. But nor would the painstaking accomplishments of the studio recordings have been possible either. Callas herself emphasized that a performance has different rules to those of recording. It was possible to take bigger risks on stage in front of an audience, but studio recording allows greater nuance and refinement of details, and magnetic tape permits as many takes as necessary. Moreover, with the arrival of stereo, Legge rethought the recording of opera as an endeavour requiring its own kind of staging, with due care for the way that the acoustic space was arranged (although he never went as far as John Culshaw at Decca, who made his name by using cinematic sound effects in the first complete recording of Wagner's *Ring* cycle). Encouraged by Legge, says Kesting, the studio recordings allowed Callas to cultivate the smallest vocal nuances, the finest inflections. According to the writer Ingeborg Bachmann, Callas had a unique way of pronouncing words 'and the record is the ideal medium for the art of sound play'.[50] The result was a *mise-en-scène* conceived in acoustic terms, a virtual space which was enhanced by stereophonic sound, a music theatre without a stage.

It is somewhat ironic to discover that the fashion icon adopted by Callas on which to model her image was that of a film star. Zeffirelli reported that during rehearsals for a Rossini opera in 1955, Callas saw *Roman Holiday*, and told him she wanted to look 'as fine and delicate' as Audrey Hepburn. The two had once met – they shared the same cosmetician in Paris – and Callas had said the same thing to Hepburn herself, much to the film star's amazement.[51] The incident only underlines a paradox: what Callas achieves through the medium of the recording continues to thrill, and no other singer has yet come near to the same qualities. Yet at the same time, for anyone who saw Callas on stage, the recording remains an *aide-mémoire* which merely evokes the memory of an extraordinary dramatic presence. It is remarkable enough that her magnetism was larger than her voice, so that even her late performances, when her voice was overstretched and sometimes awkward, remain more powerful in the memory than performances by others, however perfectly sung. The real meaning of this paradox is discovered in recordings of roles that she never performed on stage, that nobody has seen, but that no singer since has been able to match.

8

The Record and the Mix

Between the photograph and the sound recording, photography and phonography, there is both an affinity and a critical but elusive difference. It did not need photography to show people what they looked like – the image itself might surprise them, but not the fact of a visual representation, which everyone knows from reflections and mirrors, let alone human artistry in the form of drawing and portraiture. In this sense, the objective automatism of photography may be thought of as the fulfilment of aims that visual art had long entertained. But Edison, speaking of hearing the first recording he ever made, remarked 'I was never so taken aback in my life.' For no one before this moment could know what their voice sounded like. It is *still* always surprising when anyone hears their own recorded voice played back for the first time, for as Malraux once said, 'You hear other people in the ears, but your own voice in the throat.' Phonography wrested the voice from the throat and embedded it, like an echo, in a mechanical memory.[1]

Edison spoke of 'phonographing a sound', on the linguistic model of 'photographing a scene', and for decades people thought of sound recording as a kind of sound photography, meaning a technique, despite the fact that photography was recognized to be an art. Of course, as Benjamin wrote, a lot of futile thought was devoted to the question of whether it *was* an art. 'The primary question – whether the very invention of photography had not transformed the entire nature of art – was not raised.'[2] It is curious that the title of the essay containing this observation, 'The Work of Art in the Age of Mechanical Reproduction', evokes the phonographic reproduction of music, when in fact the essay deals principally with the photographic art of film – as if Benjamin thought of phonography as the paradigm of a radically new aesthetic effect, with momentous consequences for cultural attitudes, but could only analyse the process in terms of an art form that was representational.

There is a semiological puzzle here, concerning the nature of the representational sign. The automatism of the process in both media, photography and phonography, guarantees a causal relation between the signified and the signifier. In both cases, the signifier belongs to the type of sign that the American philosopher C.S. Peirce called an index – like thunder and lightning or smoke and fire – where the one is causally linked to the other. If it were true, then, that the camera cannot lie, then nor can the tape recorder. (On this reading it is not the machine which lies when the representation is mendacious, but the human being who uses it.) But the photograph is also what Peirce called an icon, the kind of signifier which represents the signified by means of a similar arrangement of certain features: a 'fitness' of resemblance, like a drawing or a map. The photograph is thus both an index and an icon at the same time. The recording process would seem analogous but is subtly different. There is no equivalent, for example, to the photographic negative, as if the recording does not so much copy the original sound as recreate it. The coded tracings which are nowadays a familiar image are not the same. Precisely what people found surprising about the record groove was that such a mechanical tracing could contain the vibrant world of sound at all.

Phonography is therefore not like taking a photograph after all. Moreover, if the reproduction of a scene in photography is a logical property of the medium, in the process, non-artistic or even unartistic objects are fashioned by the medium into artistic representations (and in the medium of film, these representations are cut up and reassembled to produce the art of dramatic montage). In phonography, however, as long conceived, such artistic ideas were shut out; the purely documentary vocation of the medium, its mimetic objectivity, completely predominated. And in its most naïve form – as if photography and film had not turned documentary into a highly poetic artistic genre. As Douglas Kahn, an American audio artist, puts it, 'Art photography is commonplace, but an art phonography? When compared to the photographic arts, the phonographic arts are retarded.'[3]

'Audio artist' is a term that signifies a new moment in phonographic culture, a new kind of artistic endeavour, belonging to the 1980s alongside the rise in performance art and installation art; in fact it is one of the links between the two, since audio technology allows sound signals to be incorporated into both. Let us define it for the moment as an art of sonic montage, something like a cross between experimental radio and *musique concrète*. It is also a movement in the interstices of mass communications, in the form, among other things, of mail-order audio cassettes. And according to Kahn, it has been a long time coming.

The reasons for the delay are not just technical – the ease of access and operation of the new gear in comparison to the earlier – but also institutional and aesthetic. There were individual experiments and proposals between the wars by artists of the avant-garde like the photographer Moholy-Nagy or the film-maker Dziga Vertov, as well as by a number of composers, like Milhaud and Cage – although Kahn insists that audio art is not primarily, or even essentially, musical. Later would come a few small spaces provided by the cultural channels of public service radio stations for essays in the form of experimental drama. The central artistic problem that they all faced was the weight of the documentary status of the recorded sound, the vocation of the recording for overt mimesis: its dogged faithfulness to the original, its empirical matter-of-factness. This is a capacity for copying which phonography shares with photography but hardly at all with music. (Which is not to say that there is no imitative music, just as there are onomatopoeic words, but rather that the ability of music to imitate non-musical sound is marginal to its primary mode of expression.) But phonography had been captured by music and non- or extra-musical uses were marginalized and downgraded. (Edison's notions about recording the dying for posterity, for example, were totally ignored by the record companies. The idea of a historical archive was none of their business; the notion belongs to the newsreel or broadcasting.) In short, the absence of an art of mimetic sound is the converse, says Kahn, of the presence of music as the universal art of sound. Audio art can only arise when this is acknowledged and then worked upon, to produce a sonic equivalent to the visual poetry of photography and film; a process that includes the creative distortion of the sound image.

Raw sound too, which interests the audio artist for a variety of reasons, is also musically alien. It seemed inescapable that if non-musical sounds were to acquire the potential of becoming artistic symbols, then by the same count they became music – unless music were to change. Kahn considers audio art, though composed, as something different from music, but it needed the work of composers like John Cage, who did things with noise, to challenge the ingrained habits of musical hearing and open up our ears. In this the relationship with noise is critical.

The first intimations of a new attitude towards noise occurred well into the age of the phonograph but were strangely independent of it. The immediate inspiration for Russolo's noise instruments, which he presented at concerts in Milan, Paris and London in 1913, came from fellow Italian Futurists like Marinetti, for whom noise signalled the ascendancy of the modern age. Sound is defined (wrote Russolo) as the result of a succession of regular and periodic vibrations, while noise is caused by irregular motion. But the distinction is not a sharp one.

> We know that the production of sound requires not only that a body vibrate regularly but also that these vibrations persist in the auditory nerve until the following vibration has arrived, so that the periodic vibrations blend to form a continuous musical sound. At least sixteen vibrations per second are needed for this. Now, if I succeed in producing a *noise* with this speed...

Hence the rectangular wooden boxes which made up the Futurist Orchestra, containing mechanisms turned by a handle to produce a remarkable variety of distinguishable noises. (This music has now been released on CD and begun to circulate afresh.)

In the 1930s, composers as diverse as Milhaud, Hindemith, Varèse and John Cage had all experimented with discs played on variable speed turntables to create striking, though limited, transformations of sound. Cage, as a student in Schoenberg's composition class at UCLA in the mid 1930s, realized he had little talent for harmony. According to one story, Schoenberg declared that he was no composer, but an inventor of genius. The prediction was borne out in the invention of the prepared piano and the composition between 1939 and 1952 of the series called *Imaginary Landscapes*, using novel combinations of percussion and electrics: turntables playing frequency test records, contact microphones made from electric guitar pickups, and so forth. The most notorious was No. 4 for twelve radios, dating from 1951. Pierre Schaeffer, a radio sound technician in Paris, began to experiment in 'scratching' records during the war and by 1948 had formulated a method of composition which freed the sonic material from association with its origins. Taking sounds from different sources, from pianos to railway trains, he produced a series of short pieces by playing them at different speeds, forwards or in reverse, isolating fragments and superimposing them. This was *musique concrète* – concrete music as opposed to music made by putting notes on paper – and by the early 1950s Schaeffer had attracted around him a group of young musicians keen to know more, including Messiaen and his pupils Boulez and Stockhausen.

Musique concrète came of age with the introduction of the tape recorder, which allowed precise control over the techniques that Schaeffer developed on the turntable. Kahn points out that, technologically speaking, Schaeffer's first works could have been produced on similar equipment available much earlier in the form of the optical film soundtrack. Optical sound equipment was used already in the late 1920s in Germany by the experimental filmmaker Walter Ruttman and others to produce radio works, and the Russian film-maker G.V. Alexandrov experimented with techniques later associated with *musique concrète* in an experimental film of the same period, such as running the sound backwards and cutting it up. And of course, these techniques are also those of film editing.

Rudolf Arnheim, in his 1930s book on radio, lamented the lack of a radio art taking advantage of the new resources. Such artistry developed, however, in cinema, especially in the domain of animation, where it seemed to be encouraged by the absence of objective reality in the image. The pioneers were experimental film-makers like Norman McLaren in New York and the Whitney brothers in Los Angeles, who scratched and manipulated the soundtrack itself (as Alexandrov also did). Working under a different sign, in RCA's sound film operations in Hollywood in 1936, a certain Frederick Samnis dreamed of an apparatus that would automate much of this work, a photoelectric 'Singing Keyboard', using loops of optical sound film. Intended as 'a special purpose instrument for making "talkie" cartoons', it would have 'ten or more sound tracks ... featuring such words as "quack" for a duck, "meow" for a cat, "moo" for a cow ... It could as well be the bark of a dog ... or the twaddle indulged in by some of our tin pan alley song writers.'[4] Other people designed machines called the Noisegraph, the Dramagraph, the Kinematophone, the Soundograph or the Excelsior Sound Effect Cabinet. Some of these instruments employed discs, like Edwin Welte's Lichttonorgel, in which photoelectric recordings of famous European pipe organs were inscribed in concentric circles on a disc made of glass. Today, this kind of machine is called a sampler, and it employs the most advanced computer technology.

If the sampler was first put to work in the Hollywood cartoon, tape editing copied techniques developed by the film editor. Nor was it the commercial recording studio where these techniques were first applied to music but the electronic music studio, which amalgamated the techniques of *musique concrète* with combinations of acoustic tones produced by assorted electronic signal generators. Radio stations were the first centres of research and experiment in electronic music, and different schools of thought quickly began to emerge about what this new kind of music could do. The first dedicated electronic music studio in Germany was set up at the radio station in Cologne by Herbert Eimert, where he was joined in 1952 by Stockhausen; here they set out to create not *musique concrète* but electronic music proper, in which 'natural' (i.e. recorded) sounds were taboo. Pretty soon Stockhausen started to incorporate them anyway, and in Italy in 1955 Luciano Berio and Bruno Maderna set up a studio at a radio station in Milan which brought the two compositional principles together from the outset.

The results – the creation of entirely novel sonic landscapes – were broadcast on the cultural radio stations and played in small concert halls. The Dutch firm of Philips, Europe's leading electronics enterprise, commissioned the veteran avant-garde composer Edgar Varèse to create a work to be played in their pavilion at the 1958 Brussels World Exhibition, designed by Le Corbusier and equipped with 350 loudspeakers. But the wider impact came when the works that these composers produced were issued on record. They were released in small editions for aficionados of the avant-garde, but as Eimert put it, it made you wonder 'whether perhaps it is not the symphony recorded on tape or disc that is the synthetic, and electronic music the genuine article'.[5] In short, these were the first recordings that seemed to be composed for the medium, rather than the medium transparently reproducing them. What is more, being records, they began to spread beyond their immediate market and exert their influence undetected, until the media began to report stories such as that of Paul McCartney, between making *Revolver* and *Sgt. Pepper*, listening to Stockhausen.

★

Revolver, released in 1966, had already used backward tapes and splicing techniques derived from *musique concrète* and the electronic music studio. Before *Sgt. Pepper* was released in 1967, the Beatles quit touring and declared themselves a studio band. Paul McCartney announced that the Beatles were not only working on new songs but new sounds, and all was ready for *Sgt. Pepper* to be received as the first of a new kind of studio rock album, composed for recording rather than performance. As the Beatles were then in their heyday, these two albums became the pivot of a new brand of 'art rock', a genre that evolved along with the stereo LP. Established exponents of the style like Yes, Electric Light Orchestra and King Crimson concentrated on incorporating classical music styles into a popular music form. The new emphasis, with champions like the Steve Miller Band, Pink Floyd and Jimi Hendrix, was on the incorporation of experimentation with sound.

Sgt. Pepper could not have been created without a four-track tape recorder, but the Beatles were not the first popular recording artists to use these techniques, which had already cropped up on so-called novelty numbers during the 1950s. More importantly, they shared the credit for these albums with George Martin, marking in the process the emergence of a new kind of popular record producer.

Rock 'n' roll had changed the job of the producer. Not only had the corporate A&R man been eclipsed by the rise of the independents, but the producer's function had altered because rock musicians brought their own material with them – that was part of the deal: they either wrote or chose it themselves. (Creative cover versions, like 'Roll Over Beethoven', first recorded by Chuck Berry for Chess in 1955, re-recorded by the Beatles eleven years later, were becoming part of the pop tradition; other groups like the Rolling Stones and the Who also attracted attention at the beginning of their careers by demonstrating their ability to take a minor hit by an American rock 'n' roll artist and turn it into a major one.) In this respect the Beatles were true to type, though untypically celebrated for their musical originality – and not just by the pop world: distinguished music critics analysed their songs and pointed to novel constructions of melody and harmony. The sound they projected in the studio, however, was not achieved merely by musical magic. With increasing possibilities for moulding the sound, a producer like Martin, who knew what he was doing, could begin to 'direct' the musicians; not so much like a conductor in front of an orchestra, but as if they were making a film, not a record.

Or as if the studio had become a huge musical instrument at the producer's disposal. The redesign of the studio following the introduction of tape had stimulated the development of a whole series of different pieces of processing equipment – delay lines and reverberation units, equalizers, filters, compressors and limiters. At the same time, hand in hand with stereo came the introduction of the multitrack tape recorder: the first four-channel tape recorders were introduced in 1958; eight- and sixteen-track recorders were available by the late 1960s. At this point pop music became a new form of musical manufacture. Where direct recording – to disc or tape – relies on microphone placement, equalization, acoustics and mixing *before* recording, multitrack recording allows mixing to take place afterwards. It also allows overdubbing, by which different musical parts can be recorded at different times on parallel tracks, and a process of re-recording evolves, known as mixing down or remixing, which combines the different parallel tracks into a single master version. Overdubbing was not a new technique. The original form of the practice was achieved on single-track tape recorders by re-recording from one deck to another while adding in another live recording at the same time, but it was not until multitrack recorders that it became anything like standard practice.

As these techniques developed, a new generation of independent producers emerged, who would team up with a favourite engineer and particular artists and groups and take charge of them in the studio (thus helping to keep the confused executives of the record company away). At the same time, musicians no longer needed to be fully rehearsed when they went into the studio, but could use the studio in order to 'compose' as they went along. Since multitrack recording also allowed for easy 'punch-ins' – re-recording parts of individual tracks on top of what is already there – they could also spend a good deal of time correcting mistakes. Before multitracking, the objective was to do a series of takes until you had enough to be able to assemble a definitive version with editing, by splicing sections of each together. When multiple tracks are recorded on the same tape, it is no longer safe to splice it, so punching-in takes over. By the same token, however, the essential activity of the musician, the performance of music, becomes more and more fragmented.

As musicians, engineers and producers became ever more involved in different facets of the recording process, two things happened: authorship became diffused, and uncertainty in the relations of production led to power struggles for aesthetic control of the finished product; as one writer puts it, 'their titles [become] as problematic as their job descriptions'.[6] George Martin, by all accounts, was completely unlike this. He was a creative collaborator, who had learned the craft of the record producer in the 1950s, among other things working on records by the American bandleader and drummer Spike Jones, famous for his musical humour. Recording allowed Jones to add sound effects to the unorthodox instruments he used in live performance, like washboards and automobile pumps. Martin brought to recording the Beatles the same spirit of technical experiment, and something of the same sense of humour.

This process of fragmentation is one of the keys to the development of commercial popular music over the past fifty years. It induces a simplification of musical elements, a reduction in musical complexity, since the artist is relieved of the need to master anything more than basic skills. This does not of course mean a reduction in potency, but its concentration in a limited range of rhythmic, melodic and harmonic gestures. The procedure originates in the practices of Tin Pan Alley, and it is not the purpose of this kind of music to yield enduring aesthetic riches but to be eminently consumable and readily disposable. But if this, as Adorno considered, is artistic trash, catering to certain social predispositions in the listener, then the aesthetic judgement that is made on it must take into account that trash has now become an artistic category.

Mixing, says Steve Jones in *Rock Formation*, is what distinguishes popular music from classical music, citing the comments of a recording engineer who has worked in both fields and has won Grammy awards for recordings by the likes of Quincy Jones and Michael Jackson. Speaking in 1987, Bruce Swedien explained:

> When I started recording classical music (I worked for RCA in Chicago, my gig was recording the Chicago Orchestra) I soon began to feel as if I was taking dictation, or something. In other words, the most that I could do in recording classical music was to re-create the original sound-field. On the other hand, in pop music (all types, rock, R&B, etc.), the only thing that limits the sound

image that we create is our own imagination. Mix up those reverb formats, get crazy, don't try to rationalize anything.[7]

The new recording techniques raised the status of producers and engineers in both classical and popular music, but not to the same degree. Royalties for producers became common in popular music, but as one classical record producer puts it, 'were never considered in the field of "serious" music, for the simple reason that nobody in management had even the remotest idea what classical producers actually did'.[8] In popular music the producer, whatever he did, clearly held the secret of success; in classical music the aim was the transparent rendition of a natural musical object. Opera was the height of the art because here the record could become a theatre of the imagination. However, the classical record producer preferred to speak not of mixing but of balance. The object was to achieve an aural image something like the sound perspective that might be heard from the middle of the stalls in one of the great concert halls like the Concertgebouw in Amsterdam or the Boston Symphony, or a top-price seat at La Scala, Covent Garden or Bayreuth, all of which have splendid (though different) acoustics. The skill of the engineer is partly concerned with how to achieve this kind of balance in less compliant acoustics. This whole approach is irrelevant in the case of pop music, because there is no comparable kind of space where the music originates. Indeed the gramophone itself has rendered popular music a product of loudspeakers which may be located anywhere, where they often have to compete with other sounds and noises. The ultimate aim is therefore to produce the most effective sound for reproduction of different kinds, from the jukebox and domestic record player to the car stereo and portable earphone player, which each make their own acoustic demands.

A history of mixing would include the effect credited to the Los Angeles producer Phil Spector in the early 1960s, known as the 'wall of sound'. Here, according to one account, the basic ingredients included generous instrumentation, like orchestral strings or blazing brass, underpinned by prominent percussion playing insistent rhythms, intensified by the use of echo and tape loops. In particular, the 'wall' effect was achieved by a mix which placed equal value on the disparate elements that went into it. 'The voice was another instrument, equal in value with the third tambourine, not lost in the mix, but not placed far in front of everything else.'[9]

Eisenberg, in *The Recording Angel*, considers Phil Spector to be 'the first *auteur* among producers', whose work was 'perhaps the first fully self-conscious phonography in the popular field', with an immense influence on his musical betters, from Brian Wilson of the Beach Boys to the Beatles and Frank Zappa.[10] The Beach Boys rapidly became a group whose essential sound was a function of studio recording, a combination of vocals, heavily multitracked, and studio effects, which included electronic keyboards for the underlying motor rhythm.

Multitracking adds a new dimension to mixing. Prior to the multitrack tape recorder, mixing was done in the process of recording the performer. That is, the sounds from the microphone were treated by equalization, reverberation and other effects, then sent to the tape head. Multitrack recorders allowed mixing after recording, by isolating each instrument on its own track, either by placing baffles between them in the studio or by recording them separately. These innovations affect musicians directly. Musicians who have to record in this way now need headphones to hear themselves and each other, even when they are playing together in the same studio.

The rock critic Simon Frith has argued that tape recording allowed producers and engineers to manipulate performances in the same way that it allowed musicians to manipulate sound. With multitrack recording, not only could parts of different takes be edited together but individual parts could be altered without changing others played alongside. Each track can be manipulated separately; different effects can be added; the tracks can then be recombined and balanced with other tracks and the final mix sent to another recorder. As a result, multitrack recording puts the producer and recording engineer firmly in charge of the studio, but it also creates new musical possibilities; the new mode of production therefore begins to turn the recording engineer – the mixer – into a musical creator of a new kind.

Mixers now came to be in as much demand as producers (and some played both roles) and their artistry expanded. Indeed, as one writer puts it, the remix 'is a unique artistic act whose artistry is produced through the technology' since the craft is in manipulating both the music and the *sound*. Remixing is 'recoding, the reanimation of familiar music by the creation of new sonic textures for different sonic contexts'.[11] For this very reason, new demands emerge to adapt the mix to the acoustic criteria of different reproduction systems. This was true even in the early 1950s. A report in *Newsweek* in 1952 called 'Men Behind the Microphones' explained that records were made 'with a slight but deliberate distortion: the volume of high frequency tones is boosted. This step is taken to over-ride needle hiss, which is a melange of high frequency noise. Phonographs are supposed to be designed to compensate for this distortion by automatically suppressing high tones. The net result, ideally, is balanced tone with reduced needle noise.'[12] By the 1980s, the history of mixing has ended up in the practice of mastering different versions of the mix for different media, and as Steve Jones puts it, the final mix is not the final product. Often several versions of a song will be released, 'one for each format; a short mix for AM radio, a longer more elaborate mix for FM radio, a long mix with many effects and edits added for dance clubs, and a version of the FM radio mix with effects and "sweetening" added specifically for combining the song with a video'.[13]

The remix has also given birth to new genres. According to one account, the development of reggae is an example. Recording engineers, says Dick Hebdige in *Cut 'n' Mix*, experimented by mixing the tracks together on the final tape in different ways. 'For instance, ska and rock-steady records were mixed differently. In ska, the vocal track had been given prominence ... but on the new rocksteady records, the singers' voices tended to be treated like any other instrument.' Pride of place was given instead to the 'dread ridims' of the bass guitar.[14]

But this is not just a question of different musical genres. What is going on, which motivates the music, is part of a wider history, that of a series of encounters between the electrification of music and cultural traditions not so much outside as at the edges of the commercial mainstream; a process driven by the record industry's need to incorporate new markets. Since the 1920s, this had largely meant black American music, in the forms of jazz, blues, and rhythm and blues. By the 1970s, the edges of this zone came to include the English-speaking Caribbean, and especially Jamaica. The result is a musical history that leads back to the practice of 'toasting', which is found at the roots of reggae, and forwards to rap, born in the hip-hop culture of urban black American youth, like the New York discos, where disc jockeys would talk to their audiences in the jive style of the old personality DJs.

In short, rap is the music of the DJ, the music that the DJ makes by rhythmically combining his voice with recorded sounds, which finds its origins, according to several writers, in Afro-American oral traditions; like reggae, where it is possible to hear echoes of old African boast songs. But the more immediate reference point is 'toasting', or talking to a rhythm in a patois, where the rhythm of the speech and the rhythm of the beat work together, a verbal style which was first married to rhythm and blues by Jamaican disco DJs. As Dick Hebdige recounts, Jamaican interest in American black music, fuelled especially by R&B stations in Florida, prompted the appearance of discotheques – large dances, indoor or outdoor, employing powerful sound systems incorporating microphones for the DJ who operated them, who not only presented the records but talked over them. They would 'add spice' to the records they were playing, says Hebdige, 'by shouting out their favourite catchphrases over the microphone. These talkovers or toasts soon became a popular feature of the blues dances.'[15] Soon, he adds, the DJs were also adding electronic sound effects like echo and reverberation, and by the end of the 1960s the first talkover records had begun to appear. These records combined the DJ's patter with a mixing technique known as dub, which consisted in using prerecorded tracks to create pulsating rhythms, distorting the original in the process in such a way that the tune is still recognizable but heavily broken up by the insistent emphasis on the drums and the bass. The technique crystallized in the records of the first talkover star, U Roy, in 1970. In Hebdige's description, 'He would take a popular rhythm track, phase out the singing and add his own stream of screeches, yelps and muttered catchphrases. The records were an immediate success...'[16]

Dub and talkover records became extremely popular with fans, but not with musicians. Jamaican radio, Hebdige tells us, was forced to ban them because of pressure from the musicians' union. The union was indignant that the musicians who recorded the original tracks of which these records made use, did not get any royalties. As one Jamaican record producer put it, 'You can copyright a song, but you can't copyright a rhythm.' But another says, 'It's not like we stealing anything from anybody. We take a ridim and update it and re-record it. And then we apply our new ideas to it. We call it 'anointing' the ridim with our own magic.'[17]

The ban – and the mixers' denial that they were violating anyone's property rights – signals the emergence of a radical new state of affairs in commercial popular music. This is not just a new kind of sound or even a new musical style, but a transformation of music, in which the 'misuse' of music becomes a new norm. The music is rough and crude, another result of a process that sees the reduction of musical content to the most basic elements, but here in a synthetic form. As Steve Jones observes, 'Many dub reggae recordings from the early 1970s, recorded on low quality equipment, contain examples of tape hiss boosted at rhythmic intervals to sound as if the hiss was part of the music.'[18] But dub and talkover records are not so much recordings composed for the medium, like the studio albums of art rock groups, they are rather composed out of it. And they become a kind of *musique concrète*, the creative distortion of the sound image using recorded musical materials as sonic objects. Naturally it is a kind of music that belongs to a very different idiom from that of the trained composer, for here, without access to the sophisticated electronics of the avant-garde composer's studio, popular artists are making music without any traditional instrument except the voice.

Rap artists take this a step further, turning mass-produced replay equipment into their instruments. All a rap band needs is a dual turntable, a drum machine if they can afford it, and a microphone. The method, which is simple, though requiring considerable dexterity, involves scratching the discs on the turntable, manipulating them to produce their own rhythmic sound. This is, of course, another fundamental example of misuse, a transgression of the normal purpose for which turntables and needles and records are designed. The result is a form that foregrounds fracture and disruption. As a description in a book on the subject, called *Microphone Fiends*, puts it, rappers call out to the DJ to 'lay down the beat' which it is expected will be interrupted. 'The flow and motion of the initial bass or drum line in rap music is abruptly ruptured by scratching ... or the rhythmic flow is interrupted by other musical passages.'[19] In short, according to another writer in the same book, materially deprived and culturally despised youths have seized on the products of advanced technology for their own purposes. They have combined some of the oldest African–American oral traditions with some of the newest technological gadgetry. 'Defamed and despised ... they [have] found a way to contest their erasure, to reintroduce themselves to the public by "throwing out" a new style that made other people take notice...'[20]

9

Global Corporations

and 'World Music'

Reproduction has produced the unhappy effects on musical perception of disembodiment and the destruction of what Walter Benjamin called the traditional aura of the artwork. The record industry has stimulated the formation of an enormous production sector of trite ephemera which damages musical sensibilities, if not our very ears. The musical world, like the cultural ethos that envelops it and to which it makes a major contribution, has been transformed. On the one hand, reproduction makes *all* music equally worn out and done to death; on the other, with the multiplication of media and the means of replication, the mechanism of the market has itself created a condition in which all music circulates more and more freely beyond its control – as *musica practica* has always done. In the new phase which develops by stages in the second half of the century, reproduction and the equipment associated with it begin to constitute a parallel agency of cultural production alongside traditional *musica practica*, and accordingly reproduction nurtures new creative potential of its own. And because this involves the increasing technification of musical production, this potential in turn extends the attack on the old traditions, while the endlessly expanding circle of consumption and reproduction throws everything back into play. This is the condition that has been dubbed postmodernism, in which the echoing imitation, instead of dying away, gets louder.

To be sure, as Adorno says, exchange value exerts its power in a special way in the realm of cultural goods like music. Since the very quintessence of the aesthetic effect hangs on the thread of illusion, the artistic product, even the quasi-artistic, appears to be uniquely exempt within the world of commodities from simple reduction to monetary value, but to survive and escape its insertion into the domain of economic consumption and godless materialism. The record, the broadcast performance or music video, the concert competing with them for the consumer's favour – these are simultaneously within and yet above the world of commodities, produced for the market and aimed at the market, which they manage, however, to penetrate and escape. All this has strange effects on the behaviour of music, and the relationship of music to society. Adorno argued that every pleasure that is capable of emancipating itself from exchange value takes on subversive features. What he did not realize was that this is not only true of Schoenberg but also of rock music – which at least in principle is equally defiant.

Music continually shows its resilience by defying the prognostications of cultural pessimists like Adorno. It displayed this resilience by riding out the economic crisis that hit the West in 1974, bringing the expansive ethos of the 1960s to an end; in spite of which the post-Beatles buoyancy of the record industry continued, with worldwide sales in 1973 of $4.75 billion rising to nearly $7 billion in 1978. The first glitch only came the following year when the market was overtaken by inflation with the second oil crisis of the decade. Sales in 1979 dropped suddenly, according to one source, by 20 per cent across the board. According to another, although the singles market remained buoyant, albums fell in Britain by 'a staggering 25–30 per cent', and in America, which constituted half the world market, by 40–50 per cent. A third source says that total record sales between 1978 and 1983 fell by 15 per cent.[1]

The effect was to reinforce the process by which the record industry coalesced with the globalization of media, electronics and telecommunications. The 1970s were dominated by six major companies and another half dozen minors, which included new groups and new labels. The minors were mostly American but included the German Bertelsmann group, one of Europe's major magazine publishers. The big six were CBS, EMI, Polygram, WEA, RCA and MCA. EMI and Polygram were European, the other four American: all of them had diverse interests. For CBS these included radio and television broadcasting, and for EMI, television, cinema and electronics. Polygram was a joint subsidiary set up in 1962 by the German and Dutch electronics giants, Siemens and Philips. WEA (Warner–Elektra–Atlantic) was part of the Warner empire which had been acquired in 1967 by the Kinney Corporation, a conglomerate with diversified interests in funeral parlours, supermarkets, cleaning firms, plumbing and car parks. RCA remained a media giant encompassing both television and electronics, while MCA (Music Corporation of America) originated in a pre-war artists' booking agency attached to Pye Records which had moved in on the movie agency business in 1938 and set up its own television production subsidiary, Revue, in 1949. MCA became the biggest independent television producer in Hollywood and in 1959 acquired the American Decca company and its Hollywood subsidiary, Universal.

One of the factors that has affected survival is a company's attitude towards innovation. On the one hand there is the drive to expand the market, which favours improved media. On the other, the market is highly volatile and the costs of innovation are ever increasing, with the result that innovation is driven less by the manufacturers of the software than those who produce the hardware. The former, if they fall behind, are liable to be swallowed up, like Decca, which after a period of decline in the 1970s was finally sold off in 1980 to Polygram. Polygram, as a joint subsidiary of Siemens and Philips, was in a much more powerful position. It was Philips who had conquered the market for a portable tape format with the launch in 1963 of the audio cassette.

The cassette was smaller than the rival cartridge formats introduced over the preceding few years, and its operation could hardly have been simpler; to ensure its success, Philips handed out manufacturing rights to anyone who wanted to produce the cassettes, provided that they used Philips' specifications. As a result, Philips not only captured the market but hugely expanded it. At the same time, the new format intensified the problems of the disc market. The original audio cassette, monaural and using ⅛" tape, was relatively low quality and no direct competition for the high-quality stereo LP. As a cheap and small machine running off batteries, it offered the lure of expanding the market by introducing a new sector of consumption, not yet conquered by open-reel ¼" tape. But the latter, still limited to a fairly small aficionado following, nevertheless already posed a threat to the record companies, because in addition to home recording it provided for taping from disc and off air. This facility began to rupture the economic laws that the record companies exploited, because it promoted the circulation of recorded music outside the market – although in doing so it expanded the market for virgin tape and introduced a new element of competition between the record companies and the tape manufacturers.

None of this led to the demise of ¼" tape, which not only transformed studio practice but also took recording out of the studio and into the home. By the late 1960s, studio quality ¼" tape recorders were cheap enough for hi-fi enthusiasts and thereafter, says a writer on rock, the marketing of high-quality equipment for home recording was aimed at the musician trying to break into the recording industry. Typical of this strategy was an advertisement by Pioneer Electronics for a four-track tape deck in 1978: 'For the price of a few hours in a recording studio, you can own one.'[2] Ten years later, a Yamaha advertisement published in many music magazines (including titles like *Music Technology* and *Electronic Musician*) read: 'Go to your room and play ... using the MT2X Multitrack Recorder/Mixer, you can layer your recording just as you would in a real studio – one track at a time ... So if you've been wondering where you're going to get your first big break in music, now you know. At home.' The claim was not beyond the bounds of imagination. Some artists have recorded hit singles and even LPs in their bedrooms.

The spread of the cassette not only introduced a new release format, but increased the problem of piracy, as we shall see in more detail below. It also encouraged further mutations in listening behaviour, above all when Sony introduced the 'walkman' in 1979, which one writer has called 'a symbolic gadget for the nomads of modernity'.[3] The use of studio-quality headphones as a means of private listening began to develop during the 1960s, following the introduction of stereo. Headphones allowed the listener to attach their head directly to the source of the sound, dissolving the physical space of their body into the virtual space created by the music's stereo image. This has two effects: on the body of the listener, which loses its sense of location, and on the music, already disembodied, whose insertion into the listener's head is entirely illusory. As a result, the two merge together in a synthetic perceptual experience which provides the model for the computer industry's dreams in the 1990s of the creation of a helmeted virtual reality.

With the walkman it became possible to carry this virtual space around with you. Another writer likens this to 'a latter-day equivalent of the *flaneur*' described by Walter Benjamin in his study of Baudelaire, the figure who strolls through the arcades of mid nineteenth-century Paris, assimilating the stream of objects, people and movements to his own pace and experience as a defence against the shocks of mass urban existence.[4] A third commentator points out that the walkman, as a private and mobile piece of audio technology, is 'one step on from the car stereo which enables bodies to be immersed in a box of sound whilst travelling along a motorway or through a city. The walkman enables its user to take music wherever they go and exclude the external world and other human beings.'[5] It may have allowed Japanese commuters to cope with crowded subway trains, but by isolating the listener from the world through music it induces a sense of solipsism. This perhaps is the final *coup* in the negation that recording perpetrates on *musica practica*, where instead of music coming from bodies in front of the listener, it is reduced to an unreal and intangible space enveloping the isolated head.

The 1980s saw several American minors swallowed up by MCA in its efforts to catch up with its competitors, all of whom, with the threat of falling sales, poured a fortune into promotion both licit and illicit, desperate to get their records on the US 'Top 40' radio stations. According to one analysis, US record industry spending on the shady business of promotion claimed at least 30 per cent of pre-tax profits.[6] With the business inflated by this enormous level of hype, profits fell, losses were made, and the bubble threatened to burst. The first to fall was RCA, acquired by Bertelsmann in 1986. CBS fell to Sony in 1988, Warner merged with Time in 1989 and in 1990 MCA went to Matsushita. In short, three of America's four majors are now owned by foreign corporations. The whole process was accompanied by continuing exchanges of ownership among leading independent labels. EMI, for example, bought Chrysalis and a couple of music publishers, SBK and Filmtrax, while Polygram, at one time best known as the leading classical company, acquired the A&M and Island labels.

As we have already seen, the rationale for the acquisition of smaller labels is not merely concentration in the classic fashion. According to a report in *The Economist*:

> The record business divides into two: a relatively unsophisticated manufacturing and distribution business, where size and clout help, and the higher-risk 'A&R'

(Artist and Repertoire) side, where size looks relatively uncreative. To seem small and friendly to artists, the majors now all promote a variety of different labels, each of which runs its A&R separately. When a new type of music springs up – be it in Miami, Moscow or Manchester's Hacienda Club – the big record companies either buy up the new labels that produce it or invent their own. Even Britain's Virgin, the biggest independent record company [annual sales around $550m], has ten labels.[7]

In plain words, the majors are too big for their own good, they never know where and when the next trend is going to emerge because they are not really in touch with the audience, and hence their reliance on smaller fry to take the risks and test the market. But woe to any independent that proves itself, for this inevitably leads to take-over.

The history of EMI is particularly instructive. In the 1950s EMI was still a traditional record company – the world's largest – with interests in allied technologies that were not always profitable. A new management regime installed in 1954 to revitalize the company reorganized the music division, streamlined distribution and bought the Los Angeles company Capitol Records to ensure access to the new rock 'n' roll market in the United States. The real breakthrough, however, came when they signed the Beatles: in 1963 sales rocketed by 80 per cent and shares in Capitol doubled (the parent company showed its gratitude to the Liverpool group by doubling their royalty from 1d a single to 2d). EMI now began to diversify: it purchased a theatre management firm, Delfont, and a small cinema chain, and then proceeded to the £64m take-over of ABC from Associated British Pictures, which gave it another 270 cinemas, Elstree Studios and 25 per cent of Thames Television. Further purchases, including the music publisher Keith Prowse, quickly made EMI the biggest entertainment group in Britain. Its two main growth areas during the 1970s were big-budget film production (titles like *Close Encounters*, *Death on the Nile* and *The Deer Hunter*) and electronics, a field in which its defence business was supplemented by the prestigious but in the end loss-making development of brain and body scanners, which integrated computers and X-ray technology.

Turnover in 1977/78 reached £350 billion; the company's interests included record manufacturing and distribution scattered across thirty-one countries in all continents; in Britain it was also a major defence contractor, held shares in various radio and television stations, was involved in film production and distribution, and owned numerous restaurants, hotels and 'leisure centres' like the Blackpool Tower. Nevertheless, music and records remained the core element in EMI's business – as late as 1973, the release of two Beatles anthologies accounted for 16.7 per cent of total profits for the year – and the downturn at the end of the 1970s was therefore serious. Failing to develop a roster of new artists capable of matching the Beatles, EMI began to contract while competitors were growing. (In 1968, EMI accounted for 31.6 per cent of albums sold in Britain; by 1978 the figure was 21.7 per cent.) By now the company was diverting profits away from its music division, and where the record business as a whole devoted an average of 12–13 per cent of turnover to A&R, EMI's investment in this area had fallen to 7 or 8 per cent. It was symptomatic. The music division had become sclerotic, and budding new singers and bands increasingly preferred the independents, not only because they had a more 'intimate' set-up, but also because they were more flexible and more adventurous. As one journalist wrote, 'The independents don't pay out fortunes in advances and often don't do long-term deals involving guarantees for several albums. But they can afford to let a good unknown band make a single or two, and if their ear for the streets is right, they'll make money.'[8] In short, EMI had become uncomprehending of new trends. The classic instance occurred when they terminated a contract with the leading punk band, the Sex Pistols. 'A few months later, the band had sold a million records on Virgin and a sheepish EMI belatedly embraced the new wave in the more "acceptable" form of the Tom Robinson Band.'

Such responses came too late, however, and in October 1979 Britain's largest television rental group, Thorn Electrical Industries, launched a £150m take-over bid for EMI, which overnight added 30 per cent to the value of EMI's shares. Thorn's logic was simple: 'Thorn has cash, EMI needs cash; EMI has high technology electronics, Thorn wants to move up the technology ladder; Thorn makes and rents TV sets, EMI makes TV, film and music products. Together ... the companies could sweep the home entertainment board in the new video age ... just around the corner.'

What was actually just around the corner was, first of all, more of the same. One of the distinctive results of these developments is the new ecology of mass culture, based on recycling. Nowadays, when a new format is introduced, the old and worn-out is made new by tarting it up and re-issuing it. The process is like a dog chasing its own tale, for with each new format the archives get bigger and bigger. The classical archives were the first to be exploited, with the introduction of the LP, when the latest 78s were re-pressed and thus remained in circulation. Some of them acquired the patina of 'classic' recordings, like those of Toscanini, and have never been unavailable since, so that the Toscanini sound, for example, is as current in 1994 as it was in 1954, the year he retired. With CDs came a new generation of re-issues, recordings that had possessed a special aura and had stuck in people's memories, like the teenage Yehudi Menuhin playing the aged Elgar's Violin Concerto; or of historic interest as being original performances of new works, like Klemperer's 1929 recording of Kurt Weill's *Kleine Dreigroschenmusik*, the orchestral suite drawn from *The Threepenny Opera*. This stage of the process was partly instigated by the exploration of their record libraries by cultural radio stations like the BBC's Radio 3. But the CD seems also to have prompted a whole new wave of rediscoveries. Not only are stereo LP albums re-issued to keep the market supplied, and the bad old cut-price LPs recycled as bad new cut-price CDs, but pre-war 78s are being dusted over and given the newest sound. You can now buy digitized transfers of the original 1913 Nikisch Beethoven Fifth. Moreover, with the CD, pop music has embarked on the same process. You can now also get digitally remastered CDs of the originals of singles covered by the Beatles.

Meanwhile, this process of economic revalorization, said to be one of the forces unleashed by postmodernism, has a number of aesthetic consequences, though not always distinct enough for the theorists of postmodernism to agree on what they are. They concur, however, that an altered state of cultural consciousness is involved, in which traditional meanings and values have been set adrift. The flux created by the reproductive technologies of previous generations is merely the precondition for this new state, which adds to the sheer proliferation of cultural products the technical ease with which they can now be recycled and placed in entirely novel contexts; a state, therefore, in which all active traces of the traditional relationship of signifier to signified disappear, as everything becomes a semblance or a simulation. In music, this is especially the vocation of the sampler.

The first modern device to fit this bill (though not yet using the terminology) was produced by the Australian company Fairlight at the end of the 1970s. A dedicated computer allowing sound to be fed in and manipulated, the software program it employed became, as one writer puts it, 'the mother and father of all sequencer software'.[9]

The sampler is a by-product of digitization, by which sound, which starts out in the shape of a continuously variable analogue wave form, is broken into discrete bits of information by sampling the wave at a rate of thousands per second. Once again, there is a long prehistory behind the digital technology employed. As the composer Hugh Davies mentions in his short 'History of Sampling', the first practical digital technique for the electrical transmission of information (though not yet binary in character like the electronic computer) was demonstrated by Samuel Morse in 1844, at the beginning of the age of telegraphy.[10] The first proposals for the digitization of sound were developed by the telephone companies in the 1920s, to improve the quality of the signal. The first system brought into operation in 1943 used the method known as pulse code modulation, devised in the late 1930s by a researcher at ITT called Alec Reeves. Pulse code modulation (other types were developed later) offers a way of transmitting signals, and amplifying them en route, with minimal noise or distortion. (It also vastly increases the capacity of the channel to carry many signals simultaneously, especially when combined with improvements in cables and the development of satellite communication links.) But for the purposes of recording, the technique remained impractical until the appearance of the microprocessor and associated systems of data storage, because of the enormous quantity of data involved. When viable methods were first introduced in the late 1970s, they reproduced the divorce between recording and replay which had been characteristic of the gramophone since the beginning of the century. At a cost of $150,000, the first digital tape recorders, produced by the tape manufacturer 3M and carrying thirty-two tracks, were used by the record companies for the remastering of the archives and for the mastering of new studio recordings. For the consumer, there was a new playback medium, the compact disc.

Digitization was to unify a whole range of evolving musical technologies, including electronic analogue instruments like the keyboard synthesizer. The prototype of the synthesizer is the electronic organ made by the American Lorens Hammond in 1929. Though not at all the first electrical instrument, it was the first one cheap and practical enough to be taken up in commercial popular music. Also, unlike the Theremin, which dates back to 1920, or the Ondes Martenot, which appeared in 1928, it was not a melodic instrument, producing a single continuous tone like a violin, say, but a harmonic one, on the model of the harmonium.[11] Hammond employed a synchronous motor to drive a series of tone-generators, using alternating current to produce the component tones which are synthesized to create the instrument's timbre. At the side of the keyboard a harmonic controller enables the player to vary the timbre, providing eight harmonics in nine gradations of intensity. The instrument was so simple to play that it was taken up after the Second World War by a new generation of untutored popular musicians, who thus acquired enough keyboard technique to speed the adoption of the electronic synthesizer which arrived in the late 1960s, when the Moog and other similar instruments appeared. By the early 1970s, the synthesizer was a fully fledged popular performing instrument, its sound familiar from the keyboard wizardry of performers like Rick Wakeman of Yes.

The late 1950s had seen devices like the Mellotron, a small keyboard in which the keys operated individual tape loops, designed to produce the sound of, say, a string orchestra, and intended not for the studio but to provide backing in performance. The synthesizer is as far from such devices as it is from, say, a mechanical fairground organ. More than just an electronic organ or piano, the synthesizer became a instrument in its own right, which employs electronic circuitry to generate both the imitation of the sounds of other instruments and newly synthesized tones of its own making. It then underwent a new transformation when Yamaha, which now dominates the market, incorporated digital means to replace the oscillators of the original design. The appearance of the Yamaha DX7 in 1983, says one writer, signalled the rise to dominance of Japanese computer-based technologies. The technique employed in this instrument came from an American academic and composer, John Chowning: Yamaha took it on when he found no American company prepared to put in the necessary investment to bring the idea to the point of mass production. The success of the new instrument was extraordinary. 'In 1989', says Andrew Blake in his book on *The Music Business*, 'a series of eight BBC television programmes, "Under African Skies", featured music from all over Africa. Among the many different percussion instruments, brass, and guitars, the DX7 appeared on all the programmes, as the only electronic performance keyboard in popular music groups from Ethiopia to South Africa.'[12]

Samplers and sequencers, on the other hand, are not performing instruments so much as gizmos which allow any digitally recorded sound to be fed into another device, including a synthesizer. Since 1982, this transfer of digital information is accomplished by means of MIDI (Musical Instrument Digital Interface). MIDI, which was promoted by Yamaha through the singular method of making the patent freely available, solved the problem of standardization in the handling of data which continues to plague the rest of the computer industry, and together with the progress and decreasing cost of microprocessors and miniaturization, radically altered the mode of production of music in the process. By 1984, groups like Frankie Goes to Hollywood, and producers like Stock, Aitken and Waterman, were issuing records that were fabricated according to a new formula. As Andrew Blake put it, 'Holly Johnson's voice was sampled a few times singing a few words, the rest of the band did little or nothing, and the magic fingers of producer Trevor Horn did the rest, producing seven remixed versions in all of "Relax", the biggest single of 1984, with all seven featuring the massive drum sound which others have copied – usually by sampling the sound itself off CD.'[13] These techniques became diffused very quickly. 'Once upon a time', says another recent writer, Jeremy Beadle, 'if you wanted a decent rhythm track, you had to play it, or hire session men to play it for you … Usually it would be necessary to try and get at least one full performance of every element of a song that you wanted to record down on tape. With a sampler and a sequencer, two bars of a basic beat is more than a luxury; it's a positive extravagance.'[14] As an article in *Keyboard* magazine in 1987 explained, this finally cuts the direct link between making music and muscular activity which began to break down in the late 1960s, 'when multi-track taping made it possible for musicians who had never even met to "play together" by laying down overdubs, punching in phrases and even single notes so as to perfect their product'.[15]

Sampling has raised an extensive series of questions about musical originality and inventiveness, as well as issues about authors and owner-ship which had been gestating for a long time, with the result, among other things, that long-standing scholars of commercial popular music have begun to turn their attention to the complex problems of copyright.

Sampling, says Simon Frith in a recent collection of essays on the subject, can be seen as a form of creative arrangement, or of creative exploitation, or indeed of creative criticism.[16] It is also a 'threat to orderly ways of making money out of music'. Samplers (the people), says Frith, adopted the long-established rule of thumb about 'folk music' – a song is in the public domain if its author is unlikely to sue you. To avoid the risks of sampling something too easily recognizable, they began to make extensive use of sounds lifted from obscure old tracks, or from the repertoire of 'world music', which it seemed could be lifted without needing clearance. But if the argument that a tune is in the public domain, and there is no one who can claim to be its author, is a familiar one in the copyright courts, then sampling, says Frith, suggests another reading: that certain sounds exist in the public soundscape, and records are as much 'found' sounds as recordings of a dog barking or a police siren. Moreover, 'Some samplers have argued that their music represents not only a "democratic" challenge to corporate control but also a new aesthetic.'[17]

The effects of sampling are thoroughly paradoxical. On the one hand, this is the ultimate negation of *musica practica*; on the other, it is like a new form of *musica practica* arising out of microchips and cables. Now it is possible for someone to create audible music without moving from their chair; not a score, like a composer at a desk, but a digitally constructed audile work; and not, like the composer in an electronic music studio, for a small discerning audience, but for a mass market. Bands like the Pet Shop Boys or Art of Noise appear, which start out as a solitary singer and a single computer programmer who, if they go on to perform live, are happy to appear, as Blake puts it, with not a guitar or drum kit in sight. 'Musical power is now in the hands of the technologically aware, of the producer, sound engineer, mixer and remixer.'[18]

At the same time, sampling produces the effect that existing pieces are no longer fixed nor clearly authored; nor is sample music notated. Added to the practice of multiple mixes for different formats and media, sampling thus brings the manipulated echo of previous records, as if the new is simply another possible version of the old. Exactly the condition described by Adorno, where everything is new and yet the same. It is a paradox that these symptoms also suggest a return to the conditions of *musica practica*, in which music circulates freely, and tunes are adopted and adapted without restraint by the issue of ownership.

It also seems like the domain of *musica practica* when Frith quotes approvingly a writer who says that the art of sampling is dependent on the sampler's musical knowledge: 'being good on the sampler is a matter of knowing what to sample, what pieces to lift off what records; you learn that by listening to music'.[19] He adds, however, that this makes it an extension more of fandom than musicianship, and the qualification is critical. For the evidence is that the technology of sampling has deepened the process of musical fragmentation induced, as we have already seen, by the machinery and procedures of the recording studio at least since the late 1950s.

Ironically, what samplers permit is for a sound of any type and from any source to be treated by the software to forms of manipulation which are logically indistinguishable from traditional musical principles like transposition, augmentation, diminution and the rest. But while real musical knowledge might be thought an advantage, it is far from necessary. This, in Jeremy Beadle's words, is 'music-making made supremely easy, if not supremely cheap'. (It is not that expensive: no more costly today, says Beadle, than 'the standard guitar, bass and drums necessary to start your own "beat" group in the 1960s or punk group in the 1970s'.)[20] These possibilities, then, come to be employed by young and musically inexperienced tyros, who are often motivated by the rebelliousness of contemporary youth but constrained by limited musical skills, with a limited vocabulary of musical gestures, and musical horizons confined by the accelerated cycles of popular musical fashion. It is the product of an irrepressible desire for music-making among a young populace with restricted access to the means of musical education but easy access to mass-produced musical reproduction.

Conflict with authority is almost inevitable. The corporations have placed on the market devices that invite people to transgress the laws on which the market operates. The issue is not whether the idea of using existing music in new pieces is in any way original to the technology of sampling. It is not whether popular artists have always drawn their material from an existing repertoire of songs, which they adapt and mix with their own original material. It is not that the musical idiom itself consists of rhythmic, melodic and harmonic motifs which are constantly recombined in new permutations, a form of artistry which is second nature. Nor is quotation, reference and sometimes downright plagiarism foreign to the classical tradition, which on the contrary made an art of it even before the twentieth century, when it became a major trait of composers from Stravinsky to Berio. However, if these practices were in some measure always in potential conflict with copyright, then now that the domain of copyright has been expanded by successive international conventions to cover the products of technology, the issue assumes a new prominence. Digital technology not only blurs the boundaries between production and consumption, but also between the different kinds of artistic rights through which music as a commodity is defined.

In 1992, a US federal judge declared sampling to be theft, in a decision against Warner's WEA for using a sample from a Gilbert O'Sullivan track on a Biz Markie album called 'I Need a Haircut'. In Britain, writes Beadle the following year, 'no case of breach of copyright involving sampling has reached trial. To date every such case has been settled out of court.'[21] These out-of-court settlements have established the parameters. Beadle cites the case that arose in 1989 when a release by The Beloved, 'The Sun Rising', took eight notes from a CD of compositions by the medieval religious composer Abbess Hildegard of Bingen issued by the specialist independent classical label Hyperion.

> Hyperion's case would have revolved around the contention that the contribution of their Hildegard of Bingen disc gave The Beloved's single its distinctive quality. The case to be put forward by East West, the WEA subsidiary, was that the sample was 'too brief to constitute a copyright issue'. The matter had got as far as a preliminary hearing [when] Hyperion backed down, aware that unsuccessful litigation – or even successful litigation which didn't come up with a large enough award and full payment of costs – might be cripplingly expensive.[22]

He adds wryly that Hyperion's releases will undoubtedly last longer than those of The Beloved, and 'indeed, the sample may even have won the Abbess Hildegard some new and unlikely admirers'. Perhaps. In any event, the record companies began in 1990 to impose the obligation on all recording artists to identify and clear all samples before release. 'Most record companies now stipulate in their artists' contracts that if a recording is issued without copyright clearance and, as a result, money has to be paid out in compensation, then that money will be deducted entirely from the artists' royalties.'[23]

Meanwhile, digitization and the home recording studio have converged. Once again these developments led in various, sometimes opposite directions. On the one hand, owing to the malleable nature of the digital signal, it became possible to alter radically the musical material even in late stages of production, where producers could re-impose their own values. On the other, they threatened the established roles and identity of the producer and the recording engineer, as musicians themselves took over the control of the apparatus either in self-interest or the interests of expanding the frontiers of musical creation. Peter Gabriel has said that 'the real pleasure in having a studio setup of my own is that I can experiment in a way that I could never afford to do in a commercial studio'.[24] In this case the experiments are not primarily technical but come from buying time, allowing Gabriel to collaborate with other musicians, including some from Third World countries, without needing the say-so of the record companies. Other musicians, like Frank Zappa, gave up recording on tape altogether, storing the composition in the sequencer, which serves as a tapeless tape recorder. The successful musician who sets up their own recording studio has parallels in the screen star who becomes the producer and/or director of their own film. It helps them to control their own creation. Zappa was totally his own man, composing, producing, engineering and mastering his own highly idiosyncratic music. But these are only the most visible examples. According to the *New York Times* journalist Jon Pareles, writing in 1987, 'affordable recording technology ... has made it possible to turn a bedroom or a kitchen into a studio for less than $1,000' and given rise to a large expansion in non-commercial recording which he calls a 'cassette underground'.[25] The gear is more basic and the musical results less sophisticated, but the results are readily diffused and just as influential.

This underground included hip-hop. Rappers and DJs, says Tricia Rose, a professor of Black Studies in New York, 'disseminated their work by copying it on tape-dubbing equipment and playing it on powerful, portable "ghetto-blasters"'.[26] She adds that this creative adoption of consumer electronics by disadvantaged inner-city youth occurred at a time when budget cuts in school music drastically reduced access to traditional instruments. But while hip-hop 'articulates a sense of entitlement, and takes pleasure in aggressive insubordination', this process takes place neither outside nor in opposition to the commodity system: 'the hip hop DJ frequently produces, amplifies and revises already recorded sounds, rappers prefer high-end microphones, and both invest serious dollars for the speakers that can produce the phattest beats'.[27]

This music is also about the location of the individual in urban space. As Public Enemy's Chuck D explained in an interview in 1990, 'rap has different feels and different vibes in different parts of the country'. For example, since people in New York City do not drive very often, rap music in New York is 'a headphone type of thing' with not too much heavy bass, while in Long Island or Philadelphia 'where in order to get anywhere you gotta drive so people have cars by the time they're sixteen or seventeen years old', it is not only much more bassy, but also much more of a 'wraparound' sound. As George Lipsitz explains in *Microphone Fiends* where he quotes these remarks:

> Large car speakers adjusted to pump-up-the-bass 'jeep beats' of rap music travel freeways and city streets, claiming space by projecting out sound, while boom boxes similarly reconfigure street corners and subway cars through the invasive properties of amplified sound. It is no accident that while heavy metal videos tend to privelege stadium and arena concerts as ideal spaces of representation, hip hop videos more often take place on the streets of ... urban inner-city neighborhoods, reclaiming them as sites of self-affirmation.[28]

Nor is it an accident that, in the same spirit, DJs in the South Bronx in the 1970s wired their turntables and speakers to street lamps to provide themselves with power, as if they were living in a Third World shanty town.

According to a report in *The Economist* in 1990, Wall Street entertainment analysts devote rather more space to the film business than the record labels, yet the record business is more profitable. In 1989 Warner's film division made profits of $312m on revenues of $2.7 billion, while profits from its recording activities were £500m, on revenues of $2.5 billion.[29] Moreover, the trend has been constantly upwards. Between 1980 and 1992, says the same magazine four years later, 'sales of recorded music in the five biggest markets (America, Britain, Japan, France and Germany) increased from $9 billion to $20 billion, a rise of more than 40% in volume terms'.[30] And in 1993, worldwide sales, according to another source, reached $30.5 billion, with the United States accounting for nearly a third. The United Kingdom saw nearly $2 billion worth, or 6.5 per cent of the total. The UK artists' share of the international market was much larger, at about 18 per cent.[31]

The recovery of the record industry in the 1980s came about partly through technological renovation in the shape of digital recording and the compact disc; the results, in other words, of computerization. With the classical market as the chosen proving ground for the launch, the new format was touted as a superior technology employing miniature lasers. The difference in the quality of reproduction, if compared with the difference between acoustic and electrical recording, is minimal. The CD, like computers, is not trouble-free, and discerning musicians tend to complain that the sound is too analytic and clinical. (Film-makers often feel the same about the video image as compared to that of film.) But it enjoys the chic of high-tech and the result was to reconstruct the market – more radically than at any time since the introduction of electrical recording in the 1920s – and once again to enable the record industry to buck the trend of worldwide recession. In 1990, while many consumer sectors had contracted, *The Economist* estimated that CDs accounted for roughly half of the market.[32] At the same time, the financial pages reported that a 'Resurgent EMI calls the tune despite the Thorn in its side'[33], and in March 1992, EMI bought Virgin Records from the entrepreneur Richard Branson, which put it back in third position globally.

The current rate of profit in the record industry comes very largely from the better margins on CDs than vinyl; sufficiently so that in Britain in 1994 it became the subject of a parliamentary inquiry, chaired by one of several record-collecting MPs (the newspapers never explained how they had time to listen). Also, said *The Economist* in 1990, because 'like previous hardware revolutions, it allows the record companies to reissue old hits … One record company says that its back-catalogue of old songs accounts for around a third of its turnover.'[34] This is not only true of the pop charts; it has become a major trend in the classical field as well. According to a television report in 1992, classical sales in the United Kingdom doubled in the 1980s, and re-issues formed a large proportion.[35] But the market has expanded in several directions, including some rare spectacular successes. Nigel Kennedy made a mint as the lovable punk violinist, and the 1990 World Cup Three Tenors Concert has sold more than eleven million copies (CDs, LPs and cassettes). Remembering, says *The Economist*, 'that the average annual sale of a classical recording from the big companies is rather less than 10,000 units, the effect of this success on record company bosses is easy to imagine.'[36]

The arithmetic, says the report, goes like this:

In Britain, at British Musicians' Union rates, a full orchestra plus expenses and a 12% management fee works out at £8,500 ($12,750) a session. When recordings were made for LPs, three or four sessions were usually required to record music lasting 35–40 minutes. Because CDs can play for longer, they have to – buyers expect it. So four or five sessions are now usual.

Hire of an acoustically suitable venue, such as a concert hall, can cost up to £1,300 a day. Five sessions last three days because of union regulations on working times. With the cost of a recording team (say £300 a day), tapes (£500) and editing the recorded music (on digital equipment), the bill reaches £50,000 for the recording alone. Add in £10,000 for design, artwork and the printing of covers, plus the writing and printing of a booklet of notes in three languages ... The record company earns around £4 (before paying royalties) from each recording sold. Even if no royalties were payable, a symphony would have to sell 15,000 units to break even. Few titles do that in less than three years. Many never do.

Why they bother, the magazine explains, is because a company lives off its backlist, which in the case of EMI's international classical division represents about 70 per cent of its business. The American black independent producer Carmen Ashhurst-Watson, of Def Jam, says the same: 'a record company can't survive without groups that have *catalogue* and *future*'.[37]

An expanding market, however, encourages risk-takers – which is what capitalists used to be in the nineteenth century – on the sole condition that they can find effective ways of cutting costs. The result (says *The Economist*) is that 'in America, France, Germany and perhaps most of all in Britain, enthusiasts-turned-businessmen have established their own record companies', with more than three hundred such independents worldwide.[38] Like their cousins, the 'independent' television programme makers, whose numbers have also mushroomed since the early 1980s with the deregulation of television, these new entrepreneurs depend on the hire of the latest professional facilities at economic prices, including the use of the majors' own pressing plants. But the key to their success, we are told, is knowing how to make money while selling a small volume of each release. Five hundred units a year 'is about average for many of them', but the number of their releases equals those of the market leaders. 'They know they cannot pay the fees demanded by the most successful musicians. They also know that buyers exist for music which the majors, with their higher costs, cannot risk recording.'[39] They therefore concentrate on a certain repertoire, effectively ignoring the rule that says the artist is more important than the music. These new classical independents have now themselves been hit by a new generation of price-cutters; the founder of one, Chandos, which started in 1979 and is now the largest independent classical label in the world, with 1,200 titles, admits to a journalist in 1994 that he has been hit hard by budget recordings from companies like Naxos. Naxos was set up in 1987 by a distributor of electronic hardware based in Hong Kong, as a series of standard repertoire recordings on CD but at LP prices. The idea, says *The Economist*, was to use 'unknown musicians' and therefore avoid paying union rates. Whatever this means, it is also a market strategy based on repertoire rather than artists. The result is that 'at Tower Records in Manhattan the shopper can choose from more than 22,000 classical musical titles',[40] but only about fifty in every duty-free shop in the world.

For the rank-and-file musician in a country like Britain the effect of such developments is not at all positive. The CD provided an opportunity for enterprise by a variety of dedicated bands and ensembles, like those of the early-music movement, who learnt to launch themselves on the market, seek the grants and sponsorship needed to enable them to stay together, and build up a following; and one result is a very considerable growth in the range of musics now available. But another paradox is at work, for this was not to translate into the improvement of conditions for the working musician. One recent report says that freelance musicians in London whose mainstay is session work have suffered a serious contraction of employment, although recording sessions by the main full-time orchestras rose over the course of the 1980s by 87 per cent.

Many of the same conditions operate in the popular market (for which many of these session musicians also used to record), which has been severely shaken up by the terminal decline of the seven-inch vinyl single in the face of the multiplicity of other formats (and rivals for teenager money like video games). In 1989 the British Phonographic Industry changed the rules for the award of silver, gold and platinum discs: now, instead of one million, you only need 600,000 to score platinum, and there are precious few of them (one hit of 1992 arrived at number one in the top ten on weekly sales of less than 30,000). The fate of the industry now lies almost entirely in the hands of the album, and there the majors are in equal trouble, leaving large holes in the market. As one independent producer puts it, 'Some major labels won't consider re-issuing an album if it will sell less than 2,000 copies, but our overheads are lower, so it's more feasible for us.' Another says the business is a creative one because 'financial entry is not so daunting ... There are still studios where you can make a record for £10,000. There are dance records being made in people's living rooms for nothing.'[41] Here too, according to Ashhurst-Watson, small companies do distribution deals with big ones, and some have production deals on top; the best (from some points of view) is the joint venture deal, when the major and the independent split the costs fifty-fifty.[42]

But there is also a much more artisanal level of independent operators, who release their own mixes which cater to very specific markets, such as the labels that started up in Detroit and elsewhere in the late 1980s to bring out a sub-genre of disco music called techno. This completely synthetic dance music is largely directed at club DJs (who in turn, in order to get gigs, make demo tapes of their scratching technique). It has achieved worldwide diffusion in small editions by mail order through specialist magazines, or even by printing the information on the records. There is lively debate among aficionados of the clubs around this music, not about its musical qualities (or lack of them) but about the future of vinyl. One of the more successful of these labels, +8, has now bought its own vinyl pressing plant to guarantee production.[43]

In the midst of this extremely fragmented market, the major players are now engaged in launching new digital recording formats, such as DAT recorders, DCCs (digital compact cassettes) and the MD, or minidisc, as well as CD-ROMs for computers. One of them, Sony, has meanwhile run into another kind of trouble, in the form of a high-profile court case brought against them by one of the artists they acquired when they bought CBS. In 1993, George Michael sued for release from his contract on the grounds that it unreasonably restrained him. Judgement was made against the singer in 1994, but as I write, the case has gone to appeal.

It was not entirely Sony's fault: they had not just acquired artists when they bought CBS but inherited the problems of a contractual system evolved in the 1950s, when the explosive rise of rock 'n' roll had first changed the ground rules. Where previously artists were paid session fees, they began to claim royalties. The level of the royalty and the size of the advance was related to market potential, and when an artist scored a hit a renegotiation followed, in which both might be raised. In the process the record companies, perfectly aware of the risks involved, extended the obligations of the artist by extending the duration of the contract: more money up front in return for more albums. The result? As George Michael himself summed up the situation, 'Even though I both created and paid for my work, I will never own it or have any rights over it. There is no such thing as resignation for an artist in the music industry. Effectively, you sign a piece of paper at the beginning of your career and you are expected to live with that decision, good or bad, for the rest of your professional life.'[44] According to the newspapers, Michael became convinced that he was being treated as software rather than creative talent.

The newspaper reports were accompanied by a breakdown of the sums of money involved. The figures confirm the enormous stakes at issue. The case cost Michael £3m. His gross worldwide royalties between 1987 and 1992 amounted to £16.89m. Sony's earnings from his records over the same period were £95.5m, thus confirming the rule that, however much the artist earns, the company always earns more.[45] In a television interview a few days later, he said that he intended to take the case to appeal, not for his own sake but for that of artists who had been caught up in the same difficulties but lacked the funds to fight the companies. That the problems are indeed widespread is confirmed by Carmen Ashhurst-Watson.[46] 'Artists on all labels get exploited,' she says, 'some get exploited less than others. Really big-name stars get exploited less but what they get paid is not commensurate with the profits that they generate, and their creative control expands only as much as the company feel they can sell this new product.'

'Most acts', says Ashhurst-Watson, 'do not make it through the first contract. So the record company locks you up for a significant portion of your career, because the average pop group rarely makes it through half of an average contract. If a pop group makes three records, that's a successful act!' The new group arrives with little negotiating power, and promotion and distribution costs a lot of money:

> To get the record distributed nationally – to get twenty copies of every record into every record store in the country – is a big financial undertaking. To get radio stations to play this record – every radio station has a forty-song cap on its three-week play list – to get your record to be one of those forty costs money...

Moreover, she continues, there are different formats, and new trends, like rap, require special treatment.

> For rap, you have to put a lot of energy into underground stuff – making sure that DJs get it and play it in clubs so that people will start demanding it. You might have to put a lot of money into getting the video done so that it will be on TV and people will start demanding it.

The artist is sucked into a system with its own synergies much too fast to understand how it operates, and ends up signing away the income they will generate if they succeed in making a hit. The stories are legion and were widely quoted in the press coverage following the ruling in the George Michael case: Richard Berry, author of 'Louie Louie', is said to have given his rights away for the price of a wedding suit, while Little Richard, possibly apocryphally, handed over 'Good Golly Miss Molly' for the keys of a Cadillac. Peter Jenner, manager of the English singer Billy Bragg, sums up: 'I went to Cambridge, I got a first in economics, I've been looking at rock contracts for 25 years, and every day I'm still learning about the slippery stuff they put in them.'[47]

It becomes very difficult for an artist to break out of these lengthy contracts. Small companies do deals with larger companies for distribution and even production, the larger companies they deal with are affiliates or subsidiaries of the majors, and the industry, says Carmen Ashhurst-Watson, becomes 'very plantation-like. Every rung down gets less and less of the pie, and the artists are at the bottom.'[48] And small artist-controlled labels, she concludes, are not going to change the balance of power in the industry,

> especially now that the industry is owned by these multinational conglomerates who are utilising the entertainment industry to fuel much bigger enterprises. Sony bought Columbia records to help them sell hardware. It's not as if they had this burning desire to sell Public Enemy records. [Mutual laughter] They're trying to sell electronic equipment. Artists' work sells interactive television, it sells video games – each artist is a pindrop, a pinhead on this much bigger mosaic. The record industry is worried about its strategic positioning in relationship to the film industry or records versus television versus telecommunications versus phone companies; that's the kind of jockeying they're doing. They're not talking about Public Enemy versus Bruce Springsteen.[49]

★

The chronic crisis of the record industry is compounded by a constant paradox, apparently inherent in the technology of reproduction, by which music is turned into a commodity only to see it escape. Every technique of reproduction is also a technique of recording, therefore of copying, of re-recording, yet the law of maximization of profits always drives the manufacturer to market the technology in both forms, adapting the latter to the mass market just as the technology becomes more capable and simple to operate at the same time. What happens to music in these conditions can be seen with particular clarity in the effects of the introduction in the 1960s of the audio cassette, which hugely increased the circulation of recorded music – and thus the products of the record industry – beyond the confines and control of the market, through both private re-recording and commercial piracy, and not only in the highly developed countries of the West but also in the Third World. The scale of both is enormous; the pattern varies in markets of different kinds.

In the developed countries of the West, when the record industry was hit by recession at the end of the 1970s, and the value of gramophone record sales fell by hundreds of millions of dollars while those of blank tape cassettes remained pretty constant, it became obvious what was happening: people were not only buying cassettes and recording off air, but also borrowing records and cassettes from friends and copying them. There can hardly be a reader of this book who has not done it – and the hardware industry colluded by making portable machines incorporating two cassette decks.[50] The record companies claimed that it costs them serious revenue, and brazenly demanded of governments that a special levy be placed on the sale of blank tape in order to compensate them for loss of sales (they generally remain silent about those entitled to royalties for the music itself). But legal or illegal, licensed or unlicensed, the real effect every time a piece of music is copied privately is to promote the circulation of the music. The significance of the individual act of copying seems to be dwarfed by the size of market, yet it affirms the music's autonomy. And it quickly mounts up.

In underdeveloped countries, meanwhile, organized piracy has had dramatic effects. According to a study by the ethnomusicologist Peter Manuel, citing reports published in the late 1980s, African countries have been hit particularly hard, 'especially since their governments have been largely unable, and in some cases unwilling, to enforce copyright laws'.

Cassette piracy has effectively destroyed the formerly lively Ghanaian record industry, inducing multinationals like HMV and Decca to abandon the country. Pirate cassettes made in Hong Kong, Singapore, Taiwan and South Korea are said to constitute 70–80 per cent of the market in Nigeria, Morocco, Algeria, Zambia and Guinea. In Kenya, the former centre of the East African music industry, the proportion is the same or even more. The phenomenon 'has contributed to the wholesale migration of much of the legitimate African music industry to Europe, where recordings are made and marketed for emigrant Africans and European enthusiasts.[51]

The diffusion of the audio cassette followed that of the transistor radio: it quickly penetrated to the most isolated village in the Sahara or the Andes – not to mention the shanty towns of Lima or Johannesburg – before such places might come to enjoy running water or mains electricity. Local centres of production and distribution have grown up in every capital city of the world. The authors of a study of the music industry in small countries, Roger Wallis and Krister Malm, cite the example of 'the managing director of Polygram Kenya in his office in Nairobi [who] bemoans the fact that home-taping is undermining his attempts to sell records and pre-recorded cassettes. But in another wing of the same building a conveyor belt is churning out Philips radio cassette recorders, i.e. the very hardware that makes home-taping possible.'[52] They also report a sophisticated version of the practice, a variant of piracy, found in the 'record bars' of Sri Lanka: 'A customer gives the shop a list of favourite songs in the morning and collects a cassette with his or her personal compilation in the afternoon'.[53] Other writers report similar practices in places as far apart as Guadaloupe and Ghana; the latter, formerly a centre of commercial highlife recording, instead by 1989 hosted over 2,700 such dubbing shops.

On the other hand, in several countries the same technology has produced the growth of small, grassroots cassette producers, recording and disseminating genres whose commercial markets were in many cases too localized and specialized for multinationals and even regional record companies to survive. In the Andes, for example, where piracy has bankrupted many record companies and cassettes are in the process of altogether replacing vinyl, the rise of the cassette has been associated with a new genre of dance music, stylistically derivative of the traditional *huayno* and *cumbia,* and known by the Aymara word for maize beer as *chicha* music. In the Middle East, the cassette has enabled local musics to develop independently of radio. In Israel, Manuel reports, *rock misrahi* or 'Eastern rock', associated with Oriental Jews, enjoyed ample dissemination on cassettes at a time when it was scorned by radio stations run by Ashkenazim (Jews of European origin). On the other side of the globe in Indonesia, an extant record industry has been entirely replaced by a vibrant and flourishing cassette scene. 'As inexpensive cassettes and players spread throughout Indonesian villages and cities,' writes Manuel,

> they precipitated, as elsewhere, an exponential expansion of the recording industry as a whole ... the output of the state record industry, Lokananta, grew from 41,508 vinyl discs in 1970, to 898,459 cassettes (and 290 records) in 1975. Many of the several dozen private cassette companies that emerged in the seventies and eighties specialised in regional musics [but they] were instrumental in the emergence of at least one indigenous pop genre, the Sundanese *jaipongan*.[54]

The effects of cassettes in Indonesia, he continues, are representative of many other countries as well. Regional musics began to acquire a new legitimacy, especially when they had never been marketed before. Local stars arose, and new standards of professionalism developed. At the same time, the proliferation of regional musics beyond their original domain has promoted stylistic borrowing and cross-fertilization between different traditions, which both enriches the music and leads to a certain homogenization.

Inevitably these new musical forms feed into the same global network as music like reggae and rap. According to Wallis and Malm, 'Small countries fulfil a dual role for the music industry. They provide marginal markets for international products. They also, by virtue of their unique cultures, can provide the sort of talent that comprises invaluable raw material for international exploitation.'[55] In many of these countries, the threat of being flooded by a characterless transnational music culture led to cultural resistance, allied with the political denunciation of cultural imperialism. Yet this could turn into very good news for the record companies. The only problem for EMI under the Popular Unity government in Chile at the beginning of the 1970s was being unable to get the millions of pesos they were making from popular protest music out of the country.[56] No matter. They made plenty more abroad after the *coup* by General Pinochet, when worldwide solidarity created a global market for Chilean music. And while Pinochet tried to ban traditional ethnic instruments as subversive, exiled or emigré groups of Andean musicians busking on the streets of London, Paris or San Francisco started selling their own cassettes on the sidewalk.[57]

Whatever the political sympathies of the executives who run the corporations, the potential for political mobilization through music is ever present. It can be measured not only in the size of the worldwide audience claimed by the satellite transmission of events like the Free Mandela concert, but also in the concentration of energy in the live audience present at the event, whose excitement inevitably infuses the music. There is no question but that this event helped to hasten the end of Apartheid in South Africa, by bringing about an unparalleled demonstration of popular feeling throughout large parts of the world. Music here returns to one of its primary functions, the affirmation of society, but on a scale previously unimaginable. No longer at the local or even regional level but vastly enlarged by the global reach of the media which at the same time threaten its freedom.

This is the most visible part of what is happening. What goes on every day without drawing political attention to itself is the progressive transformation of the musics of different cultures which the market blindly throws into contact with each other. Musicians have always travelled but now recorded music does so too. Wallis and Malm offer an example going back to the 1940s and 1950s, when records of Caribbean music began to find their way to Africa through black intellectuals from either side of the Atlantic who met at universities in England and France and exchanged musical experience. Back in the capital cities of Africa, Afro-Caribbean music caught on, especially in Zaïre (then called Congo), to produce the new musical forms that provide the basis for East African popular music today. At the same time,

> Musicians from Zaïre migrated to East Africa where a new cultural exchange process took place when the Tanzanians infused elements of local music into the Zaïrean sounds, producing Swahili jazz. This in its turn has been adopted by many Zaïrean musicians ... In the late 60s records [of this music] started appearing mainly in Zaïre and Kenya ... Some of these records found their way to the Caribbean [and] were eagerly devoured by young musicians who, in the wake of the black power movement, were seeking their African roots...[58]

This is the same kind of musical round-trip that reinfuses jazz with Afro-Latin rhythms and melody, mixes in a dose of *zouk* from Martinique, conquers New York and other growing Hispanic population centres in the United States, and then appears on the 'world music' menu as salsa. The term 'world music' is a marketing concept, which originated among a group of record producers and other interested parties meeting in London in 1987, a catch-all devised to try to exploit the proliferation of local cultural traditions in the interstices of the market. Borrowed from the ethnomusicologist Japp Kunst, and intended as a marketing term to be used on shelf dividers in the record stores, the producers were themselves surprised by the speed and breadth with which the term caught on.[59] But the notion corresponds to the globalization of mass culture at a particular stage of development: the moment when the same corporations that tout the 'information revolution' become integrated with the established entertainments industry on the transnational level. A charity rock concert in a London sports stadium becomes a major international event, beamed live to television sets in Moscow, Los Angeles, Rio de Janeiro, Hong Kong and Sydney. An English protest singer joins a young radio DJ to hit the trail with television cameras in the Andes; a Hollywood studio is bought by a Japanese electronics giant. The process produces a profound transformation, for when musical traditions come full circle and return to their sources in the ways I have described, they are no longer the same. Under the impact of electro-acoustic reproduction, musical cultures of every type develop new dynamics. Techniques are extended, new instrumental combinations are tried, fusions and hybrids appear and proceed to reproduce independently, in musical revenge against technological alienation.

A crucial set of questions arise. If our encounter in the North with the musics of Asia, Africa and Latin America is a product of the times, what are the forces that have created this trend? Is 'world music' only a commercial phenomenon, or does it represent an authentic cultural undercurrent? Is the idea just another form of cultural expropriation and exploitation or could it possibly represent a true growth of awareness of other musics? Is there any real cultural exchange involved? Is it changing our musical consciousness?

What could the answers to these questions tell us about the place of music in our lives? And about which forms of music are signs of social health, and which are symptomatic of alienation, frustration and resentment? And whether music is becoming denuded or truly being democratized?

These are the questions that arise from a position within the heart of the developed world. What they point to is an absence in the way that the history of the media in the twentieth century is usually told: another history which has had a merely shadowy presence in the present volume, in passing mentions to obscure figures like the Venezuelan Anzola, or musical styles like the Arabic *dwar*. A history written from any of these other perspectives would amount to a very different account of contemporary music but would reach the same conclusion. In the words of the American composer Elie Siegmeister at the end of the 1930s, in a pamphlet for the Worker's Music Association, capitalism has created the most magnificent apparatus for the production, distribution and consumption of music that the world has ever seen. Yet this apparatus is so riddled with contradictions, which are basically economic in origin, that it continually negates its own potentialities.[60] Nevertheless, music somehow continually manages to negate this negation, to shake off the bonds of commercialization and escape to freedom: because it has its own inner resources for overcoming the contradictions of this, our disturbed and disturbing reality.

Notes

1 Record Culture

1. As the captain explained when Pantagruel, on the high seas, hears voices and other sounds in the air:

> My lord, don't be afraid. This is the edge of the frozen sea, and at the beginning of last winter there was a great and bloody battle here between the Arimaspians and the Cloud-riders. The shouts of the men, the cries of the women, the slashing of the battle-axes, the clashing of the armour and the harnesses, the neighing of the horses and all the other frightful noises of battle became frozen on the air. But just now, the rigours of winter being over and the good season coming on with its calm and mild weather, these noises are melting, and so you can hear them.'
>
> Then he drew on the deck before us whole handfuls of frozen words, which looked like crystallized sweets of different colours…. When we warmed them a little between our hands, they melted like snow, and we actually heard them, though we did not understand them, for they were in a barbarous language.

François Rabelais, *The Histories of Gargantua and Pantagruel*, Fourth Book, Chapters 55 and 56, trans. J.M.Cohen, Penguin Books, Harmondsworth 1985, pp. 566–9.

2. See Charles Grivel, 'The Phonograph's Horned Mouth', in Douglas Kahn, ed., *Wireless Imagination: Sound, Radio and the Avant-Garde*, MIT Press, Massachusetts and London 1992, p. 43.

3. Oliver Read and Walter T. Welch, *From Tin Foil to Stereo: Evolution of the Phonograph*, Howard W. Sams, New York 1976, p. 4.

4. Quoted in Roland Gelatt, *The Fabulous Phonograph 1877–1977*, Cassell, London 1977, p. 29.

5. Quoted in Brian Winston, *Misunderstanding Media*, Routledge & Kegan Paul, London 1986, p. 331.

6. Derek Jewell, 'Popular Marriage Begets Golden Children', *The Times*, 18 April 1977.

7. Roland Gelatt, p. 118.

8. Walter Benjamin, 'The Work of Art in the Age of Mechanical Reproduction', in Hannah Arendt, ed., *Illuminations*, Schocken, New York 1969.

9. Ibid., p. 235.

10. Federico García Lorca, *Obras Completas*, Aguilar, Madrid 1986, vol. III, p. 579.

11. Ibid., p. 296.

12. Quoted in Gelatt, p. 301.

13. Luciano Berio, *Two Interviews*, Marion Boyars, London 1985, pp. 38–9.

14. Joseph Kerman, *Musicology*, Fontana/Collins, London 1985, p. 337.

15. See Michael Chanan, *Musica Practica: The Social Practice of Western Music from Gregorian Chant to Postmodernism*, Verso, London 1994.

16. Theodor W. Adorno, 'Perennial Fashion – Jazz', *Prisms*, Neville Spearman, London 1967, pp. 121–32.

17. F.W. Gaisberg, *Music on Record*, Robert Hale, London 1946, p. 58.

18. Jane Jarvis, 'Notes on Muzak', in H. Wiley Hitchcock, ed., *The Phonograph and Our Musical Life; Proceedings of a Centennial Conference*, ISAM Monograph No. 14, City University, New York 1977, pp. 13–15.

19. Ibid.

20. Jacques Attali, *Noise*, Manchester University Press, 1989, pp. 111–12.

21. Geoffrey Oord, 'Signals Beyond the Dreams of Edison', *The Times*, 18 April 1977.

22. Attali, p. 106.

23. Simon Frith, 'Music and Morality', in Simon Frith, ed., *Music and Copyright*, Edinburgh University Press, 1993, p. 6.

24. Simon Frith, 'The Industrialisation of Popular Music', in J. Lull, ed., *Popular Music and Communication*, Sage, London 1987, p. 72.

25. T.W. Adorno, *Philosophy of Modern Music*, Seabury Press/Sheed & Ward, London 1973, pp. 5–6.

26. Benjamin, p. 227.

27. David Harvey, *The Condition of Postmodernity*, Blackwell, Oxford 1990, p. 240.

28. Quoted in Stephen Kern, *The Culture of Time and Space 1880–1918*, Weidenfeld & Nicolson, London 1983, p. 118.

29. Sigmund Freud, *Civilisation and its Discontents*, Hogarth Press, London 1969, pp. 25, 27–8.

30. See *Quiet*, Journal of the British Tinnitus Association, vol. 4, no. 1, 1994.

2 From Cylinder to Disc

1. Oliver Read and Walter T. Welch., *From Tin Foil to Stereo: Evolution of the Phonograph*, Howard W. Sams, New York 1976, p. 10.

2. Quoted in Jacques Attali, *Noise*, Manchester University Press, 1989, p. 91.

3. Quoted in Douglas Kahn, 'Death in Light of the Phonograph', in Douglas Kahn, ed., *Wireless Imagination: Sound, Radio and the Avant-Garde*, MIT Press, Massachusetts and London 1992, pp. 86-7.

4. See Stephen Kern, *The Culture of Time and Space, 1880–1918*, Weidenfeld & Nicolson, London 1983, p. 69; and Brian Winston, *Misunderstanding Media*, Routledge & Kegan Paul, London 1986, p. 353.

5. Quoted in Matthew Josephson, *Edison*, Eyre & Spottiswoode, London 1961, p. 326.

6. Quoted in Roland Gelatt, *The Fabulous Phonograph, 1877–1977*, Cassell, London 1977, p. 38.

7. Quoted in ibid., p. 63.

8. Ibid., p. 115.

9. Quoted in ibid., p. 142.

10. For details of this process, see Michael Chanan, *The Dream That Kicks: The Prehistory and Early Years of Cinema in Britain*, Routledge & Kegan Paul, London 1980; second edition forthcoming.

11. See Read and Welch, p. 392.

12. Linda Martin and Kerry Segrave, *Anti-Rock: The Opposition to Rock'n'Roll*, Da Capo, New York 1993, p. 10.

13. Personal communication from Alfredo Anzola, director of *El misterio de los ojos escarlata*, Venezuela 1993.

3 'Polyhymnia Patent'

1. Erik Barnouw, *Tube of Plenty*, Oxford University Press, 1975, p. 13.

2. Ibid., p. 17.

3. See Peter Ford, 'Audio in Retrospect', *Hi-Fi News*, London, January 1960–July 1963.

4. In Carolyn Marvin, *When Old Technologies Were New: Thinking About Electric Communication in the Late Nineteenth Century*, Oxford University Press, 1988, p. 75.

5. Ibid., p. 203.

6. Robert Hopper, *Telephone Conversation*, Indiana University Press, 1992.

7. Ibid., pp. 79–80.

8. Thomas Mann, *The Magic Mountain*, trans. H.T. Lowe-Porter, Penguin, Harmondsworth 1960, p. 637.

9. Ibid., pp. 640–3.

10. Jean-Paul Sartre, *Nausea*, trans. Robert Baldick, Penguin, Harmondsworth 1965, pp. 37–8.

11. Nelson George, *The Death of Rhythm and Blues*, Omnibus, London 1989, p. 8.

12. Christopher Small, *Music of the Common Tongue*, Calder, London 1987, p. 241.

13. Walter Benjamin, 'Moscow', in *One Way Street*, NLB, London 1979, p. 195.

14. Russell Sanjek and David Sanjek, *American Popular Music Business in the 20th Century*, Oxford University Press, 1991, p. 20.

15. Luc Sante, 'The Genius of the Blues', *New York Review of Books*, 11 August 1994, p. 50.

16. Evan Eisenberg, *The Recording Angel*, Picador, London 1988, p. 116.

17. Mike Hobart, 'The Political Economy of Bop', *Media, Culture & Society*, vol. 3, no. 3, 1981, p. 267.

18. Eisenberg, pp. 118–19.

19. Francis Newton, *The Jazz Scene*, Penguin, London 1959, p. 185.

20. David Baker, 'The Phonograph in Jazz History and its Influence on the Emergent Jazz Performer', in H. Wiley Hitchcock, ed., *The Phonograph and Our Musical Life*, ISAM Monograph No. 14, City University, New York 1977, p. 46.

21. Newton, p. 186.

22. Ibid., p. 47.

23. On the introduction of the electric guitar see Michael Chanan, *Musica Practica: The Social Practice of Western Music from Gregorian Chant to Postmodernism*, Verso, London 1994.

24. Baker, p. 46.

25. Paul Oliver, 'Blues', in P. Oliver, M. Harrison and W. Bolcom, *The New Grove Gospel, Blues and Jazz*, Macmillan, London 1986, p. 116.

26. See Small, p. 401.

27. Paul Oliver, pp. 116–17.

28. Quoted in Small, p. 243.

29. Quoted in Joseph Horowitz, *Understanding Toscanini*, Alfred A. Knopf, New York 1987, pp. 415–16.

30. Small, pp. 45–6.

31. Small, p. 244.

4 Recording Electrified

1. S.T. Williams quoted in Roland Gelatt, *The Fabulous Phonograph 1877–1977*, Cassell, London 1977, p. 220.

2. Oliver Read and Walter T. Welch, *From Tin Foil to Stereo: Evolution of the Phonograph*, Howard W. Sams, New York 1976, pp. 237–8.

3. F.W. Gaisberg, *Music on Record*, Robert Hale, London 1946, p. 81.

4. Akio Morita with Edward Reingold and Mitsiko Shimomura, *Made in Japan*, Collins, London 1987, pp. 15–16.

5. Read and Welch, p. 238.

6. Kurt Weill, *Ausgewählte Schriften*, Suhrkamp, Frankfurt am Main 1975, pp. 110–14.

7. See Paddy Scannell, 'Music for the Multitude? The Dilemmas of the BBC's Music Policy, 1923–1946', *Media, Culture & Society*, vol.3, no.3, July 1981, pp. 243–60.

8. Quoted in Erik Barnouw, *Tube of Plenty*, Oxford University Press, 1975, p. 65.

9. Figures according to Mike Hobart, 'The Political Economy of Bop', *Media, Culture & Society*, vol.3, no.3, 1981.

10. Personal communication from Alfredo Anzola.

11. 'Long Playing', *El Nacional*, Caracas, 22 August 1951, in Alejo Carpentier, *Ese musico que llevo dentro*, vol. II, Editorial Letras Cubanas, Havana 1980, p. 249.

12. Read and Welch, p. 238.

13. Quoted in Read and Welch, p. 247.

14. Transmitted on Channel Four, 9 July 1994.

15. Read and Welch, p. 239.

16. William McClellan, in H. Wiley Hitchcock, ed., *The Phonograph and Our Musical Life*, ISAM Monograph No. 14, City University, New York 1977, p. 5.

17. Arthur Loesser, *Men, Women and Pianos*, Simon & Schuster, New York 1954.

5 Enter the Talkies

1. The details in this section are drawn from Patrick Ogle, 'The Development of Sound Systems: The Commercial Era', *Film Reader* No. 2, Northwestern University, Evanston 1977, and Steve Neale, *Cinema and Technology: Image, Sound, Colour*, BFI, London 1985.

2. On the strange relationship between De Forest and Case, see Douglas Gomery, 'The Coming of Sound: Technological Change in the American Film Industry', in Elisabeth Weis and John Belton, eds, *Film Sound: Theory and Practice*, Columbia University Press, 1985.

3. See Rick Altman, 'Sound History', in Altman, ed., *Sound Theory, Sound Practice*, Routledge, London 1992, p. 121.

4. Cited in Mary Ann Doane, 'Ideology and the Practice of Sound Editing and Mixing', in Weis and Belton, p. 59.

5. Quoted in Rick Altman, 'Sound Space', in Altman, ed., pp. 49–50.

6. Cited in Mary Ann Doane, p. 233.

7. Altman, 'Sound Space', p. 53.

8. Walter Benjamin, 'The Work of Art in the Age of Mechanical Reproduction', in Hannah Arendt, ed., *Illuminations*, Schocken, New York 1969, p. 233.

9. Walter Legge, 'An Autobiography', in Elizabeth Schwarzkopf, *On and Off the Record: A Memoir of Walter Legge*, Faber, London 1982, p. 57.

10. Interview with Frank Lee held in the British Library National Sound Archive. See *Developments in Recorded Sound: A Catalogue of Oral History Interviews*, The British Library, London 1989, pp. 26-7.

11. James Rorty, quoted in Erik Barnouw, *Tube of Plenty*, Oxford University Press, 1975, p. 74.

12. Quoted in Joseph Horowitz, *Understanding Toscanini*, Alfred A. Knopf, New York 1987, pp. 154–5.

13. Russell Sanjek and David Sanjek, *American Popular Music Business in the 20th Century*, Oxford University Press, 1991, p. 52.

14. Francis Newton, *The Jazz Scene*, Penguin, London 1959, p. 172.

15. Quoted in Christopher Small, *Music of the Common Tongue*, Calder, London 1987, p. 407.

16. Quoted in ibid.

17. Quoted in Oliver Read and Walter T. Welch, *From Tin Foil to Stereo: Evolution of the Phonograph*, Howard W. Sams, New York 1976, p. 395.

18. Mike Hobart, 'The Political Economy of Bop', in *Media, Culture & Society*, vol. 3, no. 3, 1981, p. 275.

19. Wole Soyinka, *Aké*, Arrow, London 1983, p. 108.

20. Mustapha Chelbi, quoted in Lizbeth Malkmus and Roy Armes, *Arab and African Film Making*, Zed Books, London and New Jersey 1991, p. 9.

6 Of LPs, EPs, DJs and Payola

1. Alejo Carpentier, *Ese musico que llevo dentro*, vol. II, Editorial Letras Cubanas, Havana 1980, pp. 250–1.

2. Ibid., pp. 262–3.

3. John Culshaw, *Putting the Record Straight*, Secker & Warburg, London 1981, p. 83.

4. Interview with Martin Camras in Kenneth A. Brown, *Inventors at Work*, Tempus, Washington DC 1988, p. 73.

5. Roland Gelatt, *The Fabulous Phonograph 1877–1977*, Cassell, London 1977, pp. 299–300.

6. Russell Sanjek and David Sanjek, *American Popular Music Business in the 20th Century*, Oxford University Press, 1991, p. 81.

7. Nelson George, *The Death of Rhythm and Blues*, Omnibus, London 1989, p. 31.

8. Charlie Gillett, *Sound of the City*, Souvenir, London 1970, p. 10.

9. Quoted in Charlie Gillett, *Making Tracks*, Dutton, New York 1974, p. 27.

10. Jerry Wexler and David Ritz, *Rhythm and the Blues: A Life in American Music*, Jonathon Cape, London 1994, p. 77.

11. George, p. 26.

12. Steve Chapple, *Rock 'n' Roll Is Here to Pay*, p. 235, cited in Linda Martin and Kerry Segrave, *Anti-Rock: The Opposition to Rock 'n' Roll*, Da Capo, New York 1993, p. 11.

13. Gillett, *Making Tracks.*

14. Wexler and Ritz, p. 82.

15. Ibid.

16. Charlie Gillett, 'The Producer as Artist', in H. Wiley Hitchcock, ed., *The Phonograph and Our Musical Life*, ISAM Monograph No. 14, City University, New York 1977, pp. 51–6.

17. Ibid.

18. George, p. 37.

19. Gillett, 'The Producer as Artist'.

20. Gillett, *Making Tracks*, p. 152.

21. Quoted in Steve Jones, *Rock Formation – Music, Technology and Mass Communication*, Sage, London 1992, p. 178.

22. Andrew Blake, *The Music Business*, Batsford, London 1992, p. 75.

23. Erik Barnouw, *The Golden Web: A History of Broadcasting in the United States, Vol. II – 1933 to 1953*, Oxford University Press, New York 1968, p. 217.

24. See Asa Briggs, *The BBC: The First Fifty Years*, Oxford University Press, 1985, p. 72.

25. A. Lloyd-James, quoted in Theo van Leeuwen, 'Rhythm and Social Context: Accent and Juncture in the Speech of Professional Radio Announcers', in P. Tench, ed., *Studies in Systemic Phonology*, Pinter, London 1992, p. 256.

26. Quoted in Barnouw, p. 8.

27. Ibid.

28. See van Leeuwen.

29. Cited in Barnouw, p. 217.

30. Barnouw, p. 218.

31. See van Leeuwen.

32. George, p. 29.

33. Quoted in Ken Barnes, 'Top 40 Radio', in Simon Frith., ed., *Facing the Music: Essays on Pop, Rock and Culture*, Mandarin, London 1990, pp. 9–10.

34. See George, p. 61.

35. Sanjek and Sanjek, p. 89.

36. Quoted in Martin and Segrave, p. 88.

37. Ibid., p. 89.

38. Ibid., p. 90.

7 The Microphone and Interpretation

1. Quoted in John Willett, *The New Sobriety 1917–1933*, Thames and Hudson, London 1978, p. 104.

2. T.W. Adorno, *Introduction to the Sociology of Music*, Seabury Press, New York 1972, p. 134.

3. Quoted by Glenn Gould, 'The Prospects of Recording', *The Glenn Gould Reader*, Faber, London 1987, p. 346.

4. Igor Stravinsky, *An Autobiography*, Steuer, New York 1958, pp. 248–9.

5. Quoted in Joseph Horowitz, *Understanding Toscanini*, Alfred A. Knopf, New York 1987, p. 239.

6. David Hamilton, 'Some Thoughts on Listening to Records' in H. Wiley Hitchcock, ed., *The Phonograph and Our Musical Life*, ISAM Monograph No. 14, City University, New York 1977, p. 69.

7. Quoted in ibid., p. 231.

8. T.W. Adorno, 'On the Fetish-Character in Music and the Aggression of Listening', in *The Essential Frankfurt School Reader*, p. 284.

9. There is extraordinary confirmation of Adorno's description of Toscanini in an anecdote recounted by the record producer Walter Legge. He once visited Toscanini at home in the north of Italy with his wife, the soprano Elizabeth Schwarzkopf. Toscanini was explaining the difference between his own beat and that of German and Austrian conductors playing Mozart. He hummed a tune and turning to the assembled company, instructed them

> 'Now you sing it and follow my beat,' and with his terribly penetrating eyes and this old, slightly bent first finger, he conducted … And we had to sing. I understood in that moment why he had this power over orchestras. We compared notes afterwards, and my wife and I both felt as if we had had steel belts around our waists, slightly elastic steel belts, which were held on to the point of that finger and that finger made it impossible to move more than the tiny liberty that he would allow you.

(Elizabeth Schwarzkopf, *On and Off the Record: A Memoir of Walter Legge*, Faber, London 1982, pp. 98–9).

10. Roger Sessions, *Questions about Music*, Harvard University Press, Cambridge, Mass. 1970, p. 52.

11. Hamilton, p. 69.

12. See Adorno, 'On the Fetish Character in Music'.

13. Gould, p. 311.

14. Horowitz, p. 198.

15. Ibid., pp. 338, 367n.

16. Peter Heyworth, *Otto Klemperer: His Life and Times*, vol. 1, *1885–1933*, Cambridge University Press, 1983, p. 293n.

17. Horowitz, p. 339.

18. Quoted in Horowitz, p. 278.

19. Quoted in ibid., p. 343.

20. Samuel Lipman, 'Stravinsky: Rerecording History' in *The House of Music: Art in an Era of Institutions*, David R. Godine, Boston 1984, pp. 123ff.

21. Richard Taruskin, 'The Pastness of the Present and the Presence of the Past', in Nicholas Kenyon, ed., *Authenticity and Early Music*, Oxford University Press, 1988, p. 206.

22. Ibid., p. 183.

23. Ibid., p. 156.

24. Will Crutchfield in ibid., p. 21.

25. Taruskin in ibid., pp. 155–6, citing Daniel Leech-Wilkinson.

26. Jürgen Kesting, *Maria Callas*, Quartet Books, London 1992, p. 65.

27. Howard Mayer Brown, 'Pedantry or Liberation?' in Kenyon, ed., p. 45.

28. Walter Benjamin, 'The Work of Art in the Age of Mechanical Reproduction', in Hannah Arendt, ed., *Illuminations*, Schocken, New York 1969, p. 233.

29. Lipman, p. 130.

30. Suvi Raj Grubb, *Music Makers on Record*, Hamish Hamilton, London 1986, pp. 56–7.

31. *BBC Yearbook*, 1928, p. 92; Paddy Scannell, 'Music for the Multitude? The Dilemmas of the BBC's Music Policy, 1923–1946', *Media, Culture & Society*, vol. 3, no. 3, July 1981, p. 248.

32. Alejo Carpentier, *Ese musico que llevo dentro*, vol. II, Editorial letras Cubanas, Havana

1980, pp. 245–6.

33. Simon Frith, quoted in Steve Jones, *Rock Formation – Music, Technology and Mass Communication*, Sage, London 1992, p. 125.

34. Roland Gelatt, *The Fabulous Phonograph 1877–1977*, Cassell, London 1977, pp. 282–3.

35. John Culshaw, *Putting the Record Straight*, Secker & Warburg, London 1981, p. 69.

36. Horowitz, p. 282.

37. Ibid., p. 341.

38. Ibid., p. 415.

39. Carpentier, p. 270.

40. Culshaw, *Putting the Record Straight*, p. 164.

41. Quoted in Steve Jones, p. 178.

42. Leonard Warren cited in 'Recording in Italy', *Time*, 29 July 1957.

43. Gould, p. 337.

44. Gould, p. 332.

45. 'Concert-goers Put Parking Before Light Shows', *The Independent*, 13 October 1994.

46. Gould, passim.

47. Schwarzkopf, p. 73.

48. Kesting.

49. Ibid., p. 67.

50. Quoted in ibid., p. 67.

51. See ibid., pp. 133 and 156.

8 The Record and the Mix

1. Douglas Kahn, 'Audio Art in the Deaf Century', in Dan Lander and Micah Lexier, eds, *Sound by Artists*, Art Metropole, Toronto 1990, pp. 301–2.

2. Walter Benjamin, 'The Work of Art in the Age of Mechanical Reproduction', in Hannah Arendt, ed., *Illuminations*, Schocken, New York 1969, p. 227.

3. Kahn, p. 301.

4. See Kahn, p. 308.

5. Herbert Eimert, 'What is Electronic Music?', Die Reihe 1, p. 10.

6. Steve Jones, *Rock Formation – Music, Technology and Mass Communication*, Sage, London 1992, p. 177.

7. Quoted in ibid., p. 173.

8. John Culshaw, *Putting the Record Straight*, Secker & Warburg, London 1981, p. 205.

9. Jeremy Beadle, *Will Pop Eat Itself?*, Faber & Faber, London 1993, pp. 32–3.

10. Evan Eisenberg, *The Recording Angel*, Picador, London 1988, p. 103.

11. Jones, p. 171, citing J.D. Tankel, 'The Practice of Recording Music: Remixing as Recoding', *Journal of Communication*, vol. 40, no. 3, 1990.

12. Quoted in ibid., p. 175.

13. Ibid., p. 172.

14. Dick Hebdige, *Cut 'n' Mix*, Methuen, London 1987, pp. 71–2, 82.

15. Ibid., p. 83.

16. Ibid., p. 84.

17. Quoted in ibid., pp. 82, 87.

18. Jones, p. 169.

19. Tricia Rose in Andrew Ross and Tricia Rose, eds, *Microphone Fiends*, Routledge, London

and New York 1994, p. 81.

20. George Lipsitz, 'We Know What Time It Is', in Ross and Rose, p. 20.

9 Global Corporations and 'World Music'

1. See Phil Hardy and Dave Laing, 'Hard Day's Night at EMI', *Time Out*, 26 October–1 November 1979; Robin Denselow, 'The Sound of Falling Platters', *The Guardian*, 2 October 1979; and 'Janus of the Turntable', *The Economist*, 11 August 1990.

2. See Steve Jones, *Rock Formation – Music, Technology and Mass Communication*, Sage, London 1992, pp. 138–9.

3. Iain Chambers, 'A Miniature History of the Walkman', *New Formations*, vol. 11, 1990, pp. 1–4.

4. S. Hosokawa, 'The Walkman Effect', *Popular Music*, vol. 4, 1984, pp. 165–80.

5. Keith Negus, *Producing Pop, Culture and Conflict in the Popular Music Industry*, Edward Arnold, London 1992, p. 35.

6. Fredric Dannen, *Hit Men*, Vintage Books, London 1991, p. 15.

7. 'Janus of the Turntable'.

8. Denselow.

9. Jeremy Beadle, *Will Pop Eat Itself?*, Faber & Faber, London 1993, p. 126.

10. Hugh Davies, 'A History of Sampling', *unfiled: Music Under New Technology*, RER, London 1994.

11. For a more detailed account of these instruments see Michael Chanan, *Musica Practica: The Social Practice of Western Music from Gregorian Chant to Postmodernism*, Verso, London 1994.

12. Andrew Blake, *The Music Business*, Batsford, London 1992, pp. 50, 54.

13. Ibid., p. 79.

14. Beadle, p. 129.

15. 'MIDI & Music', *Keyboard*, June 1987, p. 32.

16. Simon Frith, 'Music and Morality', in Simon Frith, ed., *Music and Copyright*, Edinburgh University Press, 1993, p. 13.

17. Frith, p. 15.

18. Blake, p. 82.

19. Quoted in Frith, p. 19.

20. Beadle, p. 137.

21. Ibid., p. 199.

22. Ibid., p. 200.

23. Ibid., p. 206.

24. *Music Technology*, August 1986, p. 20.

25. Quoted in Jones, p. 168.

26. Andrew Ross and Tricia Rose, eds, *Microphone Fiends*, Routledge, London and New York 1994, p. 78.

27. Ibid., p. 82.

28. George Lipsitz, 'We Know What Time It Is', in Ross and Rose, p. 21.

29. 'Janus of the Turntable'.

30. *The Economist*, 25 December 1993–7 January 1994, p. 122.

31. Roger Trapp, 'Dance of the Music Majors and Minors', *The Independent*, 24 June 1994.

32. 'Janus of the Turntable'.

33. *The Guardian*, 20 November 1991.

34. 'Janus of the Turntable'.

35. Quoted on 'The Media Show', Channel Four Television, 10 March 1992.

36. *The Economist*, 25 December 1993–7 January 1994.

37. Tricia Rose, 'Contracting Rap', in Ross and Rose, p. 125; italics in the original.

38. *The Economist*, 25 December 1993–7 January 1994.

39. Ibid.

40. Ibid.

41. Alan Robinson of Demon, which has the pre-Warners recordings of Elvis Costello in its catalogue, and Miles Copland of Pangea, a label set up by Sting and distributed by A&M, which is owned by Polygram; quoted by Trapp, 'Dance of the Music Majors and Minors'.

42. Tricia Rose, 'Contracting Rap: An Interview with Carmen Ashhurst-Watson', in Ross and Rose, p. 135.

43. In the summer of 1994 these are almost the only vinyls still sold in leading outlets like the record stores on the Ku'dam in Berlin.

44. *The Guardian*, 22 June 1994.

45. 'Judge Backs Star's "Slave Contract"', *The Guardian*, 22 June 1994.

46. Rose, 'Contracting Rap', in Ross and Rose, pp. 122–4.

47. Jim White, 'Where There's a Hit there's a Writ, A Rock Star's Guide to Staying out of Court and in the Money', *The Independent*, 24 June 1994.

48. Rose, 'Contracting Rap', p. 136.

49. Ibid., p. 137.

50. See *What They Telling Us It's Illegal For?*, videotape by Birmingham Film Co-op, 1985.

51. Peter Manuel, *Cassette Culture, Popular Music and Technology in North India*, University of Chicago Press, 1993, p. 30.

52. Roger Wallis and Krister Malm, *Big Sounds from Small Peoples*, Constable, London 1984, p. 77.

53. Ibid., p. 56.

54. Manuel, p. 32.

55. Wallis and Malm, p. xv.

56. Ibid., p. 100.

57. The latest group of this kind that I encountered, on a visit to Berlin while completing this book in August 1994, was also selling its own CDs.

58. Ibid., pp. 297–8.

59. Personal communication from Steve Stanton.

60. Elie Siegmeister, *Music and Society*, Workers Music Association, London, undated.

Index

Warner–Electra–Atlantic (WEA)
    Records 152, 155, 164
Waterman, Pete 161
wax cylinders 6
Weber, Carl Maria von 13
Webern, Anton 20
Weill, Kurt 49, 63, 116, 122, 158
Welch, Walter T. 2, 24, 58, 59, 67, 69
Well-Tempered Clavier (Bach) 132
Western Electric 4, 38, 65, 81
    electrical recording 56–7, 58
    on sound films 71, 72, 73, 76
Western Union 4
Westinghouse (company) 61, 62
Wexler, Jerry 101, 104, 105, 106
When Old Technologies Were New
    (Marvin) 40
Whiteman, Paul 110

The Who 143
Wilkinson, Kenneth 81
Wilson, Brian 147
Wolf, Hugo 14
    see also Hugo Wolf Society
Wood, Henry 63, 81
Woolworth's 66
World Cup Three Tenors Concert 167
world music 15, 177–8
Wyatt, S. 16

Yamaha (company) 154, 160–61
Yes (band) 143, 160

Zappa, Frank 147, 165
Zeffirelli, Franco 136
Zonophone 65
zouk music 176–7